MW00778441

# Volodymyr Zelenskyy

## *War Speeches I*

## *February — March 2022*

LMVERLAG 2022

L M V E R L A G
B   E   R   L   I   N
A         M         S
T   E   R   D   A   M

Some minor spelling errors corrected.
Names have not been changed from the original text.
Net proceeds go to the Ukrainian Red Cross:
https://www.icrc.org/en/donate/ukraine
www.lmverlag.shop for print copies and ebook

NUR: 6 8 9   ISBN: 9 7 8 - 9 0 - 8 3 1 7 2 7 - 8 - 1   L M V E R L A G 0 2

# Index

# On the unity of Ukrainian society
## 14 February 2022—20:53

Great people of a great country!

I am addressing you at this tense moment.

Our state is facing serious external and internal challenges that require responsibility, confidence, and concrete actions from me and each of us.

We are being intimidated by the great war and the date of the military invasion is being set again. This is not the first time.

The war against us is being systematically waged on all fronts. On the military one, they increase the contingent around the border. On the diplomatic one, they are trying to deprive us of the right to determine our own foreign policy course. On the energy one, they limit the supply of gas, electricity, and coal. On the information one, they seek to spread panic among citizens and investors through the media.

But our state today is stronger than ever.

This is not the first threat that the strong Ukrainian people have faced. Two years ago, we, like the rest of the world, looked confused in the eyes of the pandemic. However, we united and with clear systemic steps practically defeated it. In this difficult time, the strong Ukrainian people have shown their best qualities—unity and the will to win.

Unlike the pandemic two years ago, today we clearly understand all the challenges we face and what to do about them. We are confident, but not self-confident. We understand all the risks. We are constantly monitoring the situation, working out different scenarios, preparing decent responses to all possible aggressive actions.

We know exactly where the foreign army is near our borders, its numbers, its locations, its equipment, and its plans.

We have something to respond with. We have a great army. Our guys have unique combat experience and modern weapons. This is an army many times stronger than eight years ago.

Along with the army, Ukrainian diplomacy is at the forefront of defending our interests. We have managed to gain diplomatic support from almost all leaders of the civilized world. Most of them have either already visited and supported Ukraine or will do so in the near future. Today, everyone recognizes that the security of Europe and the entire continent depends on Ukraine and its army.

We want peace and we want to resolve all issues exclusively through negotiations. Both Donbas and Crimea will return to Ukraine. Exclusively through diplomacy. We do not encroach on what's not ours, but we will not give up our land.

We are confident in our Armed Forces, but our military must also feel our support, our cohesion, and our unity. The foothold of our army is the confidence of their own people and a strong economy.

We have formed sufficient reserves to repel attacks on the hryvnia exchange rate and our financial system. We will not ignore any industry that will need government support. As it happened the other day with airlines. And evidence of this is a stable hryvnia exchange rate and open skies.

An important front of defence is the objective coverage of the situation by the domestic media. And now I want to address our Ukrainian journalists. Some of you sometimes have to perform the tasks of media owners. Most of them have already fled their own country.

Work for Ukraine, not for those who fled. The fate of the country today depends on your honest position.

And now I want to address not those who stayed with Ukraine and in Ukraine, but those who left it at the most crucial moment. Your strength is not in your money and planes, but in the civic position you can show. Return to your people and the country due to which you got your factories and wealth. Today, everyone passes a real test for a citizen of Ukraine. Pass it with dignity. Let everyone understand for whom Ukraine is really the Homeland, and for whom it is just a platform for money making.

I address separately all representatives of the state: civil servants, people's deputies of all levels who have fled the country or plan to do so. The people of Ukraine have entrusted you not only to govern the state, but also to protect it. It is your direct duty in this situation to be with us, with the Ukrainian people. I urge you to return to your homeland within 24 hours and stand side by side with the Ukrainian army, diplomacy, and people!

We are told that February 16 will be the day of the attack. We will make it the Day of Unity. The relevant decree has already been signed. On this day, we will hoist national flags, put on blue and yellow ribbons and show the world our unity.

We have one great European aspiration. We want freedom and are ready to fight for it. 14,000 defenders and civilians killed in this war are watching us from the sky. And we will not betray their memory.

We all want to live happily, and happiness loves the strong ones. We have never known what it is to give up and we are not going to learn that.

Today is not just Valentine's Day. It is the day of those in love with Ukraine. We believe in our own strength and continue to build our future together. Because we are united by love for Ukraine, united and unique. And love will win. Yes, now you may think it's darkness all around. But tomorrow the sun will rise again over our peaceful sky.

Love Ukraine!

We are calm! We are strong! We are together! Great people of a great country.

# Speech at the 58th Munich Security Conference
## 19 February 2022—18:14

Ukraine wants peace. Europe wants peace. The world says it doesn't want to fight, and Russia says it doesn't want to attack. Someone is lying. This is not an axiom, but it is no longer a hypothesis.

Ladies and Gentlemen!

Two days ago, I was in Donbas, on the delimitation line. Legally—between Ukraine and the temporarily occupied territories. In fact, the delimitation line between peace and war. Where on the one side there is a kindergarten, and on the other side there is a projectile that hit it. On the one side there is a school, on the other side there is a projectile hitting the school yard.

And next to it there are 30 children who go... no, not to NATO, but to school. Someone has physics classes. Knowing its basic laws, even children understand how absurd the statements that the shelling is carried out by Ukraine sound.

Someone has math classes. Children can calculate the difference between the number of shelling occasions in these three days and the occasions of mentioning Ukraine in this year's Munich Security Report without a calculator.

And someone has history classes. And when a bomb crater appears in the school yard, children have a question: has the world forgotten its mistakes of the XX century?

What do attempts at appeasement lead to? As the question "Why die for Danzig?" turned into the need to die for Dunkirk and dozens of other cities in Europe and the world. At the cost of tens of millions of lives.

These are terrible lessons of history. I just want to make

sure you and I read the same books. Hence, we have the same understanding of the answer to the main question: how did it happen that in the XXI century, Europe is at war again and people are dying? Why does it last longer than World War II? How did we get to the biggest security crisis since the Cold War? For me, as the President of a country that has lost part of the territory, thousands of people and on whose borders, there are now 150,000 Russian troops, equipment and heavy weapons, the answer is obvious.

The architecture of world security is fragile and needs to be updated. The rules that the world agreed on decades ago no longer work. They do not keep up with new threats.

They are not effective for overcoming them. This is a cough syrup when you need a coronavirus vaccine. The security system is slow. It crashes again. Because of different things: selfishness, self-confidence, irresponsibility of states at the global level. As a result, we have crimes of some and indifference of others. Indifference that makes you an accomplice. It is symbolic that I am talking about this right here. It was here 15 years ago that Russia announced its intention to challenge global security. What did the world say? Appeasement. Result? At least—the annexation of Crimea and aggression against my state.

The UN, which is supposed to defend peace and world security, cannot defend itself. When its Charter is violated. When one of the members of the UN Security Council annexes the territory of one of the founding members of the UN. And the UN itself ignores the Crimea Platform, the goal of which is to de-occupy Crimea peacefully and protect the rights of Crimean's.

Three years ago, it was here that Angela Merkel said: "Who will pick up the wreckage of the world order? Only all of us, together." The audience gave a standing ovation.

But unfortunately, the collective applause did not grow into collective action. And now, when the world is talking about the threat of a great war, the question arises: is there anything left to pick up? The security architecture in Europe and the world is almost destroyed. It's too late to think about repairs, it's time to build a new system. Mankind has done this twice, paying too high a price—two world wars. We have a chance to break this trend until it becomes a consistent pattern. And start building a new system before millions of victims. Having the old lessons of the First and Second World Wars, not our own experience of the possible third, God forbid.

I talked about it here. And on the rostrum of the UN. That in the XXI century there are no more foreign wars. That the annexation of Crimea and the war in Donbas affects the whole world. And this is not a war in Ukraine, but a war in Europe. I said this at summits and forums. In 2019, 2020, 2021. Will the world be able to hear me in 2022?

This is no longer a hypothesis, but not an axiom yet. Why? Evidence is needed. More important than words on Twitter or statements in the media. Action is required. It is the world that needs it, not just us.

We will defend our land with or without the support of partners. Whether they give us hundreds of modern weapons or five thousand helmets. We appreciate any help, but everyone should understand that these are not charitable contributions that Ukraine should ask for or remind of.

These are not noble gestures for which Ukraine should bow low. This is your contribution to the security of Europe and the world. Where Ukraine has been a reliable shield for eight years. And for eight years it has been rebuffing one of the world's biggest armies. Which stands along our borders, not the borders of the EU.

And Grad rockets hit Mariupol, not European cities. And after almost six months of fighting, the airport in Donetsk was destroyed, not in Frankfurt. And it's always hot in the Avdiivka industrial zone—it was hot there in the last days, not in Montmartre. And no European country knows what military burials every day in all regions are. And no European leader knows what regular meetings with the families of the deceased are.

Be that as it may, we will defend our beautiful land no matter if we have 50,000, 150 or one million soldiers of any army on the border. To really help Ukraine, it is not necessary to say how many servicemen and military equipment are on the border. Say what numbers we have.

To really help Ukraine, it is not necessary to constantly talk only about the dates of the probable invasion. We will defend our land on February 16, March 1 and December 31. We need other dates much more. And everyone understands perfectly well which ones.

Tomorrow in Ukraine is the Day of the Heroes of the Heavenly Hundred. Eight years ago, Ukrainians made their choice, and many gave their lives for that choice. Eight years later, should Ukraine constantly call for recognition of the European perspective? Since 2014, Russia has been convincing that we have chosen the wrong path, that no one is waiting for us in Europe. Shouldn't Europe constantly say and prove by action that this is not true? Shouldn't the EU say today that its citizens are positive about Ukraine's accession to the Union? Why do we avoid this question?

Doesn't Ukraine deserve direct and honest answers?

This also applies to NATO. We are told: the door is open. But so far authorized access only. If not all members of the Alliance want to see us or all members of the Alliance do not want to see us, be honest. Open doors are good, but we need open answers, not open questions for years. Isn't the right to the truth one of our enhanced opportunities? The best time for it is the next summit in Madrid.

Russia says Ukraine seeks to join the Alliance to return Crimea by force. It is gratifying that the words "return Crimea" appear in their rhetoric. But they inattentively read

Article 5 of the NATO Charter: collective action is for protection, not offensive. Crimea and the occupied regions of Donbas will certainly return to Ukraine, but only peacefully.

Ukraine consistently implements the Normandy agreements and the Minsk agreements. Their foundation is the unquestionable recognition of the territorial integrity and independence of our state. We seek a diplomatic settlement of the armed conflict. Note: solely based on international law.

So, what is really going on in the peace process? Two years ago, we agreed with the Presidents of France, the Russian Federation, the Chancellor of Germany on a full-scale ceasefire. And Ukraine is scrupulously adhering to these agreements. We are as restrained as possible against the background of constant provocations. We are constantly making proposals in the framework of the Normandy Four and the Trilateral Contact Group. And what do we see? Shells and bullets from the other side. Our soldiers and civilians are being killed and wounded, and civilian infrastructure is being destroyed.

The last days have become especially illustrative. Hundreds of massive shelling occasions with weapons prohibited by the Minsk agreements. It is also important to stop restricting the admission of OSCE observers to Ukraine's TOT. They are threatened. They are intimidated. All humanitarian issues are blocked.

Two years ago, I signed a law on the unconditional admission of representatives of humanitarian organizations to detainees. But they are simply not admitted to the temporarily occupied territories. After two exchanges of captives, the process was blocked, although Ukraine provided agreed lists. Inhuman torture at the infamous Isolation Prison in Donetsk has become a symbol of human rights abuses.

The two new checkpoints we opened in November 2020 in the Luhansk region still do not function—and here we see outright obstruction under contrived pretexts.

Ukraine is doing everything possible to reach progress in discussions and political issues. In the TCG, in the Minsk process, we've put forward proposals—draft laws, but everything is blocked—no one talks about them. Ukraine demands to unblock the negotiation process immediately. But this does not mean that the search for peace is limited to it alone.

We are ready to look for the key to the end of the war in all possible formats and platforms: Paris, Berlin, Minsk. Istanbul, Geneva, Brussels, New York, Beijing—I don't care where in the world to negotiate peace in Ukraine.

It does not matter if four countries, seven or a hundred participate, the main thing is that Ukraine and Russia are among them. What is important is the understanding that peace is needed not only by us, but the world also needs peace in Ukraine. Peace and restoration of territorial integrity within internationally recognized borders. This is the only way. And I hope no one thinks of Ukraine as a convenient and eternal buffer zone between the West and Russia. This will never happen. Nobody will allow that.

Otherwise—who's next? Will NATO countries have to defend each other? I want to believe that the North Atlantic Treaty and Article 5 will be more effective than the Budapest Memorandum.

Ukraine has received security guarantees for abandoning the world's third nuclear capability. We don't have that weapon. We also have no security. We also do not have part of the territory of our state that is larger in area than Switzerland, the Netherlands or Belgium. And most importantly—we don't have millions of our citizens. We don't have all this.

Therefore, we have something. The right to demand a shift from a policy of appeasement to ensuring security and peace guarantees.

Since 2014, Ukraine has tried three times to convene consultations with the guarantor states of the Budapest Memorandum. Three times without success. Today Ukraine will do it for the fourth time. I, as President, will do this for the first time. But both Ukraine and I are doing this for the last time. I am initiating consultations in the framework of the Budapest Memorandum. The Minister of Foreign Affairs was commissioned to convene them. If they do not happen again or their results do not guarantee security for our country, Ukraine will have every right to believe that the Budapest Memorandum is not working, and all the package decisions of 1994 are in doubt.

I also propose to convene a summit of permanent members of the UN Security Council in the coming weeks with the participation of Ukraine, Germany, and Turkey to address security challenges in Europe. And elaborate new, effective security guarantees for Ukraine. Guarantees today, if we are not a member of the Alliance and in fact are in the grey zone—in a security vacuum.

What else can we do now? Continue to effectively support Ukraine and its defence capabilities. Provide Ukraine with a clear European perspective, the tools of support available to candidate countries, and clear and comprehensive timeframes for joining the Alliance.

Support the transformation in our country. Establish a Stability and Reconstruction Fund for Ukraine, a land-lease program, the supply of the latest weapons, machinery, and equipment for our army—an army that protects the whole of Europe.

Develop an effective package of preventive sanctions to deter aggression. Guarantee Ukraine's energy security, ensure its integration into the EU energy market when Nord Stream 2 is used as a weapon.

All these questions need answers.

So far, we have silence instead of them. And if there is silence, there will be no silence in the east of our state. That is—in Europe. That is—in the whole world. I hope the whole world finally understands this, Europe understands.

Ladies and Gentlemen!

I thank all the states that supported Ukraine today.

In words, in declarations, in concrete help. Those who are on our side today. On the side of truth and international law. I'm not calling you by name—I don't want some other countries to be ashamed. But this is their business, this is their karma. And this is on their conscience. However, I do not know how they will be able to explain their actions to the two soldiers killed and three wounded in Ukraine today.

And most importantly—to three girls from Kyiv. One is ten years old, the second is six, and the third is only one. Today they were left without a father. At 6 o'clock in the morning Central European Time. When the Ukrainian intelligence officer, Captain Anton Sydorov was killed because of artillery fire prohibited by the Minsk agreements. I don't know what he thought at the last moment of his life. He didn't know what agenda someone needs to meet to end the war.

But he knows exactly the answer to the question I asked at the beginning. He knows exactly who of us is lying.

May his memory live forever. May the memory of all those who died today and during the war in the east of our state live forever.

Thank you.

# Address by the President of Ukraine
## 24 February 2022—18:01

Citizens of Ukraine.

What do we hear today? It's not just rocket explosions, battles, the roar of aircraft. It is the sound of a new Iron Curtain lowering and closing Russia away from the civilized world. Our national task is to make this curtain pass not through our Ukrainian territory, but at the home of Russians.

The Ukrainian army, our border guards, police, and special services stopped the enemy's attacks. In the language of conflict, this can be called an operational pause.

In Donbas, our Armed Forces are doing great, the Kharkiv direction is very difficult, the forces for the defence of the city are working, they are reliable, they are our men. The most problematic situation today is in the south. Our troops are fighting fierce battles in the suburbs of Kherson. The enemy is pushing out of the occupied Crimea, trying to advance towards Melitopol.

In the north of the country, the enemy is slowly advancing in the Chernihiv region, but there are forces to hold it. Reliable defence is built in the Zhytomyr region. Enemy paratroopers in Hostomel are blocked, troops are ordered to destroy them.

Yes, we, unfortunately, have losses, losses of our heroes. Yes, we have captured Russian soldiers. Our doctors are helping some of them—those who have surrendered. Many Russian aircraft and many armoured vehicles were destroyed.

Yes, we see that many Russians are shocked by what is happening. Some Russians are already calling on social media that they are against the war. We see it. But the leadership of the Russian Federation is unlikely to see it.

So please.

If you hear us, if you understand us, if you understand that you are attacking an independent country, please go out to the squares and address the President of your country.

We are Ukrainians. We are on our land. You are Russians. Now your military has started a war. The war in our state. I would very much like you to speak on Red Square or somewhere else on the streets of your capital, in Moscow, St. Petersburg and other cities in Russia. Not only in Instagram—but it is also very important.

What do we see at this hour? For the world community, Russia is becoming an analogue of the so-called DPR—this is complete isolation.

I am in constant contact with the leaders of partner countries and international organizations. Russia has already begun receiving the first sanctions from a large package of sanctions, the most powerful in world history.

No one will be able to convince or force us, Ukrainians, to give up our freedom, our independence, our sovereignty. But it seems that the Russian leadership is trying to do this by destroying the potential of their country. Everything that Russia has done since 2000 can now be burned live in front of the world.

We emphasize that Ukraine did not choose the path of war. But Ukraine offers to return to peace.

What can Ukrainians do? Help the national defence. Join the ranks of the Armed Forces of Ukraine and territorial defence units. Any citizen with combat experience will now be useful. It is up to you and all of us whether the enemy will be able to advance further into the territory of our independent state. Please help the volunteer community and the medical system, for example by donating blood.

Politicians and community leaders—help people, ensure normal life on the ground as much as possible. Everyone should take care of their loved ones and take care of those neighbours or acquaintances who need it. The duty of journalists, an important duty, is to defend democracy and freedom in Ukraine.

I spoke today with many leaders—the United Kingdom, Turkey, France, Germany, the EU, the United States, Sweden, Romania, Poland, Austria, and others.

If you, dear European leaders, dear world leaders, leaders of the free world, do not help us today, then tomorrow the war will knock on your door.

Glory to the Armed Forces of Ukraine! Glory to Ukraine!

## Address at the end of the first day of Russia's attacks
## 25 February 2022—01:10

Glory to the Armed Forces of Ukraine!

Men and women, our defenders! You are brilliantly defending the country from one of the most powerful countries in the world.

Today Russia attacked the entire territory of our state. And today our defenders have done a lot. They defended almost the entire territory of Ukraine, which suffered direct blows. They regain the one that the enemy managed to occupy. For example, Hostomel near Kyiv. This gives more confidence to the capital.

According to preliminary data, unfortunately, we have lost 137 of our heroes today—our citizens. 10 of them are officers. 316 are wounded.

On our Zmiinyi Island, defending it to the last, all the border guards died heroically. But did not give up. All of them will be posthumously awarded the title of Hero of Ukraine.

May the memory of those who gave their lives for Ukraine live forever.

I am grateful to everyone who saves people right now and helps maintain order in the state.

The enemy strikes not only at military facilities, as it claims, but also at civilians. They kill people and turn peaceful cities into military targets. This is vile and will never be forgiven.

I know that a lot of fakes are being produced now. In particular, that I allegedly left Kyiv. I stay in the capital; I stay with my people. During the day, I held dozens of international talks, directly managed our country. And I will stay in the capital. My family is also in Ukraine. My children are also in Ukraine. My family is not traitors. They are the citizens of Ukraine. But I have no right to say where they are now.

According to our information, the enemy marked me as the number one target. My family is the number two target. They want to destroy Ukraine politically by destroying the Head of State.

We also have information that enemy sabotage groups have entered Kyiv. That's why I am asking Kyivites very much: be careful, follow the rules of curfew. I remain in the government quarter together with all those who are necessary for the work of the central government.

No matter how many conversations I had with the leaders of different countries today, I heard a few things. The first is that we are supported. And I am grateful to each state that helps Ukraine concretely, not just in words.

But there is another—we are left alone in defence of our state. Who is ready to fight with us? Honestly—I do not see such. Who is ready to guarantee Ukraine's accession to NATO? Honestly, everyone is afraid.

Today we heard from Moscow that they still want to talk. They want to talk about Ukraine's neutral status.

I tell all the partners of our state now is an important moment—the fate of our country is being decided. I ask them: are you with us? They answer that they are with us. But they are not ready to take us to the Alliance.

Today, I asked the twenty-seven leaders of Europe whether Ukraine will be in NATO. I asked directly. Everyone is afraid. They do not answer.

And we are not afraid of anything. We are not afraid to defend our state. We are not afraid of Russia. We are not afraid to talk to Russia. We are not afraid to say everything about security guarantees for our state. We are not afraid to talk about neutral status.

We are not in NATO now. But the main thing—what security guarantees will we have? And what specific countries will give them?

We need to talk about the end of this invasion. We need to talk about a ceasefire.

But now the fate of the country depends entirely on our army, on our heroes, our security forces, all our defenders. And on our people, your wisdom, and the great support of all friends of our country.

Glory to Ukraine!

# Address on the second morning of the large-scale war
## 25 February 2022—07:27

The second morning of a large-scale war. At 4 am, Russian forces continued to launch missile strikes on the territory of Ukraine.

They say that civilian objects are not a target for them. This is a lie. In fact, they do not distinguish in which areas to operate.

Just as yesterday, the military and civilians are equally under Russian attack. The purpose of this attack is to put pressure on you, the citizens of Ukraine, to put pressure on our entire society. I emphasize not just on the government—on all Ukrainians. And today—even more than yesterday.

Our men and women—all defenders of Ukraine—did not allow the enemy to realize the operational plan of invasion on the first day. Ukrainians demonstrate real heroism.

The enemy was stopped in most directions. There are fights.

Therefore, Russia's attack continues with the expectation that our forces will be tired. But no one is tired.

Ukraine's air defence forces are protecting our sky. As much as possible. Enemy aircraft operate treacherously over residential areas, including the capital.

Terrible explosions in the morning sky over Kyiv, bombing, hitting a house, fire—all this reminds of the first such attack on our capital, which took place in 1941.

This morning we are defending our state alone, as we did yesterday. The world's most powerful forces are watching from afar.

Did yesterday's sanctions convince Russia? We hear in

our sky and see on our earth that this is not enough. Foreign troops are still trying to become more active in our territory.

Only the solidarity and determination of Ukrainians can preserve our freedom and protect the state. The army, border guards, the National Guard, the police, intelligence, the Territorial Defence Forces—everyone performs their tasks to the maximum.

It is very important that today our citizens also demonstrate maximum endurance and mutual support. Take care of your family and loved ones, but do not forget about the people around you. Those who are single, those who are older. Help them with food.

Help find shelter when there is an air alarm. Help with access to verified official information.

Stop the enemy wherever you see it. The fate of Ukraine depends only on Ukrainians. No one but ourselves will control our lives. We are on our land; the truth is on our side. It will not be possible to destroy our character. Kalibr missiles are helpless against our freedom.

Russia will still have to talk to us sooner or later. Talk about how to end the fighting and stop this invasion. The sooner the conversation begins, the smaller Russia's losses will be.

Dear citizens of the Russian Federation. As I said, tonight they started bombing residential areas of the hero city of Kyiv. It all reminds me of 1941. To all the citizens of the Russian Federation who come out to protest, I want to say—we see you. This means that you heard us. This means that you begin to trust us. Fight for us. Fight against the war.

Dear citizens of Ukraine.

We are defending ourselves! We do not stop! Glory to you!

# Glory to our army! Glory to Ukraine!
## 25 February 2022—13:07

Chancellor of Germany Olaf Scholz yesterday said Russia's invasion of Ukraine is something Europe has not seen for 75 years. And it's true. But this is not the whole truth.

This is not just Russia's invasion in Ukraine, this is the beginning of the war against Europe. Against the unity of Europe. Against elementary human rights in Europe.

Against all coexistence rules on the continent. Against the fact that European states refuse to divide, yes, to divide the borders by force.

The cities of Ukraine undergo rocket bombing for the second day already. Tank columns and air strikes are as similar as something Europe has already seen a long time ago—during the Second World War and talked "never again" about it. But this is it! Again. Now. In 2022. 75 years after the Second World War completion.

I'm confident you see it—all of you, entire Europe. But we do not see in full what you are going to do. How are you going to protect yourself when you help us so slowly in Ukraine?

I'd like to point out what has already happened. And for this we are grateful. Sectoral sanctions. The United States, Canada, United Kingdom, the European Union, Australia, and New Zealand introduced precisely sectoral sanctions against Russia. In particular, against all the largest banks. Against the largest Russian enterprises. Against Russia's access to Western technologies.

But Russian tanks are still shooting at residential buildings in our cities. Armoured vehicles are still attacking, including civilians. Ordinary citizens of Ukraine.

Europe has sufficient force to stop this aggression. What to expect from European states further?

Cancellation of visas for Russians? Cutting off SWIFT? Full isolation of Russia? Recalling ambassadors? Oil embargo? Closure of the sky? Today, all this should be on the table because it is a threat to us, all of us, all of Europe. You can still stop aggression. We must act without delay.

Ordinary people can also do their part of the job, I'm sure, in every country of the world, in each country of Europe. Go out on the square of your cities and demand peace for Europe, peace for Ukraine, stop this war. Go out, go out on the squares and demand to stop the war. This is our right. This is your right.

When bombs fall in Kyiv, this happens in Europe, not only in Ukraine. When missiles kill our people, it's the death of all Europeans. Require more protection for Europe, more protection for Ukraine—as part of a democratic world.

While state institutions in Europe are in no hurry with really strong decisions, every European in the capital can already come to our embassy and offer assistance.

Demand from your governments more financial, more military assistance to Ukraine. For this help is a help to you. For it is a help to Europe. You help yourself.

If you have a combat experience in Europe and do not want to look at the indecision of politicians, you can arrive in our state and protect Europe with us where it is now urgently required.

You have already been blackmailed with gas. Already humiliated. They already want to split and divide you the same way as they are trying to divide Ukraine today.

Protect yourself. Just as we protect yourself.

I want to address Russian Federation President once again. Battles take place all over the territory of Ukraine. Let's sit at the negotiating table. To stop the death of people.

And now I want to address the Armed Forces of Ukraine.

Stand firmly. You are all we have. You are everything that protects our state.

Glory to Ukraine!

## Address in the evening of the second day of the large-scale war
## 26 February 2022—00:38

Today was a hard yet courageous day. We are fighting for our state absolutely on all frontlines: South, East, North, in many cities of our beautiful country. Fighting around the clock on the diplomatic frontline as well—it's easier to say with whom I did not speak to among world leaders today. We continue this. I have been constantly working and spoke with President Macron, Scholz, Rutte, Mrs. von der Leyen, President of the United States Biden. I outlined what answer Ukrainians still expect from the West to this aggression and agreed on new assistance, new support, significant assistance for our state. I thank all the leaders and I am separately grateful to President Biden.

I was really glad to see the news from friendly Georgia. I want to thank the good, beautiful Georgian people who went out on the streets of their country and supported Ukraine. You are true friends! Thanks.

Our main goal is to end this slaughter. The enemy suffers very-very serious losses. These are hundreds, hundreds of killed soldiers who crossed our border, who came to our land.

We suffer losses as well, unfortunately. Ukrainians resist the aggression heroically. It is impossible to justify. Therefore, the invaders must come up with more and more absurd accusations to say at least something.

I am convinced that these allegations are biased, nobody will believe them. Ukrainians won't believe them, the world won't believe them, citizens of the Russian Federation won't believe them.

It's simply cannot be such a truth that could clarify why kindergartens and housing infrastructure are fired from a missile artillery. In Vorzel, Kyiv region, they fired "Grads" at an orphanage. Okhtyrka, Sumy region, was shelled by "Uragans". Housing quarters, shelter, kindergartens were under the shelling. What is this war against Ukrainian children in a kindergarten? Who are they? Are they neo-Nazis from kindergarten as well? Or were they NATO soldiers that threatened Russia? Killed and injured children are the sentence to this invasion.

Everyone, I emphasize, everyone must do everything they can to stop this war. Every day of aggression destroys normal life not only in Ukraine, but also in Russia, and in Europe, in the world.

Europeans do not imagine yet what it is like to live when there is such a confrontation next to you. I have to say absolutely frankly: this night will be harder than a day. Many cities of our state are under attack. Chernihiv, Sumy, Kharkiv, our boys, our girls in Donbas, cities of the south of Ukraine. Kyiv requires special attention. We cannot lose the capital.

I appeal to our defenders on all frontlines. This night the enemy will use all the forces available to break our resistance. Treacherously, viciously, inhumanly. This night they will make an assault upon us. We all have to understand what we are going to face.

This night we have to withstand. The fate of Ukraine is now being decided. Each civilian should be as careful as possible. Help, please, each other, especially elderly people, lonely, those for whom it is very difficult now. In case of any danger go to the shelter.

Everyone who has already joined the country's defence or

can help defend, stop the enemy everywhere you can. Remove special signs that saboteurs leave on the roads and buildings. Burn the enemy's equipment with anything you can. If even kindergartens are a permissible target for invaders, you must not leave them any chance.

All thoughts, all prayers of Ukrainians are with our military. We believe in them, take care of them. Defend our state. The night will be tough, very tough. But the morning will come.

Glory to Ukraine!

# We withstood, on the third day of the war
## 26 February 2022—12:14

I can start this address with good news. We withstood and successfully repel enemy attacks. The fighting continues. In many cities and districts of our state. But we know what we are defending. The country, the land, the future of children.

Kyiv and key cities around the capital are controlled by our army. The invaders wanted to block the centre of our state and put their puppets here, as in Donetsk. We broke their plan. They did not gain any advantage over us.

On our streets, in the skies of Kyiv, in Vasylkiv, in Vyshhorod, even in the surrounding fields, a real battle for Kyiv took place. The enemy used everything against us: missiles, fighter aircraft, drones, artillery, armoured vehicles, saboteurs, paratroopers. The invaders are shelling residential neighbourhoods, including with the use of missile artillery, trying to destroy energy facilities. They have very treacherous tactics.

Dwellings destroyed by missiles and artillery are the ultimate argument for the world to stop the occupation invasion together with us.

I say this as frankly as possible now: the people of Ukraine have already earned and have the right to become a member of the European Union. This will be the key evidence of our country's support.

It is a crucial moment to close the long-standing strategic discussion once and for all and to decide on Ukraine's membership in the European Union. I discussed this today with Charles Michel, Ursula von der Leyen, Emmanuel Macron.

The anti-war coalition is operating—defence weapons and equipment are heading to Ukraine. We already have almost full support from EU countries for disconnecting Russia from SWIFT. I hope that Germany and Hungary will have the courage to support this decision. We have the courage to defend our homeland, to defend Europe.

In each of our cities, the invaders are being severely rebuffed. Uman, Odesa, Kherson, Mykolaiv, Donbas, Kharkiv, Sumy, Chernihiv, Kyiv—wherever the enemy kills our people, the Armed Forces of Ukraine are doing everything to stop and destroy the invaders. Lviv and other cities in western and central Ukraine that are under air attacks endure firmly. Well done!

Every Ukrainian needs to remember one thing. If you can stop and destroy the invaders, do it. All those who can return to Ukraine, come back to defend Ukraine. And then we will have a lot of work with you to rebuild it!

All those who can defend Ukraine abroad, do it purposefully, unitedly, continuously! All friends of Ukraine who want to join the defence—come, we will give you weapons! All the details of how to implement this will be announced in the near future.

Glory to all those who defend Ukraine today! You are heroes!

I adopted a decision to posthumously award the title of Hero of Ukraine to Vitaliy Volodymyrovych Skakun, a sapper of the 35th Separate Marine Brigade. At the cost of his own life, he blew up the bridge.

And now I want absolutely everyone in Russia to hear me. Thousands of victims. Hundreds of prisoners who simply cannot understand why they were sent to Ukraine. Sent to be killed. The sooner you tell your government that the war must be stopped immediately, the more of your people will remain alive.

We see that there are indeed protests by your citizens against the war. We know that many in Russia are now simply shocked by the meanness and cruelty of the authorities. This is a truly correct response. I thank you for this reaction. Thanks to Leonid Parfyonov, Dmitry Muratov, Yury Dud, Liya Akhedzhakova, Valery Meladze and thousands, thousands of other Russians whose conscience is heard loud. Just stop those who lie to you, lie to us, lie to the whole world. We need to end this war. We can live in peace—in global peace, in human peace.

Our military, national guards, national police, territorial defence, border guards, special services, citizens—hold on! We will defeat everyone. Glory to Ukraine!

## Addressing the citizens of Belarus
## 27 February 2022—09:54

These words of mine will be addressed to the citizens of Belarus.

Today, all of you are called to the polls to vote in the referendum. This could look like a normal political process. But now it certainly cannot be anything normal.

Now decisions are made on a completely different level.

Last night in Ukraine was cruel. More shelling. More bombing of residential areas, civilian infrastructure. Today there is not a single object in the country that the invaders would not consider a valid target for themselves. They fight against everyone. They fight against everything that's alive—against kindergartens, against residential buildings and even against ambulances. They use rocket artillery, missiles against entire urban areas in which there has never been any military infrastructure.

Vasylkiv, Kyiv, Chernihiv, Sumy, Kharkiv and many other cities of Ukraine are surviving in conditions that were last seen on our land and your land during the Second World War.

But in the war that is going on now, you are not on the same side with us. Regretfully. From your territory, the troops of the Russian Federation launch rockets into Ukraine. Our children are being killed from your territory, our houses are being destroyed, they are trying to blow up everything that has been built over decades—and, by the way, not only by us, but also by our fathers, our grandfathers.

And all this is also a de facto referendum for you, Belarusians. You decide who you are. You decide who to be. How will you look into the eyes of your children, how will you look into the eyes of each other, your neighbours. And we are your neighbours. We, Ukrainians. Be Belarus, not Russia! You are making this choice right now. Exactly today.

Now there is a lot of news about possible negotiations between Ukraine and Russia, which can end this war and restore peace to all of us. And they often mention your capital. Minsk. As a platform for these negotiations. A place we didn't choose. And, in fact, you did not, too. The leadership of Russia chose it. And now, there is an offer to meet there again.

Four days ago, cruise missiles, planes, helicopters, and equipment came from Belarusian territory. They hit our homes, they hit our lives. The heavy equipment followed. And this is a dreadful deja vu. You know, Kyiv was attacked at 4 am.

Someone has such a sense of humour, just as in 1941. You slept, Belarusian brothers. And we woke up. But you are still sleeping. And we haven't gone to bed since that moment. Because we are fighting. We are fighting for our country. We are fighting for our freedom. Because we have every right to do so.

If there were no aggressive actions from your territory, we could speak in Minsk. In your city. When you were neutral, we spoke in Minsk, we met many times. This is right. This is truthful. To talk like neighbours. Right now, you haven't made your big choice yet. And it is ahead, it should depend only on you. Not on Russia, not on Ukraine, not on America, but on the people of Belarus.

That is why now we say—not Minsk. The venue for the meeting may be other cities. Of course, we want peace. We want to meet; we want the end of the war! Warsaw, Bratislava, Budapest, Istanbul, Baku—we proposed to the Russian side all of this. Any other city suits us in a country from whose territory missiles are not launched. Only in this way can negotiations be honest. And they can really end the war.

I sincerely wish Belarus to once again become that kind, safe Belarus that everyone saw not so long ago. Make the right choice. I am sure this is the main choice of your great people.

# Address to the citizens on the fourth day of the war
## 27 February 2022—10:21

This night was hard. What do they do? This is revenge. The people rose to defend their state, and they showed their true faces. This is terror.

They are going to bomb our Ukrainian cities even more. They are going to kill our children even more insidiously. This is an evil that has come to our land and must be destroyed.

They lied that they would not touch the civilian population. But since the first hours of the invasion, Russian troops have been hitting civilian infrastructure.

They consciously chose tactics to destroy people and everything that makes life just normal. Power plants, hospitals, kindergartens, residential buildings—all this is under attack every day.

What the invaders are doing to Kharkiv, Okhtyrka, Kyiv, Odesa and other cities and towns deserves an international tribunal. We clearly record all their crimes. And there would have been many more of these crimes if it hadn't been for our courageous defenders.

Ukrainian forces are great. Repulse attacks, breaking the enemy's plans. They do their job brilliantly.

Yes, this is truly a job. A hard, fundamental, and most importantly—fair job. A job that deserves the highest appraisal and the highest gratitude. A decision was made to significantly increase the payments to our defenders. I can honestly say that it will be expensive. But there is nothing more precious than life and the struggle for our freedom and freedom of our next generations.

And there are those who will help us. This is already real. We get weapons, medicine, food, diesel, money. A strong international coalition in support of Ukraine has been formed. An anti-war coalition.

Here is the latest summary from the diplomatic frontline. There were very substantive talks with the Prime Minister of the Netherlands, the President of Georgia, the Prime Ministers of the Czech Republic and Slovakia, Prime Minister of the United Kingdom Johnson. Each conversation added specifics to the defence capabilities of our state and the strength of our military.

Germany has announced the supply of 1,000 anti-tank grenade launchers and 500 Stingers with additional ammunition. Belgium provides 5,000 machine guns and 5 million rounds of ammunition, and another 4,000 tons of fuel.

Thanks to active diplomacy, we've convinced all European countries to disconnect Russia from SWIFT. We thank President of Poland Andrzej Duda for his personal leadership in granting Ukraine membership in the European Union. Poland's daily assistance to our country is also very much needed.

We have to call a spade a spade. Russia's criminal actions against Ukraine show signs of genocide. I talked about this with the UN Secretary General. Russia is on the path of evil. The world must deprive Russia of the right to vote in the UN Security Council.

Ukrainians! We know exactly what we are defending. We will definitely win.

Glory to each of our soldiers! Glory to Ukraine!

# Address to the citizens
## 27 February 2022—18:10

I had a phone conversation with Alexander Lukashenko. We haven't spoken to him in two years. And today I had a long substantive conversation with him.

I explained to him in detail the impossibility of our clash. I do not want missiles, planes, helicopters to fly to Ukraine from Belarus. I do not want troops to go to Ukraine from Belarus. And he assured me of that.

My task as President is to protect our state. And you have seen during these tough days how we are fulfilling this task.

Alexander Lukashenko called on the meeting of the Ukrainian and Russian delegations on the Pripyat River. I emphasize without any conditions.

I will say frankly, as always: I do not really believe in the result of this meeting but let them try. So that no citizen of Ukraine would have any doubt that I, as President, did not try to stop the war when there was even a small chance.

And while our guys are there, the President is here, the Head of the Office is here, the Prime Minister is here, the army is here, the Commander-in-Chief is here. We will all defend our state and our borders.

You and I must act pragmatically to achieve our goal. And our goal is our territorial integrity. You have seen our position one hundred percent. This is the unconditional protection of national statehood.

As regards our motivation. It is obvious that our servicemen are fighting not for money, but for today, for tomorrow. And they provide a very tough response to what happened yesterday.

But we must understand that today the most important job is to be a soldier, to defend the country. And that's why I really want the state to pay decently for this job.

We will pay our armed servicemen a hundred thousand hryvnias a month. Not to hear "thank you" from them, but to let them know that the country is definitely grateful to them. And it will be so until this war is over.

And the last thing. Yesterday, unfortunately, we lost our "Mriya". But the old "Mriya". And we are building a new one now.

Glory to Ukraine!

## Stand firm
## 28 February 2022—11:00

Good morning, Ukrainian heroes! The fifth day of Russia's full-scale war against the people of Ukraine. We stand firm. During this time, we have experienced as much as other nations may not have in decades. We have been told for a long time that there is something wrong with Ukrainians in this or that issue. That Ukrainians have to do so-called "homework" for decades. Because of this, we often did not notice what we are really capable of. And now we have shown ourselves to the fullest. And it's inspiring. For everyone.

In every conversation with our partners, I hear sincere respect. Ukrainians have shown the world who we are. And Russia has shown what it has become. Just think about it: during the Russian invasion—in just four days—sixteen Ukrainian children died as a result of the Russian shelling. Sixteen! 45 children were wounded.

Every crime, every shelling that the invaders commit against us, unites us and our partners even more. Russia did not believe in such a solidary and powerful reaction. But

Ukrainians have changed that story. The European Union has decided to supply us with weapons. We are grateful. Yesterday I spoke with Ursula von der Leyen, President of the European Commission, about further, even stronger steps. Europeans are aware that our soldiers are fighting for our country and, consequently, for the whole of Europe. For peace for all European countries, for the lives of children, for equality, for democracy. And this gives us the full right to do the following.

We appeal to the European Union for Ukraine's immediate accession under a new special procedure. We are grateful to our partners for being with us. But our goal is to be with all Europeans and, most importantly, to be equal. I am confident that is fair. I am confident we deserve it. I am confident that all this is possible.

Yesterday I spoke with the Presidents of Portugal, Lithuania, President of France Emmanuel Macron and President of Poland Andrzej Duda. I am especially grateful to Andrzej Duda for our fruitful work. I spoke with the Prime Ministers of Belgium, Spain, and Prime Minister of the United Kingdom Boris Johnson. Support of our anti-war coalition is unconditional and unprecedented.

Europe has closed the sky to all Russian planes. Global business refuses any ties with Russian companies. Let's see how this week will end for the Russian currency—what will be the fall of the ruble. If this criminal invasion of Ukraine continues, the Russian state is suffering losses as if the war passed through their territory. Do you need all this? Russian mothers, Russian teachers, Russian entrepreneurs, ordinary people. For what?

Four and a half thousand Russian soldiers have already been killed. Why did you all come here? Why do the columns of your armoured vehicles go against us? From our Crimea. From Yalta, Yevpatoriya, Sudak, Simferopol... These are not the names of military camps for tankers. Once again: four and a half thousand Russian invaders killed. Throw away your equipment. And leave. Do not believe your commanders. Do not believe your propagandists. Just save your lives. Leave.

We dedicate every hour to strengthening our state. Anyone who can join the fight against the invaders must do so. Therefore, a decision was made—not easy from a moral point of view, but useful from the point of view of our protection. Under martial law, participants in hostilities—Ukrainians with real combat experience—will be released from custody and will be able to compensate for their guilt in the hottest spots of war. All sanctions are lifted from some people who took part in the anti-terrorist operation. The key now is defence.

When I ran for presidency, I said that each of us is the President. Because we are all responsible for our state. For our beautiful Ukraine. And now it turns out that each of us is a warrior. The warrior in his or her own place. And I am confident that each of us will win.

Glory to Ukraine!

## Address to the citizens
## 28 February 2022—23:48

Russian forces today brutally shelled Kharkiv with rocket artillery. This is definitely a military crime. A peaceful city. Peaceful residential areas. No military objects. Dozens of eyewitness records prove that this is not a separate false shot, it is a conscious destruction of people. Russians knew where they were shooting.

For this crime there will definitely be a tribunal. International. This is a breach of all conventions. No one in the world will forgive you the murder of peaceful Ukrainian people. Here is Ukraine. Here is Europe. Here is 2022. Evil, armed with rockets, bombs and artillery, must be stopped immediately. Destroyed economically. We must show that humanity is able to protect themselves. I believe that it is necessary to consider the full closure of the sky for Russian missiles, airplanes, helicopters. In five days of invasion, already 56 missile strikes have been carried out against Ukraine. 113 cruise missiles were fired. This is their "fraternal friendship". And the world knows what to do. I spoke about this with partners today.

The state committing military crimes against civilians cannot be a member of the UN Security Council. The entrance to all ports, channels, airports in the world must be closed for this state. Such a state must not receive hundreds of billions for energy exports. Buying Russian goods now is to pay money for murdering people.

Peaceful, proud, strong Kharkiv. You have always been such. You will always be such. We will withstand this as well. We will defend Ukraine. We will help everyone affected by inhuman invasion. Chernihiv, Okhtyrka, Sumy, Hostomel, Vasylkiv, Kherson, Mariupol, Donetsk and all other cities and towns of our native country will see a peaceful and safe life. Sincere condolences to all who lost their relatives and loved ones in this war. Eternal memory to those who died. Eternal glory to everyone who defends our freedom!

Before addressing you, I signed a decree on awarding the title of the Hero of Ukraine to twelve our defenders:

Lieutenant Colonel Eduard Mykolayovych Vahorovsky (posthumously). He died saving our aircraft from a missile strike. Gave others the opportunity to take to the air.

Major Dmytro Valeriyovych Kolomiets (posthumously). He rescued his brothers-in- arms, diverted enemy aircraft fire and was shot down by an enemy plane.

Lieutenant Colonel Hennadiy Vasyliovych Matulyak

(posthumously). Hostomel. Destroyed the group of enemy equipment.

Lieutenant Vitaliy Anatoliyovych Movchan (posthumously). In an air battle he destroyed two enemy aircraft.

Colonel Oleksandr Yakovych Oksanchenko (posthumously). He died in an air battle, distracting enemy aircraft.

Senior Lieutenant Vyacheslav Denysovych Radionov (posthumously). Thanks to his courageous actions, the entire crew of the brigade's planes took to the air in Vasylkiv, and this saved ours from a missile strike.

Senior Lieutenant Andriy Andriyovych Gerus. Over the city of Kropyvnytskyi he shot down an enemy IL-76, which prevented the landing of Russian troops with weapons.

Brigadier General Dmytro Serhiyovych Krasylnykov, Commander of the Operational and Tactical Group "North". For two days he has been fighting off the continuous assault, saved people and equipment. And did not let the enemy into Kharkiv from the Luhansk region.

Lieutenant Colonel Andriy Mykolayovych Kruhlov. He withdrew the Buk SAM unit from the enemy attacks and personally destroyed two Russian helicopters and one plane.

Colonel Oleksandr Volodymyrovych Mostov. He shot down a Russian IL-76 near Vasylkiv, as well as two Mi-24 helicopters, which prevented the landing of paratroopers and weapons.

Lieutenant General Yuri Ivanovych Sodol. In the battles for Volnovakha, he saved our men from the encirclement and organized a successful counterattack. He brought people out of the enemy's attack. Defends Mariupol extremely effectively.

Colonel of medical service Eduard Mykolayovych Khoroshun. He personally organized the defence of the besieged military medical centre and carried out the evacuation of the wounded.

Now about Kyiv, our beautiful capital, the basis of our

state, our security. For an enemy, Kyiv is the key target. They want to break our national statehood. Therefore, the capital is constantly in danger. Three rocket-bombing strikes are carried out only today. TETs-6 is the target. They want to damage a power station and leave our city without light. We did not allow them to break the defence of the capital. And they send saboteurs to us. Constantly. Hundreds. All they are being neutralized.

In addition to defence, we are thinking about the rear as well. Provide people with everything necessary. We formed a round-the-clock coordination headquarters that collects all requests from regional administrations regarding the lack of the most necessary stuff. Products, medicines, fuel, equipment. The headquarters directly finds suppliers that can quickly and qualitatively meet such needs. This is the restoration of supply chains, interrupted by the war.

Today, at the initiative of the Russian side, the first round of negotiations between Ukraine and Russia took place. These negotiations took place against the background of bombing and shelling of our territory, our cities. Synchronization of shelling with a negotiation process could be seen. I believe that Russia is trying to put pressure on us in such a way. Don't waste time. We do not perceive such tactics. Fair negotiations are possible when one side does not hit the other side with rocket artillery precisely at the moment of negotiations.

So far, we do not have the result we would like to get. Russia has declared its position. We have outlined positions in response—to end the war. Some signals we received.

When the delegation returns to Kyiv, we will analyse what we've heard and then determine how to move to the second round of negotiations.

Another thing that is very important to say. We've been waiting 30 years for this. Today I signed an application for Ukraine's membership in the European Union. We have gained the right to be together with everyone in Europe. The application has already been delivered to Brussels, officially registered. The time has come.

Glory to Ukraine!

# The missile at the central square of Kharkiv is terrorism, and Russia must be held accountable for this in international courts
1 March 2022—12:37

Kharkiv. A cruise missile strike. At the largest square of Europe. Freedom Square. Dozens of victims. This is what the price of freedom is. This is what the morning of the people of Ukraine is.

Ukrainian Kharkiv and Russian Belgorod have always been close cities. In many ways. Even the border between them was only conditional, only on maps, but not in the soul. Not in the soul. Now everything has changed. After the cruise missile that struck Kharkiv from Belgorod. The missile that hit Freedom Square. The face of our Kharkiv. This is terror against the city. There was no military target on the square. Just as in those residential areas of Kharkiv hit by rocket artillery. The rocket aimed at the central square is an outright, undisguised terror. No one will forgive. No one will forget.

This attack on Kharkiv is a war crime. This is state terrorism of the Russian Federation. After that, Russia is a terrorist state. Obviously. And it must be official. We call on all countries of the world to respond immediately and effectively to this criminal tactic of the aggressor and to declare that Russia is committing state terrorism. We demand full responsibility for terrorists in international courts.

Kharkiv and Kyiv are currently the most important targets for Russia. Terror is meant to break us. To break our resistance. They are heading to our capital, as well as to Kharkiv. Therefore, the defence of the capital today is the key priority for the state. All cities of Ukraine must do everything to stop the enemy. The military and civilian authorities of each city are responsible for this. But Kyiv is special. If we protect Kyiv, we will protect the state. This is the heart of our country. And it must keep beating. And it will keep beating. So that life triumphs.

Dear Kyiv residents! Defence of the capital is above all. That's why I decided to appoint a professional military person as the Head of the Kyiv City Military Administration for the period of war. To guarantee the defence of the city. To block the enemy's approaches to our capital. To ensure that the people of Kyiv have everything they need. The Head of the Military Administration will be General Mykola Mykolayovych Zhyrnov, who served as commander of the support forces. At a high level he organized the engineering support of combat operations of the Armed Forces of Ukraine in 2014- 2015. He is currently a state expert of the Military Security Service at the National Security and Defence Council. Vitali Klitschko remains mayor of Kyiv. He will have his own sphere of responsibility. And now it is a joint work of the mayor and the Head of the Military Administration. After the war, we will return everything to its place in the capital.

Regarding our diplomats. Right now, our diplomats are implementing fair and necessary decisions in relation to those states that have betrayed their word and international law. We immediately recall the Ambassador from Kyrgyzstan for consultations. For justifying aggression against Ukraine. We immediately recall the Ambassador from Georgia. For the obstacles to volunteers who want to help us. For an immoral attitude towards sanctions.

And now I want to speak about those whose feat is an example of the highest moral strength. These are our doctors. You save people around the clock. Always. And now your work is one of the key lines of our defence. You keep it brilliant. Thousands of lives have been saved in 5 days. I am also grateful to everyone who provides our people with everything they need for life in these extremely difficult conditions. Food, energy, medicine. And I thank the ordinary people of Ukraine, who stop tanks with their bare hands, expel the invaders from administrative buildings by force of spirit and make their stay in Ukraine shameful. To prove that they are all strangers here. This is what the people's war is. This is what the people of Ukraine is.

Glory to Ukraine!

## Address: Ukrainians are a symbol of invincibility
## 2 March 2022—09:32

Good health to you, united country! I did not accidentally say "united". The seventh day of this terrible war began. A war we feel the same way. During this time, we have had more unity than for over thirty years before. At first, we were equally scared, then we felt equally painful. And now we do not care. Except for victory. Except for the truth. Except for peace. Except for the tranquillity we want to achieve. Except for the lives of our people, for whom we are worried. Except for Ukraine. During this time, we have truly become one. We forgave each other a lot. We started loving each other. We help each other. We are worried for each other. Yesterday morning on Freedom Square, we were all Kharkiv residents. Then the enemy destroyed us all by striking at residential buildings in Borodyanka. We were all bombed in Kyiv last night. And we all died again in Babyn Yar—from a missile strike. Although the whole world promises constantly—never again.

For any normal person who knows history, Babyn Yar is a special part of Kyiv. A special part of Europe. A place of prayer. A place of remembrance for the hundred thousand people killed by the Nazis. The place of old Kyiv cemeteries. Who should you be to make it a target for missiles? You are killing Holocaust victims for the second time. During the Soviet era, a TV centre was built on the bones there. And also, a sports complex. Outbuildings. They built a park there. To erase the true history of Babyn Yar. But why was it bombed? This is beyond humanity. Such a missile strike shows that for many people in Russia, our Kyiv is completely foreign. They know nothing about our capital. About our history. But they have an order to erase our history. Erase our country. Erase us all. On the first day of the war, Uman was brutally bombed, where hundreds of thousands of Jews come every year to pray. Then—Babyn Yar, where hundreds of thousands of Jews were executed. I am now addressing all the Jews of the world—don't you see what is happening? That is why it is very important that millions of Jews around the world do not remain silent right now. Nazism is born in silence. So, shout about the killings of civilians. Shout about the killings of Ukrainians.

Last night and tonight they continued to bomb our cities. Bombs. Missiles. Artillery. Machine guns. Targeting peaceful people. Again. Targeting residential areas. Again. Mariupol, Kharkiv, Kyiv, Zhytomyr and other cities and towns of Ukraine. This cannot be explained by any human reason. Any reason of God. What then, if Babyn Yar was attacked? What other military facilities threaten Russia? What other "NATO bases"?

Saint Sophia Cathedral? Lavra? St. Andrew's Church?

Whatever they dream of there—damn them! Because God is with us!

During this time, we have united the European Union already on a new level. Higher than formal. Higher than interstate. At the level of ordinary people. Millions and millions of Europeans. From the Atlantic Ocean to the suburbs of Kharkiv, where fierce fighting continues. When the European Parliament stood and applauded us, our struggle, it was an assessment of our efforts. Our unity. Six days of war like thirty years. That is why the European Union answers "yes" to us. We have started a special accelerated accession procedure. Our diplomats and our friends unite the world for the sake of Ukraine and peace even more. Neutral Switzerland has supported EU sanctions against Russian oligarchs, officials, the state and companies. Once again: neutral Switzerland! So, what do some other countries expect? Our anti-war coalition has already been joined by the countries that Moscow relied on a week ago. This is an extraordinary result. You can't stay neutral right now!

And what is the result for Russia? The flag of this state will no longer be seen in sports tournaments. Modern world culture will now be closed to them. Russian goods are being removed from store shelves around the world. Russian banks are disconnected from the global system. Russian citizens are losing their savings, losing all prospects. Russian mothers are losing their children in a completely foreign country. Think of this number: almost six thousand Russians died. Russian military. In six days of war. This is without counting the losses of the enemy last night. Six thousand. To get what? Get Ukraine? It is impossible. This is not to be changed by missiles. Bombs. Tanks.

Any blows. We are on our native land. And for the war against us there will be an International Tribunal for them.

Ukrainians! Another night of Russia's full-scale war against us, against the people, has passed. Hard night. Someone spent that night in the subway—in a shelter. Someone spent it in the basement. Someone was luckier and slept at home. Others were sheltered by friends and relatives. We've hardly slept for seven nights. Or we sleep, but anxiously. My dears, the time will come when we will be able to sleep. But it will be after the war. After the victory. In a peaceful country, as we need. Which we have always appreciated. And which we have never destroyed. I ask all of you to take care of your loved ones. Take care of your brothers-in-arms. I admire you! The whole world admires you. From Hollywood stars to politicians. Today you, Ukrainians, are a symbol of invincibility. A symbol that people in any country can become the best people on earth at any moment.

Glory to Ukraine!


## For us, this is a patriotic war, and we know how such wars end for the invaders
3 March 2022—01:14


Good health to you, dear Ukrainians! Strong and kind! But — kind NOT to enemies.

We are a nation that broke the enemy's plans in a week. Plans that have been built for years. Treacherously. Deliberately. With hatred of our country, of our people—of any people who have heart and freedom. But we stopped them. We beat them. Our military, border guards, territorial defence. Even ordinary farmers capture the Russian military on a daily basis. And they all say one thing: they don't know why they're here. Even though their quantity is ten times bigger, the morale of the enemy is deteriorating. More and more invaders are fleeing back to Russia. From us. From you.

From all who drive out the enemy with javelins, stugnas, guns, tanks, planes, helicopters. Everything that shoots.

But Ukrainians are beating the enemy even without weapons. I sincerely admire the heroic civilians of Konotop, Bashtanka, Energodar, Melitopol. Other towns and villages. Who do not let the invaders in by blocking the roads? People come out in front of enemy vehicles. This is extremely dangerous. But this is brave. It is also salvation.

I'm sure you saw a video from Melitopol where Ukrainians protested against Russians who entered our city. Temporarily. I am sure of this: if they entered somewhere, it is only temporarily. We'll drive them out. With shame. As those people, ordinary people who drive the invaders out of grocery stores when the Russian soldiers are trying to find food do. These are not warriors of the superpower. These are confused children who were used. Take them home.

Ukrainians! Every invader should know they will not get anything here. No one will be conquered. Even if they can accumulate more equipment and more people, it doesn't change anything for them. Wherever they enter. They will be destroyed everywhere.

They will not have peace. They will have no food. They will not have a single quiet moment. The invaders will receive only a rebuff from Ukrainians. Fierce rebuff. Such a rebuff that they will forever remember that we will not give up what's ours. That they will remember what the patriotic war is. Yes, for us it is a patriotic war. We remember how patriotic wars begin. And we know how they end. For the invaders.

Our army is doing everything to break the enemy completely. Almost nine thousand Russians were killed! In one week! In the Mykolaiv direction invaders have to take away the "two hundred" and "three hundred" with tens of helicopters. 19 years, 20 years ... What did they see in life, apart from this invasion? But most of them remain everywhere. Ukraine does not want to be covered with military corpses. Go home.

Your whole army. Tell your commanders that you want to live. Not to die. To live. The war must be stopped, and peace restored as soon as possible.

Today was, as usual, an active day of negotiations with the leaders of the member states of our anti-war coalition. I held talks with the heads of government of Norway and Israel. With the President of Kazakhstan. With the Emir of Qatar Tamim Bin Hamad al Thani. With President of the European Council Charles Michel. With Prime Minister of Canada Justin Trudeau. With President of Poland Andrzej Duda. Brilliant result at the UN General Assembly. 141 countries supported the resolution, which calls on Russia to withdraw troops from Ukraine immediately. 141 states stand for us! And for Russia—only four states that voted against. Here is the list: North Korea, Eritrea, Syria and Belarus. This is the list. These are the friends. And there will be no others for the state that does not know how-to live-in peace.

Today I held a meeting with the heads of regions and cities of Ukraine. The new head of the Odesa regional state administration is already working. Maksym Marchenko. Military. Professional. Our guys on the ground are working hard to organize "green corridors". To take out civilians. To bring medicine. Volnovakha, cities of the Kyiv, Sumy, Kharkiv regions, south of Ukraine. This is very difficult. Extremely difficult. We are opposed by terror. But terror loses. Thanks to our heroes.

Today I signed a decree awarding the title of Hero of Ukraine to fifteen of our defenders:

Senior Lieutenant Maksym Vitaliyovych Bilokon. Posthumously. He took part in repelling the enemy's attack during the defence of Chernihiv, destroyed the enemy's subversive group and two enemy tanks.

Lieutenant Colonel Oleksandr Valeriyovych Kapichun. Posthumously. Thanks to his heroic actions, the enemy column was stopped, equipment and enemy soldiers were destroyed.

Soldier Oleksandr Volodymyrovych Lukyanovych. Posthumously. During the battle he neutralized up to three dozen units of enemy equipment. He was fatally wounded by an air strike.

Junior Sergeant Mykhailo Mykhailovych Nesolyony. Posthumously. He died in close combat with enemy forces while evacuating people.

Soldier Andriy Valeriyovych Nikonchuk. Posthumously. He protected the Kyiv HPP from Russian air raids and missile strikes.

Lieutenant Vitalii Romanoviyh Sapyl. Posthumously. Tank platoon commander. Neutralized three dozen enemy vehicles. Killed by an air strike.

Chief Sergeant Oleksiy Oleksandrovych Senyuk. Posthumously. He defended Chernihiv, destroyed two enemy IFVs and captured a T-72 tank. Killed by an air strike.

Lieutenant Vladyslav Petrovych Ukrainets. Posthumously. He covered the retreat of brothers-in-arms when the enemy attacked.

Major Stepan Ivanovych Choban. Posthumously. The pilot of the Su-27 distracted the enemy aircraft over Kropyvnytskyi.

Major Ihor Vasyliovych Mykhalchuk. Head of the tank battalion unit. Destroyed numerous enemy armored vehicles.

Colonel Serhiy Mykolayovych Musienko. Head of the Missile and Artillery Division. Inflicted devastating blows on the enemy in the Kharkiv direction.

Lieutenant Yevhen Mykhailovych Palchenko. Tank platoon commander. Covered the exit of the brigade from the encirclement.

Major Vladyslav Yuriyovych Prokopenko. Head of the tank battalion. Withdrew personnel and equipment from the encirclement without loss.

Lieutenant Colonel Pavlo Yuriyovych Fedosenko. Head of the unit of the 92nd brigade. For the effective defence of Kharkiv.

Senior Lieutenant Dmytro Petrovych Chavalakh. For heroic participation in the defence of the Kherson region.

All 40 million are like these fifteen heroes!

## Glory to Ukraine! They wanted to destroy Ukraine so many times, but failed
### 3 March 2022—11:20

Unbreakable people of invincible Ukraine!

Exactly two years ago, the first case of COVID-19 was recorded in Ukraine. The first weeks of fighting it were extremely difficult. But we were united, and therefore strong, and therefore we withstood. Exactly a week ago, Ukraine was attacked by another virus. Another disease. By those who suffer from severe annexation and occupation of foreign lands. One week ago, at 4 am, Russia invaded our independent Ukraine, our land. Acute fit of aggression, megalomania, delusion of persecution. Heavy psychological complexes and as a result—missile systems. Rocket artillery. Tanks and other armoured vehicles—simply like locusts. The first hours and days of full-scale war were extremely difficult. But we were united, and therefore strong, and therefore we withstood. And it will be so. And we will continue to stand.

We stand so that the invaders were forced to change tactics. Russia's missile and bomb strikes at Ukrainian cities are a confession that they could not do anything significant on land. All lines of our defence are preserved. The enemy has no success in any of the strategic directions. They are demoralized. They are doomed. Kyiv survived this night and withstood another missile and bomb strike. Our air defence worked. Kherson, Izyum, all other cities where the invaders carried out strikes from the air, did not give up anything. Chernihiv, Sumy, Mykolaiv holds the line. Odesa. They also want to destroy Odesa. But they will see only the bottom of the Black Sea. The target of Russia was the Assumption Cathedral in Kharkiv. One of the oldest Orthodox monuments of the city, monuments of Ukraine. During the war, the cathedral is a shelter for Kharkiv residents. Shelter for all people: believers and non-believers. For everyone, because everyone is equal. Holy place. Now it is damaged by war. They are not afraid of even that! They enjoy the fact that God does not give an instant rebuff. But he sees. And he answers. Answers so that you cannot hide. There is no such bunker to survive God's response. And we will restore the cathedral so that no trace of war remains there. And even if you destroy all our cathedrals and churches, you will not destroy our sincere faith in God, in Ukraine. Faith in people. We will restore every house, every street, every city. And we say to Russia: learn the words "reparations" and "contributions".

You will repay everything you did against Ukraine. In full. And we will not forget those who perished, and God won't.

You have come to destroy our cities. Destroy our people. Take away from us everything that is dear to us. You cut off electricity, water and heating to civilians in Ukraine. You leave people without food and medicine. You are shelling routes of possible evacuation. There is no weapon that you would not use against us, against the free citizens of Ukraine. And now you are telling your propagandists that you are going to send so-called humanitarian columns to Ukraine... Remember, godless men: when millions of people curse you, you have nothing to save yourself.

Ukrainians in all war-torn regions will receive everything they need from us. Coordination headquarters are working in full. Real humanitarian goods are on the way. Our government has already prepared a program of special assistance for all Ukrainians who have lost the opportunity to work. Now. Because of the war. Where there is fighting! Every employee, every sole proprietor, every citizen of ours, from whom Russia has taken away the opportunity to work, will receive six and a half thousand hryvnias without any conditions. I especially emphasize this for older Ukrainians. Despite the war, we ensure full payment of pensions. Indexed pensions. As it should be in accordance with the law. From March 1, pensions for Ukrainians are indexed by 14%. The money has already gone to the banks. All payments will be made in full.

Ukraine receives weapons from its partners on a daily basis. From real friends. More and more powerful weapons every day. Ukraine is already meeting foreign volunteers who are going to our country. The first of sixteen thousand. They are going to defend freedom. Defend life. For us. For all. And it will be successful. I'm sure.

We have survived in our history and on our land two world wars, three Holodomors, the Holocaust, Babyn Yar, the Great Terror, the Chornobyl explosion, the occupation of Crimea and the war in the east. We do not have a huge territory—from ocean to ocean, we do not have nuclear weapons, we do not fill the world market with oil and gas. But we have our people and our land. And for us—it's gold. That is what we are fighting for. We have nothing to lose but our own freedom and dignity. For us, this is the greatest treasure. They wanted to destroy us so many times. They failed. They wanted to wipe us off the face of the earth. They failed. They backstabbed us. And we are on our feet. They wanted us to be silent. But the whole world heard us. We've been through so much! And if someone thinks that having overcome all this, Ukrainians—all of us—are scared, broken or will surrender, he knows nothing about Ukraine. And he has nothing to do in Ukraine. Go home. To your home. Protect Russian-speaking people. Not all over the world. In your country. There are almost 150 million of them. And here...

Glory to Ukraine!

# We have survived the night that could have stopped the history of Ukraine and Europe
## 4 March 2022—11:21

People of Ukraine!

We have survived the night that could have stopped history. History of Ukraine. History of Europe.

Russian troops attacked the Zaporizhzhia nuclear power plant. The largest in Europe. It alone could be like six Chornobyl's. Russian tankers knew what they were firing at.

Direct aiming at the station. This is terror of an unprecedented level.

There are 15 nuclear units in Ukraine. And the Russian servicemen have completely forgotten about Chornobyl. About this world tragedy.

Russian people, I want to address you. How is that even possible? Together in 1986 we struggled with the consequences of the Chornobyl disaster. You must remember the burning graphite scattered by the explosion. Victims. You must remember the glow above the destroyed power unit. You must remember the evacuation from Pripyat and the 30 km zone. How could you forget it? And if you have not forgotten, then you cannot be silent. You must tell your authorities, go to the streets, and say that you want to live. To live on earth without radioactive contamination. Radiation does not know where the border of Russia is.

All night I was in touch with partners, with the leaders of other countries, so that the world could react. I felt that the world leaders were shocked. Britain is convening a UN Security Council over the attack. The IAEA is launching its 24-Hour Incident and Emergency Center. Immediate sanctions against the nuclear terrorist state are needed. Immediate closure of the sky over Ukraine is needed, because only this can guarantee that Russia will not strike at least missiles and air bombs at nuclear facilities.

I am grateful to our heroes from the National Guard who guarded the station and tried to stop the enemy. I am grateful to the rescuers who extinguished the fire. But a lot depends on the common people of Energodar. You understand the threat to the station better than anyone else. You live there. Next to it. And you see the invaders directly.

Drive them away. Let them know that Energodar is Ukraine. That Ukraine is not a place for nuclear ashes.

Ukrainians! The enemy has brought the vast majority of its troops into the territory of our state. Almost the entire Russian army is thrown against our people. But the heroic resistance of Ukrainians has been saving our country from this invasion for the ninth day. Ukrainian cities have not seen such inhuman cruelty since the Nazi occupation.

Chernihiv, Okhtyrka, Kharkiv, Mariupol. They are purposefully destroying civilian infrastructure. Destroying people. Residential neighbourhoods. Just yesterday, Russian bombs killed 47 people in Chernihiv. Peaceful people. Kharkiv... Kharkiv is simply being destroyed by rocket artillery and air strikes. Russia. Destroys. Kharkiv. How could this happen? This morning in Zhytomyr, the rocket hit the school building. Hit children. This is the reality when "fraternal" Russia comes.

Yesterday, during talks in Belarus, we managed to agree on the creation of humanitarian corridors where people suffer the most. Today we will see whether the agreement works.

Our defence inflicts maximum losses on the enemy. Almost 9,200 invaders were killed. As of the morning of the ninth day of the war. We beat them near Mykolaiv. We beat them near Kharkiv. We beat them near Kyiv. The capital remains a key target for the invaders. But they will not break us, they will not break our statehood. Never. No matter what they do, they will still lose. Because we are at home. We are on our own land.

They are constantly preparing provocations. A provocation is being prepared in Kherson. They are going to put up a performance of a kind of rally for Russia. To do this, they brought strangers to the city. They are looking for local traitors. They want to make a TV picture as if Kherson is no longer Ukrainian. I want to remind you that this is how they started the so-called "DPR" and "LPR". You understand what happened to them later. This must be stopped. Kherson residents, show that this is your city. You can stop everything, any plan of the invaders. Do not listen to anyone—listen to your children, listen to your heart. You are Ukrainians.

I urge Kherson residents to get rid of any despair. Ukraine will not give up what is ours. We are fighting against a powerful enemy that outnumbers us. Which outnumbers us in the amount of equipment. But which is thousands of light years away from normal people who have dignity. Show it. Our national flag. Our national anthem. Our national spirit. Be sure to let the occupiers know that they can only be in Kherson temporarily. And they will never be able to own Kherson. Like any other city in Ukraine. Let the occupiers know that they can only stay in Kherson temporarily.

And they will never be able to own your city, Kherson. Like any other Ukrainian city—the city of our state.

Glory to Ukraine!

We continue to fight; we will protect our state and liberate our land thanks to our heroes.
4 March 2022—23:06

Great people of a great country!

A country of power. A country of freedom. The people of absolute moral leadership.

We have endured nine days of darkness. Nine days of evil. This is three times more than darkness and evil expected.

We responded to the invasion as we can in times of greatest danger. Responded with heroism. Solidarity. Mutual assistance. We responded in Ukrainian. So that the history of Europe will remember it forever. It will tell children about it. Show it to grandchildren.

The whole continent will know the city of Kharkiv. The city of Chernihiv. The city of Sumy. The city of Volnovakha. The city of Mariupol. The city of Mykolaiv. And many other of our beautiful cities. Living cities! Cities that have withstood the worst invasion since World War II.

I say this specifically as a fait accompli. Withstood. No matter what the situation is at the moment, strategically, everything is clear.

Ukrainians are united from Uzhhorod to Kharkiv, from Kyiv to Kherson. Ukrainians are chasing the enemy near Kyiv. They are beating him for Okhtyrka. Punishing him for Hostomel. They will take revenge for Kherson. Our Kherson! Ukrainian Kherson. Which they tried to humiliate today.

They failed. They were not allowed. Ukrainians have shown themselves.

They did not allow themselves to be deceived in a cheap cynical show. With a handout instead of help. With propaganda instead of sincerity.

Russian propagandists thought of our people as of themselves. And they saw that Kherson residents are proud. And respect themselves. Respect Ukraine.

I understand how difficult the decision is. When in the occupation they come out against armed enemies.

I feel how risky it is.


But I see how our people refuse to play by the rules of the invaders. How our people remain Ukrainians. How our people stay with our state, even temporarily finding themselves in the darkness.

If Russian politicians still have their eyes, they will be able to see what Ukraine is. What our freedom is.

The invaders thought they could turn off our television to Ukrainians. Our connection. They thought they could take away products, shut off the electricity. They thought it would force Ukrainians to submit.

But even if you deprive us of oxygen, we will breathe deeply, to say: get out of our land! Even in complete darkness we see the truth.

And we will fight until it darkens in our eyes.


Because we are the warriors of light. And today no one on Earth will be able to say that this line is pathos.

The 9th day of the war. Many of us have a tradition to remember those who are not with us on the 9th day.

Eternal memory to everyone who died for Ukraine!


Unfortunately, today there is a complete impression that it is time to give a funeral repast for something else:

Security guarantees and promises. Determination of alliances. Values that seem to be dead for someone.

The NATO summit took place today. Weak summit. Confused summit.

Summit, which shows that not everyone considers the struggle for freedom to be Europe's number one goal.

All NATO intelligence offices are well aware of the enemy's plans. They also confirmed that Russia wants to continue the offensive. As best it can.

For 9 days we have seen a brutal war. They are destroying our cities. They are shelling our people, our children, and residential neighbourhoods. Churches. Schools. They destroy everything that ensures a normal life. And they want to continue it.

Knowing that new strikes and casualties are inevitable, NATO deliberately decided NOT to close the sky over Ukraine.

We believe that NATO countries themselves have created a narrative that the closure of the sky over Ukraine would provoke Russia's direct aggression against NATO.

This is self-hypnosis. Of those who are weak, underconfident. Internally. Although they may have weapons many times more powerful than ours.

You had to think about people. About humanity itself. And what did you think about at that summit?

All the people who will die starting from this day will also die because of you.

Because of your weakness. Because of your disunity.

All the Alliance has managed to do so far is to carry fifty tons of diesel fuel for Ukraine through its procurement system. Probably so that we can burn the Budapest Memorandum. To make it burn better.

But it is already burnt for us. In the fire of Russian troops.

64

Is this NATO we wanted? Is this the Alliance you were building?

Today, the Alliance's leadership gave the green light for further bombing of Ukrainian cities by refusing to make a no-fly zone.

You could close our sky. But...

I do not know who you can protect and whether you can protect NATO countries.

You will not be able to buy us off with litres of fuel for litres of our blood. Shed for our common Europe. For our common freedom. For our common future.

But I am also grateful to our country's friends in NATO. There are many countries of our friends, our partners—most of the powerful partners. Those who help our state no matter what. From the first day of the invasion. And I'm sure, until the victory.

And that's why we do NOT feel alone.

We continue to fight. We will protect our state. We will liberate our land. Thanks to our heroes.

I awarded decorations and medals to 76 Ukrainian heroes for personal courage and selfless actions for our defence. Unfortunately, 37 of them are awarded posthumously.

I awarded the title of Hero of Ukraine to Lieutenant General Oleksandr Oleksiyovych Pavliuk, Commander of the Joint Forces Operation.

I conferred the military rank of Brigadier General on Colonel Volodymyr Vasyliovych Shvorak, Deputy Commander of the East Operational Command of the Land Forces of the Armed Forces of Ukraine.

I conferred the military rank of Brigadier General of Justice on Colonel of Justice Serhiy Mykolayovych Melnyk, Head of the Military Law Institute of the Yaroslav the Wise National Law University.

I conferred the military rank of Brigadier General on Colonel Artem Yevhenovych Bohomolov, Deputy Commander of the West Operational Command.

I conferred the military rank of General on Valerii Fedorovych Zaluzhnyi, Commander-in-Chief of the Armed Forces of Ukraine.

Glory to Ukraine!

## I am sure that soon we will be able to tell our people: come back, because there is no more threat.
5 March 2022—11:22

Free people of a free country!

It is already the tenth day of our national struggle. Sincere faith. And round-the-clock work.

The tenth day is like one infinitely long day. One infinitely long night that does not allow us to have a rest.

Today is Saturday. Saturday. This word means nothing during the war. Like Monday or Thursday or any other day. They all became the same.

We still protect the state. We still save people.

The country does not know weekends anymore. It doesn't matter what time it is. It doesn't matter what date it is. And it will be so until victory.

Late at night I spoke with French President Emmanuel

Macron. And with President of Poland Andrzej Duda. Our interaction is constant. Our conversations are daily. I am immensely grateful to each of them. I am immensely grateful to Andrzej for his determination and devotion to our common cause. Protection of people. I am grateful to Andrzej's wife— Agata. They are friends whom I sincerely consider friends and sincerely wish to everyone.

We managed to prevent a humanitarian crisis at the border. We managed to organize the situation so that thousands and thousands of Ukrainian women and children were treated decently. Nobody asks about their nationality, faith or how much money they have. In fact, we no longer have a border with Poland. Because we are together on the side of good. We do not have time for borders.

I am sure that soon we will be able to tell our people: come back! Come back from Poland, Romania, Slovakia, and all other countries. Come back because there is no more threat.

We are already thinking about the future. For all Ukrainians. After the war. About how to revive our cities. How to revive the economy. I spoke with World Bank President David Malpass, IMF Managing Director Kristalina Georgieva.

We have an agreement among the largest financial institutions to support Ukraine. There is already a decision on emergency aid and tens of billions of dollars for the reconstruction of Ukraine after the war.

And these are only the first decisions. I emphasize these are only the first. I spoke with Turkish President Erdogan. I spoke with the leaders of Saudi Arabia and the United Arab Emirates. I spoke with President of the European Council Charles Michel and President of the European Commission Ursula von der Leyen. The main topic is EU membership for Ukraine.

I am grateful to Europeans—hundreds of thousands of people in different cities of our continent. Bratislava, Vilnius, Frankfurt, Lyon, Paris, Tbilisi, Prague. They came out yesterday in support of Ukraine. In support of Europe. They came out for peace to be reached as soon as possible.

I am grateful to Americans for the unwavering bipartisan majority of ordinary people. We saw the poll. We saw the opinion of ordinary people in America who support ordinary people in Ukraine. Who demand tougher sanctions against Russia for aggression already now? Who support closing the sky now to save the lives of our people? 74 percent of Americans stand for the no-fly zone. 74! The vast majority. What else is needed to make a decision? We are sure that the result is similar in other democratic countries.

The Armed Forces of Ukraine bravely hold all key areas of our defence.

They are counterattacking the invaders near Kharkiv—defending the city. They are holding the line in Mykolaiv. Kyiv, Chernihiv region, Sumy region, Donbas. We inflict losses on the invaders they have not seen in their worst dreams.

The Russian army has not reached the planned frontiers. Yet it has reached almost 10 thousand Russian soldiers killed. 10 thousand. This is dreadful! 18-year-old, 20-year- old boys. Very young, almost children. Soldiers who were not even explained why they were going to fight. For what and why they are in a foreign land.

10 thousand. Russia could definitely give these people something else. Instead of death.

The Ukrainian people are resisting even where the invaders managed to pass. Unfortunately. But not for long. I admire every Ukrainian who is not silent. Who protests? Who takes the national flag and shows the Russian military that they will lose? They will definitely lose. Because it is impossible to win against people who stop military equipment without weapons in their hands. Who refuse to take anything from the hands of the invaders? Whose situation is tough and dangerous. But they do not lose their dignity. And will never lose it.

At the talks in Belarus, the groups agreed on the first step. To bring back at least one percent of humanity from the normal level. Surrounded cities that are being destroyed and experiencing the worst days. Humanitarian corridors must work today. Mariupol and Volnovakha. To save people. Women, children, the elderly. To give food and medicine to those who remain. Our help is already on the way. Everyone who needs help should be able to leave. Those who are willing. Everyone who can defend their city must continue to fight. Must. Because if everyone leaves, then whose city will it be?

We are doing everything—on our part—to make the agreement work. This is one of the main tasks for today. Let's see if we can go further. In the negotiation process.

Let's pray for our military. Let's help our civilians. Let's work for peace.

Glory to Ukraine!

# Ukrainians do not retreat, do not give up, do not stop the resistance
# 5 March 2022—21:40

Our free people!

You are now at the height of your spirit. At the maximum of possibilities. Every soldier on the lines of defence. Every doctor who saves lives. Every firefighter who extinguishes fire. Every entrepreneur who continues to work. Dozens and dozens of other professions. Millions of people, which became one whole. Superpower of the spirit.

Programmers who joined the information troops. Everyone

who joined the territorial defence. Teachers and educators who do not leave children. Police officers. Civil servants. We all withstood the blow together. We will all rebuild our state together.

What gives us this confidence? Where is it from? It's not just words. It's not just faith. This is our reality. Unconditional reality. Which is fuelled by the energy of our people every day. Our resistance. Our protest.

Kherson. Melitopol. Berdyansk. Konotop. The reality of all cities and towns, rural communities that expel the invaders every day. By their determination. By their unity.

Freedom Square in Kherson is the whole of Ukraine. The streets of Konotop, where locals are shouting at the invaders, are Ukraine.

Ukraine, which we know, love, protect and will not give up to any enemy.

It is a special heroism to protest when your city is occupied. Even temporarily. When you don't have a weapon and in response you receive gunshots. And you don't run.

When you don't have armour and an armoured personnel carrier is coming at you. And you do not move aside.

That is why the occupation is temporary! It is artificial.

Our people, our Ukrainians do not retreat. Do not give up. Do not stop the resistance. They shout to the occupiers—go home. Like a Russian ship!

They drive them away from our territory. They block the roads for them. Every meter of our Ukrainian land won by protest and humiliation of the invaders is a step forward, a step towards victory for our entire state. This is a chance to live.

Ukrainians! In all our cities where the enemy entered. Feel it. Go on the offensive! You need to go outside! You have to fight! Every time when there is an opportunity. As in Kherson. As in Berdyansk. As in Melitopol. As in Konotop. You need to go out and drive this evil out of our cities. To prevent the creation of new DPR and LPR where normal life is simply impossible. Only slavery. Only on the knees.

Donbas! Remember what they said about you: Nobody put Donbas on its knees! And no one will be able to do that! Everyone in Donetsk and Luhansk knows these words. They were often repeated. Earlier. What about today?

Donbas, today is the time! We appeal to all people in the temporarily occupied territory. To all who hear us. Whose memory has not been erased by propaganda. Whose eyes have not been closed by fear. Whose soul has not been mutilated by cynicism.

Fight for your rights! For your freedom. For Ukraine. Together with Kherson. Together with Berdyansk. Together with Kyiv and all other Ukrainian cities that value life and are not afraid of anything.

I know that many of you believed that Ukraine allegedly hates you. Will allegedly attack you. Will allegedly destroy you.

Liars on Russian TV talk about it every day.

Liars. It's their job to lie to you every day. But this should not be your destiny. Just compare Donetsk after 8 years of war and Kharkiv after 8 days of war.

You were told that we are destroying cities. Look at Kharkiv. At Chernihiv. At 500 kg bombs that were dropped on the houses of Ukrainians. They were killing us. They were killing children. Look at Borodyanka. Look at the destroyed schools. At the blown-up kindergartens. At the damaged Kharkiv Assumption Cathedral. Look what Russia has done.

It did it right in front of your eyes. Protect yourself! Otherwise, it will take your life, too. Your houses. Ukraine does not shoot its people. We do not blow-up residential buildings. And everyone in Donbas has always been and will be our people. Our citizens.

In Donetsk. Luhansk. Kherson. Berdyansk. Melitopol. Konotop. In all our cities. In all cities of our state. In Ukraine. Glory to Ukraine!

## Ukraine receives support from partners backed by concrete steps
## 6 March 2022—12:22

I wish you victory, Ukrainian people!

I will start with the words of support I hear from our partners. From our friends. Very important words of support backed by concrete steps.

Every day and every night I talk to the leaders of many countries, to the leaders of the business community. During all the days of the war, there is almost no hour when Ukraine does not hear what help it will receive.

I talked about it again with President Biden last night. I am grateful to him for his determination. For preparing more new solutions for Ukrainians and Europeans. More new sanctions against aggression!

And before that I spoke with American congressmen. More than two hundred representatives of both parties of the Congress. They are very sincere. They are fully interested in really helping us, providing concrete assistance.

These are conversations that increase our confidence. Because one who is on the side of light will never fall into darkness.

The world has the power to close our sky from Russian missiles. From Russian combat aircraft, helicopters.

If anyone still doubts, Ukraine needs planes. In fact, it's

simple. When you have the will. To make the sky safe. The sky of Ukraine. The sky of Europe.

I spoke with the Prime Minister of Australia. And I am grateful to Australians for their moral stance on Russian exports. There must be no port where a terrorist state can make money.

The Prime Ministers of Albania, Bulgaria, and Israel. Support for Ukraine.

Inspirational conversation with Elon Musk. With a man who creates rockets for the future. Instead of killing with rockets for the sake of the past. We talked about how to win now. About how we will cooperate later. After the victory.

Support for Ukraine from global business, from the leaders of the most advanced companies is no less important than support from leading countries. When the corporate world stands by you and is not afraid, you have double protection. Triple weaponry. You have a future.

Ukrainians!

We have already gained our future.

But we are still fighting for our present. It is very important. We are fighting for where the border will be. Between life and slavery.

And this is not only our choice.

The citizens of Russia are making exactly the same choice right now. These days. During these hours.

Between life and slavery. Today. Tomorrow. In the coming week.

This is the time when it is still possible to defeat evil without irreparable losses.

When for a position they threaten with dismissal or a paddy

wagon, not with the Gulag. With material losses but not with execution.

Don't miss this opportunity. Social networks, friends, acquaintances, colleagues, and relatives. You must be heard! We, Ukrainians, want peace!

Citizens of Russia! For you, this is a struggle not only for peace in Ukraine! This is a fight for your country. For the best it had. For the freedom that you have seen. For the wealth that you have felt.

If you keep silent now, then only your poverty will speak for you later. And only repression will answer it.

Do not be silent!

The Russian servicemen who were taken captive by our defenders started speaking. Hundreds and hundreds of prisoners. Among them are the pilots of the planes that bombed our cities. Our peaceful people. We heard their testimony. We saw the documents. Maps. Plans. Elaborated NOT yesterday.

This is NOT improvisation. This is war.

They prepared this invasion exactly this way—cruelly, cynically, consciously violating the rules of war. Therefore, Kharkiv. Therefore, Chernihiv. Therefore, Sumy.

Therefore, Mariupol. And many, many other Ukrainian hero cities have faced pure evil. Atrocity.

This was planned.

But this will not kill our humanity.

Despite everything, we treat war prisoners under the Geneva Convention. Despite everything, our missiles do not hit Russian civilian facilities in response. Or Belarusian. From where rockets fly to our territory every day. Columns of military equipment. Aviation. Against peaceful people. Against peaceful cities. Zhytomyr, Korosten, Ovruch, suburbs of Kyiv, cities in the south... They are preparing to bomb Odesa.

Odesa!

Russians have always come to Odesa. They have always felt only warmth in Odesa. Only sincerity. And now what? Bombs against Odesa? Artillery against Odesa? Missiles against Odesa?
It will be a war crime.

It will be a historical crime.

Ukrainians!

We have been fighting for 11 days. For freedom. For the state.

We withstood. We already understand how we will rebuild our country.

We are already forming special funds for reconstruction. There are already four of them.
Fund for the Restoration of Destroyed Property and Infrastructure. Fund for Economic Recovery and Transformation. Public Debt Service and Repayment Fund. Small and Medium Business Support Fund.
And many more programs to support our people. Heroes who fight for our state. And this is just the beginning.
And now we still need strength. Wisdom.
Will.

Victory.

Peace!

Peace to save Ukraine.

Glory to Ukraine!

## The audacity of the aggressor is a clear signal that sanctions against Russia are not enough
6 March 2022—23:09

Ukrainians!

Today is Forgiveness Sunday. A day when we always apologized. To each other. To all people. To God. But today, it seems, many have not mentioned this day at all. Have not mentioned the obligatory words: "Forgive me." And the obligatory answer: "God forgives, and I forgive." These words seem to have lost their meaning today. At least in part. After everything we went through.

We will not forgive the destroyed houses. We will not forgive the missile that our air defence shot down over Okhmatdyt today. And more than five hundred other such missiles that hit our land. All over Ukraine. Hit our people and children.

We will not forgive the shooting of unarmed people. Destruction of our infrastructure.

We. Will. Not. Forgive. Hundreds and hundreds of victims. Thousands and thousands of sufferings. And God will not forgive. Not today. Not tomorrow. Never. And instead of Forgiveness, there will be a Day of Judgment.

I'm sure of it.

It seems everything Russian servicemen have already done is still not enough for them. Not enough ruined destinies. Mutilated lives. They want to kill even more.

Tomorrow Russia has officially announced the shelling of our territory. Our enterprises. Defence complex. Most were built decades ago. By the Soviet government. Built in cities.

And now they are in the middle of an ordinary urban environment.

Thousands of people work there. Hundreds of thousands live nearby. This is murder. Deliberate murder.

And I have not heard a reaction from any world leader today. From any Western politician. Reaction to this announcement. Think about the sense of impunity of the invaders: they announce their planned atrocities. Why?

Because there is no reaction. Because there is silence. Not a word, as if Western leaders have dissolved tonight. For this day. I hope that at least tomorrow you will notice it.

React. Say something. We know exactly who prepared this attack. We know exactly how orders will follow the vertical command. We know everything.

And we will not forgive anything. The Tribunal is waiting for you. And God's judgment, if you try to hide.

The audacity of the aggressor is a clear signal to the West that sanctions against Russia are not enough. Because they didn't understand. Did not feel. They did not see that the world is really determined. Really determined to stop this war. You will not hide from this reality.

You will not hide from new murders in Ukraine.


There was a lot of talk about humanitarian corridors. There were talks every day about the opportunity for people to leave the cities where Russia came. Russian military.

I am grateful to every Ukrainian who stays to defend our cities, even in the encirclement. Our freedom.


But I also know that there are people who really need to get out. Who cannot stay? And we heard the promise that there would be humanitarian corridors. But there are no humanitarian corridors.

Instead of humanitarian corridors, they can only make bloody ones.

A family was killed in Irpin today. A man, a woman and two children. Right on the road. As in the shooting club. When they were just trying to get out of town. To escape.

The whole family. How many such families have died in Ukraine! We will not forgive. We will not forget.

We will punish everyone who committed atrocities in this war. On our land. We will find every bastard. Which shot at our cities, our people. Which bombed our land.

Which launched rockets. Which gave the order and pressed "start". There will be no quiet place on this earth for you. Except for the grave.

Today I decided to award orders to the heads of regional administrations and mayors who have excelled in the defence of their communities.

The Order of Bohdan Khmelnytsky of the Third Degree is awarded to:

Head of Kharkiv Regional State Administration Oleh Vasyliovych Syniehubov. Head of Mykolaiv Regional State Administration Vitalii Oleksandrovych Kim. Head of Donetsk Regional State Administration Pavlo Oleksandrovych Kyrylenko. Head of Luhansk Regional State Administration Serhiy Volodymyrovych Haidai. Head of Chernihiv Regional State Administration Vyacheslav Anatoliyovych Chaus. Head of Sumy Regional State Administration Dmytro Oleksiyovych Zhyvytskyi.

The Order of Courage is awarded to:

Mayor of Kharkiv Ihor Oleksandrovych Terekhov. Mayor of Mykolaiv Oleksandr Fedorovych Senkevych.

Mayor of Chernihiv Vladyslav Anatoliyovych Atroshenko. Mayor of Sumy Oleksandr Mykolayovych Lysenko.

Mayor of Kherson Ihor Viktorovych Kolykhayev. Mayor of Melitopol Ivan Serhiyovych Fedorov.

Mayor of Nova Kakhovka Volodymyr Ivanovych Kovalenko.

And I decided to award a special title to our heroes, our hero cities. As it has already been once. When we withstood another attack. But a similar attack.

Another invasion. But no less brutal invasion.

Hero cities will be: Kharkiv. Chernihiv. Mariupol. Kherson. Hostomel. Volnovakha.

Glory to Ukraine!

# The future of the continent is being decided by us with our resistance and by our friends with their help
## 7 March 2022—12:01

Peaceful people of a belligerent state!

We have been defending ourselves against the invasion for 12 days already. We never wanted this war. But it was brought to us. We never dreamed of killing. But we have to knock out the enemy. From our land and from our lives.

We have to endure what no other European nation has seen in 80 years.

And it is on our land that it is decided whether someone else in Europe will fall victim to the same aggression.

I'm telling this to the leaders of the world, and I hear that they agree.

We decide the future of the continent. With our resistance. And our friends—with their help.

I spoke again with Polish President Andrzej Duda. They help us. Keep working.

I spoke with Prime Minister of the United Kingdom Boris Johnson and Prime Minister of Italy Mario Draghi. With President of France Emmanuel Macron and Prime Minister of India Modi.

I received very important signals, which, I'm sure, will only strengthen Ukraine.

Our theses in conversations with partners are absolutely logical. They are fair. Honest.

If the invasion continues and Russia does not abandon its plans against Ukraine, then a new sanctions package is needed. New sanctions, new sanction steps against war and for peace.

Boycott of Russian exports. In particular, the refusal of oil and petroleum products from Russia.

This can be called an embargo. Or just morality. When you refuse to give money to a terrorist. Boycott of imports to Russia. If they do not want to follow civilized rules, they should not receive goods and services from civilization. Let the war feed them.

The international community must act even more decisively.

When someone loses their mind, we have to lose fear and forget about commerce. We need to defend ourselves.

You have to be moral. Both states and companies.

We must fight against the inhuman force that wants to destroy humanity itself.

The success of the Ukrainian army. The will of the Ukrainian people. The principled nature of international sanctions. This is the way to peace.

At night the invaders fired at Mykolaiv. Right at the residential areas. Using rocket artillery.

They fired at Kharkiv, at residential areas of a peaceful city. They fired at other cities of our state.

No military sense. Just terror.

Residents of Irpin, Bucha, Hostomel and many other towns and villages, which the invader managed to capture, are being held hostage. Temporarily. Until the invaders get punishment. And they will get it.

Our Armed Forces know how to do it.

The enemy is tired. Demoralized. They came to our land to look for something that has never been here: cowardice, consent to slavery.

Any normal person is afraid to look at burned houses. It is obvious. Destroyed panel high-rise buildings. Destroyed ordinary cars.

Missiles, air bombs, "Grads", mortars. Against people.

It feels like it's in another country. But this is in our country. In ours, not somewhere else. In ours.

Which has always wanted peace above anything else.

How many more deaths and losses are needed to secure the sky over Ukraine? How do civilians in Kharkiv or Mykolaiv differ from Hamburg or Vienna?

We are waiting for a decision. Securing the sky.

Either with the power you have or give us fighter jets and air defence systems that will provide us with the strength we need.

This is the help that the world should provide not just to Ukraine, but to itself. To prove: humanity will win. As soon as possible.

The Government of Ukraine is already working on how to restore our state after the victory.

How to give more strength to the country while we are fighting.

A special package of assistance to businesses and employees has been created. Sole proprietors of the first and second groups are completely exempt from UST.

Enterprises and sole proprietors of the third group are exempt from paying UST for employees who were drafted into the Armed Forces of Ukraine and other defence formations. In particular, the territorial defence.

Exemption from land tax and rent for state and communal land in all areas where hostilities are taking place.

All this is during martial law and at least a year after its end.

The payment of taxes for all enterprises that are unable to pay them is postponed. And this is only the first part of a large aid package. Government support.

All leaders of the central government have a clear task: to develop a system of action so that the recovery of Ukraine is rapid and focused only on people. First of all—on people.

For us all to return to peace, to normal work. When we return our land, return peace to our land.

I am grateful to all business owners and managers who continue to work and fulfil their obligations to their employees.

To pay salaries to people—even if the company does not work as before—is to protect Ukraine.

The state fulfils all its obligations.

Indexed pensions have already been provided to the people. The salary in the budget sphere is paid as it should be.
Ukrainians!

There are millions of us. And these are millions of ways to fight for our future. For our state. For our freedom. For our national flag. Blue and yellow. Not a tricolour. We defend our flag because it is our worldview.

Under the blue and yellow we gained victories at the Olympics. We unfurled this flag both in space and in Antarctica.

Under our national flag, our rescuers, firefighters, peace-keepers, medics, and everyone else came to the aid of Turkey, Greece, Israel and Georgia, Afghanistan and Montenegro, India, Italy, the Congo, and many other countries.

What we have never done under this flag is attacking other countries, seizing foreign lands, killing people, peaceful people of other nations.

We and terror are different universes.

That is why there is no blood on our flag. There are no and will never be black spots on it. There are no and will never be any swastikas on it. The Ukrainian flag is the land.

Peaceful, fertile, golden and without tanks. This is the sky. Peaceful, clear, blue and without missiles. So, it was. And so, it will be.

I believe!

I know.

Glory to Ukraine!

## Every day of resistance creates better conditions for Ukraine in the negotiations to guarantee our future in peace
## 7 March 2022—23:42

Monday. Evening. You know, we used to say: Monday is a hard day. There is a war in the country. So every day is Monday.

And now we are used to the fact that every day and every night are like that. Today is the 12th. 12th evening of our struggle. Our defence.

We are all on the ground, we are all working.

Everyone is where they should be. I am in Kyiv. My team is with me. The territorial defence is on the ground. The servicemen are in positions. Our heroes! Doctors, rescuers, transporters, diplomats, journalists...

Everyone. We are all at war. We all contribute to our victory, which will be achieved. By force of arms and our army. By force of words and our diplomacy. By force of spirit, which the first, the second and each of us have.

Take a look at our country today.

Chaplynka, Melitopol, Tokmak, Novotroitske and Kherson. Starobilsk. Everywhere people defended themselves, although they do not have weapons there. But these are our people, and that's why they have weapons.

They have courage. Dignity. And hence the ability to go out and say: I'm here, it's mine, and I won't give it away. My city. My community. My Ukraine.

Every Ukrainian man and woman who protested against the invaders yesterday, today and will protest tomorrow are heroes.

We shout at the invaders together with you. We stand in the squares and streets with you. We are not afraid with you when the invaders open fire and try to drive everyone away.

YOU do not back down. WE do not back down.

And the one who repeated: "We are one people"—certainly did not expect such a powerful reaction.

In the south of our country, such a national movement has unfolded, such a powerful manifestation of Ukrainianness that we have never seen in the streets and squares there. And for Russia it is like a nightmare.

They forgot that we are not afraid of paddy wagons and batons. We are not afraid of tanks and machine guns. When the main thing is on our side, truth. As it is now.

Mariupol and Kharkiv, Chernihiv and Sumy. Odesa and Kyiv. Mykolaiv. Zhytomyr and Korosten. Ovruch. And many other cities.

We know that hatred that the enemy brought to our cities with shelling and bombing will not remain there. There will be no trace of it. Hatred is not about us. Therefore, there will be no trace of the enemy. We will rebuild everything. We will make our cities destroyed by the invader better than any city in Russia.

Enerhodar. Chornobyl. And other places where barbarians just don't understand WHAT they want to capture. WHAT they want to control. Your work, your hard work on critical objects is a real feat. And we see it. We are sincerely grateful for it.

The Ukrainian army holds positions. Well done! It inflicts extremely painful losses on the enemy. Defends. Counterattacks. If necessary—can take revenge. Necessarily. For every evil. For every rocket and bomb. For each destroyed civilian object.

Today in Makariv, Kyiv region, they fired at the bread factory. For what? The old bread factory! Think about it—to fire at the bread factory. Who should you be to do that?

Or to destroy another church—in the Zhytomyr region. The Church of the Nativity of the Blessed Virgin built in 1862.

These are NOT people.

There was an agreement on humanitarian corridors.

Did it work? Russian tanks worked instead. Russian "Grads". Russian mines. They even mined the road, which was agreed to transport food and medicine for people and children in Mariupol.

They even destroy buses that have to take people out. But ... At the same time, they are opening a small corridor to the

85

occupied territory. For several dozen people. Not so much to Russia, as to propagandists. Directly to their TV cameras. Like, that's the one who saves. Just cynicism. Just propaganda. Nothing more. No humanitarian sense.

The third round of negotiations in Belarus took place today. I would like to say—the third and final. But we are realists. So, we will talk. We will insist on negotiations until we find a way to tell our people: this is how we will come to peace.

Exactly to peace.

We must realize that every day of struggle, every day of resistance creates better conditions for us. Strong position to guarantee our future. In peace. After this war.

Apart from the dead people and the destroyed cities, the war leaves destroyed the aspirations that once seemed very important, but now ... You don't even mention them.

Almost three years ago, as soon as the election took place, we entered this building, this office, and immediately began planning our move.

I dreamed of moving from Bankova. Together with the government and parliament. To unload the center of Kyiv and in general—to move to a modern, transparent office—as befits a progressive democratic European country.

Now I will say one thing: I stay here. I stay in Kyiv. On Bankova Street.

I'm not hiding.

And I'm not afraid of anyone.

As much as it takes to win this Patriotic War of ours.

Today I signed a decree to present state awards of Ukraine to 96 Ukrainian heroes—our military.

Including...

The Order of Bohdan Khmelnytsky of the second degree is awarded to:

Major Oleksandr Oleksandrovych Sak. Commander of the mechanized battalion who entered the battle with the battalion tactical group of the enemy and won thanks to a rational approach to combat and non-standard tactics.

Captain Rostyslav Oleksandrovych Sylivakin. Commander of the mechanized battalion, which successfully fought the overwhelming forces of the enemy, liberating Ukrainian towns and villages in the Sumy region.

The Order of Bohdan Khmelnytsky of the third degree is awarded to:

Lieutenant Ihor Serhiyovych Lozovyi. Acting as part of the group, he stopped a column of enemy vehicles numbering about 150 units, which was moving in the direction of the Zhytomyr-Kyiv route. Destroyed.

Lieutenant Vitaliy Viktorovych Poturemets. He showed exemplary courage and composure in the battle, destroying a column of enemy equipment near the city of Kyiv. He was wounded.

The Order "For Courage" of the third degree is awarded to:

Master Sergeant, Commander of the Automobile Platoon Valentyn Viktorovych Baryliuk. Thanks to his brave actions and personal determination, the tank unit received fuel in time and left the encirclement, destroying the enemy on the way.

All 96 of our heroes are like these five! Our gratitude to all the military.

Our gratitude to the Armed Forces of Ukraine!

Our gratitude is boundless.

Glory to Ukraine!

In the leading capitals, humanity must overcome fear and benefits, and then the Ukrainian sky will be safe, and the cities will be unblocked
8 March 2022—12:23

Ukrainians!

We always celebrate this holiday. The holiday of spring. We congratulate Ukrainian women, our girls, wives, mothers.

Always.

But not today.

Today, I just can't tell you the traditional words. I just can't congratulate you. I can't. When there are so many deaths. When there is so much grief. When there is so much suffering.

When the war continues. A full-scale terrorist war against our people. The people of Ukraine.

The invaders bombed Sumy again. With air bombs. Our peaceful city that has never threatened Russia in its history! Good, quiet, soulful Sumshchyna! Which is turned into hell.

Mariupol. Peaceful and hard-working city without any internal malice. It was surrounded. Blocked. And is being deliberately exhausted. Deliberately tortured. The invaders deliberately cut off communication. Deliberately block the delivery of food, water supply. Turn off the electricity.

In Mariupol, for the first time in dozens of years, perhaps for the first time since the Nazi invasion, a child died of dehydration.

Hear me, today, dear partners!

A child died of dehydration. In 2022!

We have been fighting for the thirteenth day. We destroy the invaders wherever we can. Everywhere. But there is a sky. Hundreds of Russian cruise missiles. Hundreds of fighter jets of the invaders. Hundreds of helicopters. Yes, we destroy them.

Russia has not lost as much aircraft in the past 30 years as in these 13 days in Ukraine.

But they still have enough machinery to kill. There are still enough missiles for terror. They still have enough 500 kg bombs to drop them on us, ordinary people. On Chernihiv and Kyiv. Odesa and Kharkiv. Poltava and Zhytomyr. Dozens and dozens of Ukrainian cities. On millions of peaceful Ukrainian people.

It has been 13 days of promises. 13 days when we are told that there will soon be help in the sky. There will be planes. They will be handed over to us...

The blame for every death of every person in Ukraine from air strikes and in blocked cities, of course, lies with the Russian state, the Russian military, those who give and those who carry out criminal orders, who violate all the rules of warfare, who deliberately exterminate the Ukrainian people.

The fault lies with the invaders. But the responsibility for this lies also with those who have not been able to make an obviously necessary decision somewhere in the West, somewhere in the offices for 13 days. Those who have not yet secured the Ukrainian sky from Russian murderers.

Those who did not save our cities from air strikes. From these bombs, missiles. Although they can.

Those who do not help in lifting the blockade.

Hundreds and hundreds of thousands of people in the cities are on the verge of life and death. Literally.

Not as it sounds in the comments of politicians about providing Ukraine with vital combat aircraft. Vital missile defence.

Vitally important!

We have heard many assurances and seen many agreements. In particular, on the creation of humanitarian corridors. To save our citizens in Mariupol. But they didn't work. All of them didn't work. Yet. And I have no more time to wait. We do not have. Mariupol doesn't have time to wait.

It is the invaders who want our people to die. Not us. We sent columns with humanitarian aid to Mariupol. Everything necessary is there! We sent vehicles to rescue people. Drivers understand everything. They are heroes. Brave people! They understand that Russian troops can simply destroy these vehicles on the road. Just as they did, killing people who were just trying to get to a safe territory from the war zone.

But if you fire at these vehicles, these people, you should know that it will be before the eyes of the whole world.

Everyone will be witnesses. And everyone will testify.

When everyone, I repeat this, everyone who gives and fulfils inhuman orders will be severely judged and convicted.

We have seen the concrete consent of the Russian side to organize an evacuation corridor from the city of Sumy. And not just for our people. For hundreds of foreigners. Citizens of India, China. These are students who studied in Sumy.

You know, I was told that the Red Cross, the International Red Cross, forbids us to use the emblem on vehicles carrying out humanitarian missions. The Red Cross prohibits it as if it is their property.

And this is indicative. This says a lot about the fact that some people, very influential, have decided to give up Ukrainians.

But we will not allow it. And I will not allow it. Our friends. They are next to us.

I will appeal directly to the nations of the world if the leaders of the world do not make

every effort to stop this war, this genocide.

Of course, we continue to talk to our partners, to the leaders, parliamentarians of all countries who know how to help Ukraine. We have a very busy negotiation period.

I spoke with Lithuanian President Gitanas Nauseda. The people of Lithuania always stand by Ukrainians in this struggle. We feel this help and appreciate it.

I spoke with President of the European Council, our friend Charles Michel. I also spoke with Prime Minister of India, Mr. Modi.

But there are things that are not decided in negotiations, that depend not directly on us, but on humanity, which must win in the leading capitals, must overcome fear, must overcome any benefits.

And then we will see that the Ukrainian sky is safe and the Ukrainian cities are unblocked.

We can do this together as people of the world. And if the world stands aloof, it will lose itself. Forever. Because there are unconditional values. The same for everyone. First of all, this is life. The right to life for everyone.

This is exactly what we are fighting for in Ukraine. Very fiercely, together with our military. This is exactly what these weak invaders want to deprive us of.

This is exactly what the whole world must protect.

Glory to Ukraine!

## Address to the Parliament of the United Kingdom
## 8 March 2022—20:36

Mr. Speaker! Mr. Prime Minister! Members of the government, parliament, lords.

Ladies and gentlemen!

I'm addressing all the people of the United Kingdom. All the people of Great Britain. Great people. With a great history. I'm addressing you as a citizen, as President of a great country as well. With a great dream. And a great struggle. I want to tell you about our 13 days. 13 days of fierce war, which we did not start and did not want. But we are waging it.

Because we do not want to lose what we have, what is ours—Ukraine. Just as you did not want to lose your island when the Nazis were preparing to start the battle for your great power, the battle for Britain.

13 days of our defence.

On the first day at 4 am, cruise missiles were fired at us. So that everyone woke up—we, the children, all of us, living people, all of Ukraine. And we haven't slept since. We all took up arms becoming a large army.

The next day we fought off attacks in the air, on land and at sea. And our heroic border guards on Zmiinyi Island in the Black Sea told everyone about the end of the war.

Namely: where the enemy will go in the end. When a Russian ship demanded that our guys lay down their weapons, they answered him... As firmly as one cannot say in the parliament. And we felt the power. Great power of our people who will persecute the invader to the end.

On the third day, Russian troops openly fired at people and

apartment buildings without hiding. Used artillery, air bombs. And it finally showed us, showed the world who is who. Who are great people and who are just savages?

On the fourth day, when we have already begun to take dozens of prisoners, we have not lost our dignity. We didn't abuse them. We treat them like people. Because we remained human on the fourth day of this shameful war.

On the fifth day, the terror against us has already become outright. Against cities, against small towns. Ruined districts. Bombs, bombs, bombs, again bombs on houses, on schools, on hospitals. This is genocide. Which did not break us. It mobilized each and every one of us. And it gave us a sense of great truth.

On the sixth day, Russian missiles hit Babyn Yar. This is the place where the Nazis executed 100,000 people during World War II. 80 years later, Russia killed them for a second time.

On the seventh day, we realized they were destroying even the churches. Using bombs! Rockets again. They do not know the holy and great as we know.

On the eighth day, the world saw Russian tanks firing at a nuclear power plant. The largest in Europe. And the world began to understand that this is terror against all. This is a great terror.

On the ninth day, we listened to a meeting of NATO countries. Without the desired result for us. Without courage. That's how we felt—I don't want to offend anyone—we felt that alliances don't work. They can't even close the sky. That is why security guarantees in Europe must be built from scratch.

On the tenth day, unarmed Ukrainians protested everywhere in the occupied cities. Stopping armoured vehicles with bare hands. We have become unbreakable.

On the eleventh day, when residential areas were already

bombed, when everything was destroyed by explosions, when children were evacuated from a damaged children's oncology hospital... We realized: Ukrainians became heroes. Hundreds of thousands of people. Entire cities. Children, adults—all.

On the twelfth day, when the losses of the Russian army have already exceeded 10,000 killed, the general also appeared in this number. And this gave us confidence: for all crimes, for all shameful orders there will still be responsibility before the International Court or Ukrainian weapons.

On the thirteenth day, a child died in Russian-occupied Mariupol. Died of dehydration. They do not allow food or water to people. They just blocked it—and people are in the basements. I think everyone hears people don't have water there!

In 13 days of the Russian invasion, 50 children were killed. 50 great martyrs. This is dreadful! This is emptiness. Instead of 50 universes that could live, they took them away. They just took them away.

Great Britain!

Ukraine did not strive for that. It did not seek greatness. But it became great during these days of this war.

Ukraine that saves people despite the terror of the invaders. Defends freedom despite the blows of one of the world's largest armies. Defends despite the open sky. Still open to Russian missiles, aircraft, helicopters. "To be or not to be?"—You know this Shakespearean question well.

13 days ago, this question could still be raised about Ukraine. But not now. Obviously, to be. Obviously, to be free. And if not here, where should I remind you of the words that Great Britain has already heard. And which are relevant again.

We shall not give up and shall not lose! We shall go the whole way.

We shall fight in the seas, we shall fight in the air, we shall defend our land, whatever the cost may be.

We shall fight in the woods, in the fields, on the beaches, in the cities and villages, in the streets, we shall fight in the hills ... And I want to add, we shall fight on the spoil tips, on the banks of the Kalmius and the Dnieper! And we shall not surrender!

Of course, with your help, with the help of the civilization of great countries. With your support, for which we are grateful and on which we rely. And I am especially grateful to you, Boris, my friend!

Increase sanctions against the terrorist state. Recognize it as a terrorist state finally. Find a way to make our Ukrainian sky safe. Do what you can. Do what you have to. Do what the greatness of your state and your people obliges to.

Glory to the great Ukraine! Glory to Great Britain.

# The world does not believe in the future of Russia, yet speaks about Ukraine, helps and is preparing to support our reconstruction after the war
8 March 2022—23:36

Ukrainians!

Today we have important news. The United States has taken a step that will significantly weaken the invaders. It will make them pay for aggression and be responsible for the evil they have done. For all the evil. America bans imports of oil from Russia, petroleum products, gas, coal. Prohibits US citizens from any investment in Russia's fuel and energy sector.

I am grateful personally to President of the United States

Biden for this decision. For this leadership. For this most powerful signal to the whole world. It is very simple: every penny paid to Russia turns into bullets and projectiles that fly to other sovereign states.

Either Russia will respect international law and will not wage wars, or it will not have the money to start wars. Another gas station will be found. But it's not just about the money. A ban on oil imports to the United States will weaken the terrorist state economically, politically, and ideologically. Because it is about freedom, about the future. About where the world will go.

The United Kingdom is also banning the import of oil and petroleum products from Russia.

I am grateful to Prime Minister Boris Johnson for the principled position you expect from the Prime Minister of the United Kingdom in difficult times.

Speaking today in the British Parliament, I mentioned other difficult times. Other, yet similar. 1940, when tyranny threatened what it considered a small island. And it was sure that the island would not withstand brutal blows, bombings and a blockade.

And it turned out that the island could do more than that tyranny. Because it had wisdom. And endurance. And friends. And strength. And it believed in the future, the future of its own and the future of freedom in Europe.

As we believe. As we fight. And as we will win.

Look: the world does not believe in the future of Russia, does not talk about it. Not a word, not a prospect. They understand everything. They talk about us. They help us. They are preparing to support our reconstruction.

After the war. Because everyone saw that for the people who defend themselves so heroically, this "after the war" will surely come.

There will be a new Marshall Plan for Ukraine. The West

will form this support package. The British Prime Minister said this today. A man of his word, a sincere friend of Ukraine.

We are already expecting tough decisions from the European Union. Sanctions. Against Russia. For this war. For this aggression, which its authors will regret. They will. For sure. That is why it is so important that the Russian leadership realizes that the world will follow the example of the United States, Great Britain, the European Union, Canada, Australia, Japan, and other free countries.

So, the world cannot be fooled. Sanctions cannot be avoided.

I am grateful to those Russians who support us, take to the streets and fight. They are fighting daily for us and for themselves. Because they are fighting for peace.

The war must end. We need to sit down at the negotiating table—honest, substantive, in the interests of the people, not obsolete murderous ambitions.

I spoke today with Mark Rutte, Prime Minister of the Netherlands. We have a new page in relations with the Netherlands. Thank you for your support. With Prime Minister of Israel Bennett. With Prime Minister of Luxembourg Bettel and President of France Macron. We have support. We have an understanding.

You may have seen in the news today the story that the United Nations allegedly does not consider the Russian invasion a war. I know this outraged many, and not only in Ukraine.

I am grateful to our team. We made everything clear and quickly received assurances: there will be no lies in the UN structures. There will be no playing along with the aggressor. The word "war" will be heard on this site. Because that is the truth. We will not allow anyone in the world to ignore the suffering and murder of our people, our children.

Today, when I spoke to the British Parliament, the scariest

number was 50. 50 Ukrainian children killed in 13 days of war. And in an hour, it was 52. 52 children. I will never forgive that. And I know that you will never forgive the invaders.

Like Kharkiv, Mariupol and all other cities. In the evening, they fired a missile at Korbutivka in the Zhytomyr region. Destroyed the dormitory.

How could an ordinary dormitory threaten Russia? What geopolitical interests of the nuclear state were threatened by it? Eternal memory to all the people who were killed by these savages.

Today we managed to organize a humanitarian corridor from the city of Sumy to Poltava.

Hundreds of people were saved. The humanitarian cargo was delivered. But that's only one percent of what needs to be done, of what people, blocked Ukrainians expect. We are ready. Our cargo is ready. Our transport is ready. But ... savages—they are not ready. They fire at evacuation routes. They block the delivery of essential products and medicines to people. What do they want? They want Ukrainians to take it from the hands of the invaders. This is torture. Deliberate. Systematic. Organized by their state. Foreign to us. And ruthless for everyone, even for its citizens.

Oleshky in the Kherson region. Berdyansk and Melitopol in the Zaporizhzhia region. All the cities where Ukrainians are resisting, where they are protesting against the invaders... Know: we stand with you. We are grateful. The cargo will still go. No matter how many bullets stop them. Humanitarian corridors will still work. And only time separates you from freedom. Short time. Believe it. I believe. And I really want that.

Glory to Ukraine!

# Ukrainians withstood and inspired the whole world with their determination
## 9 March 2022—12:34

Brave Ukrainians of the unconquered country!

It is already the 14th day of our defence. The 14th day of our unity. Truly all-Ukrainian. The scale of the threat to the state is maximum. The invasion contingent has already brought into our territory almost everyone who was gathered to invade Ukraine. But the scale of our answer is maximum as well. And these are two different words "maximum".

They have only equipment. At the maximum. We have our people in addition to the equipment. Up to the mark. They only have orders. To attack, to kill, to abuse. And we have a real desire of millions of Ukrainians to win. Defend ourselves. Clear our state…
And on the renewed land

There will be no enemy, adversary,

And there will be a son, and there will be a mother, and there will be people on the land.
Today is Taras Shevchenko's birthday. This is our old dream. It is his dream to clean
the land. And it is alive! And quite real. Ukrainians!
Everything is in our hands! We withstood and inspired the whole world with our determination. There is no such place on earth where they are not aware of the heroism with which the Ukrainian people defend our beautiful land. Even where we are not supported, they know well what we have achieved. And they feel what else we will achieve if we save the country. If we maintain unity. National force. If we continue to

respond wisely and boldly to the activity of the enemy who can destroy the walls of our homes, our schools, our churches, who can destroy Ukrainian enterprises, but will never reach our soul, our heart, our ability to live freely and fight boldly.

Our military and territorial defence units managed to replenish the arsenal of our equipment due to the many trophies they took on the battlefield. Enemy tanks, armoured vehicles, ammunition will now work for our defence. For our lives. For our country. What could be more humiliating for the invaders? We will beat the enemy with his own weapons. In addition to ours, which the Russian troops have already felt well, so that more and more enemy soldiers and commanders are asking themselves a simple question: why were they sent to this foreign land, to this war? And we have no answer. Except for one word—death.

Russian soldiers!

You still have a chance to survive. Almost two weeks of our resistance have shown you that we will not give up. Because this is our home. These are our families and children. We will fight until we regain our land and take revenge for all our killed people. For the killed children. You can still be saved if you just leave. Do not believe your commanders when they tell you that you still have a chance in Ukraine. Nothing is waiting for you here. Except for captivity, except for death. You take our lives and give yours. And we know—we have communications interception—that your commanders already understand everything.

This war must be ended. We must return to peace. Leave our home, go back to yours. 14 days of a full-scale brutal war. Terror against our people.

Destruction of cities, blockade of entire districts, constant bombing... 14 days of absence of a vital decision. Not our decision! We would make that decision in hours if we had to help our friends.

From the first day of the Russian invasion, Ukraine has been repeating to its partners that if you do not close the sky, you will also be responsible for this catastrophe, a large-scale humanitarian catastrophe.

Russia uses missiles, aircraft, helicopters against us, against civilians, against our cities, against our infrastructure. This is the world's humanitarian duty to respond. But... There is no decision.

We are grateful to Poland for the alternative—for its readiness to provide Ukraine with combat aircraft. The problem is in logistics. In fact, it is a technical issue. It must be solved! Immediately.

There is an official decision of Poland to transfer the planes to the relevant base—the American base. We also have confirmation—we have all heard—that the agreement between the American party and Poland has been reached. But at the same time, we hear that Poland's proposal is allegedly unfounded. And that's what they say in Washington. We also read this. So when will the decision be made? Listen: we have a war! We do not have time for all these signals. This is not ping pong! This is about human lives! We ask once again: solve it faster. Do not shift the responsibility, send us planes.

Yesterday we finally managed to organize a humanitarian corridor. From the city of Sumy to Poltava. 1,600 students and 3,500 residents were rescued. Evacuation of people from cities and towns of the Kyiv region continues. More than 18,000 people have already been rescued from Dymer, Vorzel and Irpin. Today we will do everything to continue the functioning of humanitarian corridors. Sumy—Poltava. Izyum—Lozova. Enerhodar—Zaporizhzhia. Mariupol—Zaporizhzhia. Vorzel, Bucha, Borodyanka, Hostomel to Kyiv. Our government officials are working on this, our servicemen have created all the conditions. If there is at least one shot, full responsibility lies with the invaders.

And you have already seen the world's response. Powerful. Sanction packages.

In the morning I spoke with Prime Minister of Canada Justin Trudeau. We have full understanding. Full support. Our delegation returned from Belarus last night, from negotiations. I will listen to their report. We will prepare for the next rounds of talks. For the sake of Ukraine. For peace.

And finally. Concerning our unity. This is our strength. This is what is needed at this time. We are receiving a lot of signals that someone in Ukraine has decided that he or she may not fight anymore together with everyone. And tries somehow separately, for something personal, for some personal benefit...

We are receiving various signals that some politicians are looking for threads to Russia again.

And some others are again working for a split, contrary to unity.

I want to say one thing and only once: I see what you are doing. If I hear another signal, the answer will be quick. As befits wartime.

Thank God, our people have already sorted everything and everyone out.

Glory to Ukraine!

# Europeans must tighten sanctions against Russia so that it has no chance to continue the genocide in Ukraine
## 9 March 2022—23:56

Europeans! Ukrainians! Mariupol residents!

Today is the day that defines everything. Defines who is on whose side. Russian bombs fell on a hospital and maternity hospital in Mariupol. Children's hospital. Maternity hospital that is functioning! Buildings are destroyed. As of now, there are 17 wounded. Disassembly of the debris is still ongoing. People began to hide from the air threat in time.

From 500 kg aviation bombs dropped by the invaders on Ukrainian cities. Many times, already.

Children's hospital. Maternity hospital. What did they threaten the Russian Federation with? What kind of country is this—the Russian Federation, which is afraid of hospitals and maternity hospitals and destroys them? Were there little Banderivtsi? Or were pregnant women going to fire at Rostov? Did someone in the maternity hospital abuse Russian-speakers? What was that? Was it the denazification of the hospital?

It is beyond atrocities already. Everything that the invaders are doing to Mariupol is beyond atrocities already. Europeans! Ukrainians! Mariupol residents! Today, we must be united in condemning this war crime of Russia, which reflects all the evil that the invaders brought to our land.

All destroyed cities. What they did to Volnovakha, Kharkiv, Izyum, Okhtyrka, Chernihiv, Borodyanka, Hostomel, Zhytomyr and dozens of other Ukrainian cities, which never posed any threat to the Russian Federation.

Destroyed hospitals. Destroyed schools, churches, houses.

And all the people killed. All the children killed.

The air bomb on the maternity hospital is the final proof. Proof that the genocide of Ukrainians is taking place.

Europeans! You won't be able to say that you didn't see what happened to Ukrainians, what happened to Mariupol residents. You saw. You know.

Therefore, you must increase sanctions against Russia so that it no longer has any opportunity to continue this genocide.

You must put pressure on Russia to force it to sit down at the negotiating table and end this brutal war.

Moscow knows very well that Mariupol is also the Donetsk region. We have heard so much from Russia about the inhabitants of the Donetsk region. So many accusations, so many demands... And now we see how Russia actually treats the residents of the Donetsk region. Treats ordinary people who live in the houses of Mariupol, work at the enterprises of the city of Mariupol, are treated in hospitals of Mariupol and give birth to children, imagine, people like you give birth to children in the maternity hospitals of Mariupol.

We have not done and never would have done anything similar to this war crime to any of the cities of the Donetsk, Luhansk or any other region. To any of the cities on earth. Because we are people. And you?

I spoke today with European Council President Charles Michel and European Commission President Ursula von der Leyen. We also worked and spoke with Speaker of the United States House of Representatives Nancy Pelosi, with Prime Minister of the United Kingdom Boris Johnson. Thank you for your support, Boris.

The partners are fully informed about what is happening in our Mariupol. And about the situation in all other regions of Ukraine, where hostilities continue. We are working to make Russia feel the consequences of its actions. We are doing everything to finally secure our sky. I am grateful to the vast majority of Ukrainians who support this position. Those who collect signatures, who convince their acquaintances in the West, write on social networks, organize rallies.

Together we must return courage to some Western leaders. So that they finally do what they had to do on the first day of the invasion. Either close the Ukrainian sky from Russian missiles and bombs or give us fighter jets so that we can do everything ourselves. A pause without a decision has become simply deadly.

Today we managed to organize the work of three humanitarian corridors. From the city of Sumy, from the cities and towns of the Kyiv region and from Enerhodar.

In total, about 35,000 people were rescued. We will continue tomorrow. We are preparing six corridors. We pray that people will be taken out of Mariupol, Izyum, Volnovakha, etc. Taken to safe cities of our free Ukraine.

And I am sure that every Ukrainian whose help these people need will do everything possible to make them feel our care. Until they can return home.

And finally. Every year on March 9, the winners of the Shevchenko Prize are announced. Our national award for the most significant contribution to the preservation and development of the Ukrainian spirit, our national culture.

I believe that our traditions must be observed during martial law and the fierce battles for our freedom. We must not betray them so that we preserve all ours, Ukrainian, completely while we are heading to victory. While we are heading to peace.

The decree was signed. Now I look forward to meeting the winners. But after the victory. After the victory of Ukraine.

Glory to Ukraine!

# Thanks to our defenders, Ukrainians have not become slaves and will never become
## 10 March 2022—14:08

Ukrainians!

Information about the victims of yesterday's bombing of the maternity hospital and the children's hospital in Mariupol appeared last night. We lost three people, including a child, a girl. The number of wounded is 17. These are children, women, medical workers.

You know, this topic was mentioned on Russian television. It was on their talk show. But not a word of truth was said. The Russians were lied to that there had been no patients in the hospital and no women or children in the maternity hospital. The Russians were lied to that "nationalists" had allegedly taken up positions there. They lie confidently, as always.

War crimes are impossible without the propagandists who cover them up. I want to tell them one thing: you will bear responsibility just as all those who give orders to bomb civilians. We will find all the property of the propagandists and their associates. We will do our best to confiscate it wherever it is. You love a rich life. Love prosperous countries. You will not have this anymore. And this is just the beginning.

You will definitely be prosecuted for complicity in war crimes. And then, it will definitely happen, you will be hated by Russian citizens. Everyone whom you have been deceiving constantly, daily, for many years in a row. When they feel the consequences of your lies in their wallets, in their shrinking possibilities. In the stolen future of Russian children.

War is never isolated. It always beats both the victim and the aggressor. The aggressor just realizes it later. But it always realizes and always suffers.

Today, we are once again providing humanitarian corridors

for our cities. The buses have already departed, the trucks are already on their way—with food, water, medicine.

Mariupol, Volnovakha, Izyum, Sumy and the region. Cities and towns of the Kyiv region—Bucha, Borodyanka, Irpin, Hostomel... My heart is broken by what the invaders did to our cities, to our state! And by what they want to do to our people who need urgent help.

Russian troops have already created a humanitarian catastrophe in Ukraine. But for them it is part of the plan. They want to humiliate our people. Make them take bread and water from the hands of the invaders standing on their knees. So that Ukrainians can save their lives just by going to the occupied territories or to Russia. That's why they are blocking Mariupol, that's why they are blocking Volnovakha, blocking other cities.

The invaders specially organize this torture to give their propaganda channels new material. Just for that. Monsters.

Despite everything, updated information was received every hour yesterday about people whom we managed to evacuate to the free territory of Ukraine. In total, more than 60,000 of our citizens were rescued yesterday plus those who did not have time until night and continued the evacuation in the morning.

I spoke today, in particular about that, with German Chancellor Olaf Scholz. About the torture of our cities, our people. I spoke with French President Macron.

I felt in a conversation with Prime Minister of the United Kingdom Boris Johnson that our anti-war coalition will soon become much stronger. Consequently, the pressure on Russia for peace will also be much stronger. For us, specifics in relations with world leaders, with European leaders are very important.

We are really fighting for our independence! For freedom, for equality for all on the continent! That is why we want to see from partners the decisions based on reality, not on declarations or abstract considerations.

These days, the EU leaders will convene to discuss Russia's war against Ukraine. To discuss our application for EU membership. We are waiting for a concrete signal. We look forward to strong support. Because it will be fair, real, human, European.

We know exactly the position of every leader. We know exactly who stands with us and who thinks that the European Union is just accounting, profits, expenses, and nothing more. We will work, we will persuade. Life will convince them.

Ukrainians! Our defenders!


We all have been defending our state for the 15th day. We endured. The Ukrainian army is repelling attacks in key directions. Thanks to our military, National Guards, border guards, police, territorial defence, and everyone who joined the defence of the state, we have not become slaves, and will never become!

Because this is our spirit, this is our destiny. Pride for our Armed Forces of Ukraine is boundless!

After the war, after our victory, we will rebuild everything that was destroyed.


Very quickly and with a very high quality. A special state program for reconstruction will be created for each affected city. I have already instructed the government to start the elaboration.

Chernihiv and Sumy, Okhtyrka and Zhytomyr, Izyum, Mariupol and all our beautiful cities to which evil has come will not see a single trace of the Russian invasion.

The best architects, the best companies, the best projects. For every city! I want to say this on the example of Kharkiv. Our Kharkiv, which is now experiencing the worst suffering since World War II.

Saltivka, Oleksiivka... Perhaps most Ukrainians know nothing about these names. But the people of Kharkiv will hear. Freedom Square will be such that everyone, all of us, all Europeans will be there! Poltava Way, Belgorod Highway, Myronosytska Street, Regional Children's Hospital, Kharkiv Oncology Center, Karazin University, Labor Palace, Korolenko Library.

We will rebuild everything! I promise you personally. Kharkiv residents will see that Ukraine stands with them. And it really does.

Glory to Ukraine!

## The state is doing everything to help Mariupol
11 March 2022—00:09

Ukrainians!

One of the main tasks for us today was the organization of humanitarian corridors.

Sumy, Trostyanets, Krasnopillya, Irpin, Bucha, Hostomel, Izyum. Almost 40,000 people have already been evacuated this day. They were given safety at last. In Poltava, Kyiv, Cherkasy, Zaporizhzhia, Dnipro, Lviv.

Humanitarian cargoes were also delivered. Hundreds of tons of food, medicine.

We are doing everything to save our people in the cities that the enemy just wants to destroy. Taking into account the work of humanitarian corridors in the previous two days, we have already evacuated about one hundred thousand people.

But…

Mariupol and Volnovakha remain completely blocked.

Although we did everything necessary to make the humanitarian corridor work, Russian troops did not cease fire.

Despite this, I decided to send a convoy of trucks to Mariupol anyway. With food, water, medicine. I am grateful to the drivers—brave people who were ready to fulfil this mission. An extremely important mission.

But the invaders started a tank attack exactly in the area where this corridor was supposed to be. Corridor of life. For the people of Mariupol.

They did it consciously. They knew what they were disrupting. They have a clear order to hold Mariupol hostage, to torture it, to carry out constant bombardment.

Today they destroyed the building of the main department of the State Emergency Service in the Donetsk region. Right next to this building was the place where Mariupol residents were to gather for evacuation.

This is outright terror. Blatant terror. From experienced terrorists.

The world needs to know that. It has to admit it. We are all dealing with a terrorist state.

But no matter what, we will try! Constantly! We will continue to try to bring to Mariupol the aid that people so desperately need. Ukrainians need.

The invaders are doing everything to deceive our people in the besieged cities.

They block communication. Prevent the provision of Information. The state is doing everything to help our city.

Everything to tell the people of Mariupol: we are fighting. And we will not give up this fight.

Therefore, if you have the opportunity to talk to the people of Mariupol, to write to the people of Mariupol, spread the truth. Remind them that Ukraine is with them wholeheartedly and is doing everything to stop the torture of the city.

Russian propagandists have substantially intensified their activity today. And they tried very hard.

Probably to cover up the crimes of their army in Ukraine. Crimes against Mariupol. Against Donbas. Against Kharkiv. Against dozens of other cities.

Cover them up with new accusations. New-old fakes.

They accuse us... Again us! That we are allegedly developing biological weapons. Allegedly, we are preparing a chemical attack.

This makes me really worried, because we've been repeatedly convinced: if you want to know Russia's plans, look at what Russia accuses others of.

Look, spreading such accusations in the Russian media shows that it is THEY who are capable of this. The Russian military, the Russian special services. It shows that they want it.

They have already done such things in other countries. Similar! They themselves announced, they themselves organized, they themselves complained. And they will do so again.

Again, and again. If they are not stopped.

They tore apart Moldova with Transnistria. They tore apart Georgia with Abkhazia. They tore apart Ukraine with Donbas and Crimea.

But they blame us! Those who have become victims.

Those who are forced to defend themselves. Fight for the

right to live. They themselves come to us in tanks and with missiles.

They take something that doesn't belong to them. Capture.

They are even ashamed to show their officers! They hide their generals. They conceal from their own people that they are sending conscripts to this war only to make the invasion forces larger.

But we are to blame! We are accused of attacks on allegedly peaceful Russia.

And now what? What are these allegations of preparing chemical attacks? Have you decided to carry out "de-chemicalization" of Ukraine? Using ammonia? Using phosphorus? What else have you prepared for us?

Where will you strike with chemical weapons?

At the maternity hospital in Mariupol? At the church in Kharkiv? At the Okhmatdyt Children's Hospital?

Or at laboratories, most of which have remained since Soviet times and are engaged in ordinary science. Ordinary!
NOT military technology.

We are adequate people. I am the President of an adequate country, an adequate nation. And the father of two children.

And no chemical or any other weapons of mass destruction were developed on my land.

The whole world knows that. YOU know that.

And if YOU do something like that against US, you will get the most severe sanctions response.

Ukrainians! Our defenders!

I have signed several important decrees.

About awarding the title of Hero of Ukraine to thirteen of our defenders:

Lieutenant Colonel Litun Andriy Mykolayovych. Posthumously. He died covering our troops and heroically restraining the enemy's offensive.

Captain Korpan Oleksandr Bohdanovych. Posthumously. He saved our soldiers and civilian houses when he took the falling aircraft away from them.

Junior Lieutenant Blokha Yuriy Ihorovych. Posthumously. In the battles in the Mykolaiv region, he heroically protected brothers-in-arms, saving their lives.

Senior Sergeant Ivashko Andriy Oleksandrovych. Posthumously. During the rocket fire, he personally provided information about the enemy's actions at the cost of his own life.

Junior Sergeant Volkov Yevhen Volodymyrovych. Posthumously. For courage and heroism during the evacuation of the wounded in the Donetsk region, for saving our military.

Major General Nikoliuk Viktor Dmytrovych. He skillfully led the defence in the north- eastern direction and managed to prevent the capture of Chernihiv.

Colonel Khoda Leonid Oleksiyovych. During the war, under his command, more than 50 enemy vehicles were destroyed.

Lieutenant Colonel Ponomarenko Vyacheslav Anatoliyovych. Thanks to his actions, a significant number of enemy's equipment and soldiers in the city of Hostomel were destroyed.

Lieutenant Colonel Yakovenko Oleksandr Oleksiyovych. He withdrew his units from the enemy artillery fire, thanks to which he saved personnel and continued to successfully defend the Donetsk region.

Major Bova Yevhen Petrovych. For the heroic defence of Mariupol and holding positions under constant enemy attacks.

Captain Boyechko Vasyl Vasyliovych. For the extremely

successful destruction of enemy equipment and manpower.

Sergeant Moroz Oleh Romanovych. Thanks to his heroic deeds, the enemy's offensive in the Luhansk region was stopped.

Sailor Samofalov Valeriy Mykhailovych. In one battle, for the first time in the history of this war, he shot down three enemy helicopters.

I also signed a decree awarding orders for personal courage to 39 national guardsmen, 31 policemen (9 posthumously), 14 border guards (4 posthumously) and 23 employees of the State Emergency Service.

Today the rank of Brigadier General is awarded to:

Nechayev Oleh Oleksandrovych. For the successful defence of the Kyiv region.

Lishchynsky Vladyslav Vatslavovych. For extremely successful actions against the enemy in the Kherson region.

Hutsol Volodymyr Volodymyrych. For the successful destruction of enemy airborne troops in Vasylkiv.

Demyanchyk Hryhoriy Petrovych. For the successful organization of personnel training for our military units.

And finally.

Discussions on Ukraine's future in the EU continue today and tomorrow in Europe.

I believe that our people, our state, our army did everything for us to be welcome there. As equals. For us to be invited there.

This is the final exam for Europe.

Among the leaders of the states there are those who support us. And there are also those who support only themselves. But we see how the nations of all European countries treat us. And this is the main thing.

Because I know for sure—if people decided on our membership in the EU, they would definitely choose the people of Ukraine.

Today, when I see the support of the people of each country in the squares of European capitals, I know that the Ukrainian people are already in the European Union.

And politicians... I'm sure they will adjust to that. Preferably faster.

Glory to the nations of Europe!

Glory to Ukraine! Glory to our military! Thank you!

# We have already reached a strategic turning point and are moving towards our goal, our victory
## 11 March 2022—14:19

Free people of a free country!

We have been fighting for our freedom for the 16th day already. This is four times longer than the enemy planned for his invasion.

Four times longer! Against the army, which was considered one of the strongest in the world. Which hoped that the Ukrainians would surrender. Hoped that someone would meet Russian flags on Ukrainian streets, on our streets with flowers.

But Ukrainians are proud people who always defend their land and will not give the invader a single piece of land. Not a percent of their freedom.

16 days. I know that many people have started to feel tired. I understand. Impatience. I understand.

Emotions play a bad game with people. This is life. When we mobilize, when we see our victories and the loss of the enemy on the battlefield, we expect the struggle to end sooner. We expect the invaders to fall faster. But... This is life, this is war. This is a struggle.

Time is still needed. Patience is still needed. Our wisdom, energy. The ability to do our job to the maximum so that we can win together.

It is impossible to say how many more days we must liberate our Ukrainian land. But it is possible to say—we will do it! Because we strived for that. Because we have already reached a strategic turning point. We are already moving towards our goal, towards our victory.

This is a patriotic war. War with a very stubborn enemy who does not pay attention to the thousands of his killed people, killed soldiers. Who is now gathering reservists and conscripts all over Russia to throw them into the hell of this war?

Who came up with the idea of throwing mercenaries against our people? Thugs from Syria. From the country that was destroyed in the same way as the invaders are destroying us now—our Mariupol, our Kharkiv, Okhtyrka, Chernihiv, Volnovakha, Izyum, etc.

This is how Russian troops treat Ukrainians. This is how they treat Donbas, Russian- speaking people, as they said. How they shouted to everyone about "protection", which they talked about so much in Moscow. Rockets, air bombs, artillery. And now Syrian mercenaries who do not distinguish at all who speaks what language here, what church people go to, what party people supported.

Mercenaries who simply go to kill in a foreign land—in every sense of the word.

Over the past night and morning, the invaders carried out,

as they say, "demilitarization" of the water supply system in Chernihiv. The city was left without water. We are doing everything to restore the water supply. Due to constant shelling in parts of the Sumy, Kyiv, Donetsk regions there is no electricity, yes, there are problems with heating, no gas, water. This is a humanitarian catastrophe.

Humanitarian catastrophe—two words that have become fully synonymous with the other two words—the Russian Federation.

At night, the invaders bombed a shoe factory, an apartment building and a kindergarten in Dnipro. For what? How did they threaten the Russian state? They destroyed residential houses in the villages of the Sumy region. They continued torturing Mariupol residents, Kharkiv residents.
They fired rockets at Lutsk and Ivano-Frankivsk...

If this continues, sanctions against Russia are not enough. And I expect, we are already working on this, new sanctions from our partners today.

Russia must pay for this terrible war. Pay daily!

A very important meeting of the leaders of the European Union took place yesterday. Long, substantive. We know what was said at this meeting. What all leaders said. Who specifically spoke? Who supported? Who remained silent? And who tried to make the wording insufficient—for Ukraine, Europe, and our common freedom.

How do we evaluate the decision made?

It's very simple: it must be stronger. This is not what we expect.

It is necessary that the decisions of politicians coincide with the mood of their nations, European nations. We are aware of this mood. And they are aware of this mood.

Every politician is well aware!

The numbers are different in different countries, but there are polls and support is huge. At least 60 percent stand in favour. And this is the vast majority which stands for Ukraine to be part of Europe!

Europeans are clearly talking about this. And I'm sure they will clearly tell their politicians about this. If they haven't figured it out yet.

The decision of yesterday's meeting of EU leaders now reaches the level of the European Commission.

For implementation. For specific procedures. The European Union must do more.

It must do more for us, for Ukraine. And for itself.

We are waiting for that. All European nations are waiting.

Our government officials have organized 12 humanitarian corridors today. Cargo with food, water, medicine is already on the way. Izyum, Enerhodar,

Volnovakha, Polohy, Bucha, Hostomel, Borodyanka, Andriivka, Mykulychi, Makariv, Kozarovychi, of course, Mariupol.

The Ukrainian servicemen have ensured "silence" for the humanitarian corridors to work.

If the invaders shoot and disrupt the rescue of people again, they will eventually receive such a response from the world that they themselves will need humanitarian corridors.

Our government officials, despite difficulties, are doing everything to ensure that there is fuel, products, medicines and all goods people need throughout the country.

Gasoline, diesel—everything is imported.

This morning I was asked a question at a daily conference call. Logical question. Given the spring. What about sowing?

How to start it, especially in those areas that are temporarily occupied?

My answer is very simple: all over our land, no matter what, we have to organize a full- fledged sowing campaign this spring. Of course, as much as possible. It all depends on the people and the situation. Because it's about life. Life is more important. It's about our life. About our dreams. About our future. And therefore, about our victory.

I repeat again and again: when we defend freedom, everyone must be like a full- fledged army.

Do everything we can in our place to get the result we all deserve. That's fair. To win. Necessarily.

Be sure to hold on. Be sure to fight. Be sure to give your all strength.

It will not be easy with such a neighbour. But with us, it will not be easy, too. As it already turned out.

Glory to Ukraine!

# Speech in the Sejm of the Republic of Poland
## 11 March 2022—19:26

Dear Mr. President, my friend Andrzej!

Dear Mrs. Marshal of the Sejm! Dear Mr. Marshal of the Senate! Ladies and gentlemen deputies and senators!

Dear Sirs!

Polish brothers and sisters!

When I became President in 2019, it felt like we had a long way to go with Poland.

Because our relationship was pretty cold, our attitude towards each other wasn't too warm.

This was the situation. But I wanted to go this way fast. The path to warmth. Because we are such nations. I knew that we were akin by nature—Ukrainians, Poles.

I remember my first meetings with Andrzej Duda. From meeting to meeting everything changed. The coolness disappeared. We understood each other. As a Ukrainian and a Pole. As Europeans. As friends. As parents who love their families and realize that our children must live in a world of equal good values. Our shared values.

They must live in a world where nations are independent, where freedom reigns, where the family matters, and where no one ever has the right to war, to invasion.

It is believed that the number seven brings happiness. That is how many neighbours God has given to Ukraine. Does it bring us happiness? The whole world knows the answer today.

And 78 Ukrainian children who died from rockets and shelling of the Russian Federation know it better than others. A neighbour who brought trouble and war to our land. A neighbour who obviously acts without God.

When there is someone who beats like a savage, it is very important to have someone who will lend a hand. And when the foot of the enemy enters your house, he will lend you a helping hand.

On the morning of February 24, I had no doubt who it would be. Who will say to me: "Brother, your people will not be left alone with the enemy."

And so, it happened. And I'm grateful for that. Polish brothers and sisters are with us. And this is natural.

Just in one day, on the first day of the war, it became clear to me and to all Ukrainians, and, I am sure, to all Poles that there are no more borders between us, between our nations. No physical ones. No historical ones. No personal ones.

During the 16 days of this war, Ukrainian pride and Polish honour, Ukrainian courage in battles and Polish sincerity in helping us allow me to say very important words now.

Words that there is real peace between our nations. Peace between relatives. Peace between brothers. And now I really want these words to be heard by our common Belarusian neighbours.

Peace between relatives, peace between neighbours, peace between brothers. We have to come to this with them as well! We will definitely come!

Dear Sirs! Polish brothers and sisters!

For a long time, various "stakeholders" tried to create an impression that Ukrainians and Poles live differently. And separately. Why did they do all this?

I will recall the words of President of the Republic of Poland Lech Kaczynski said in Tbilisi in 2008: "We know very well: today—Georgia, tomorrow—Ukraine, the day after tomorrow—the Baltic countries and then, perhaps, the time will come for my country—Poland".

On February 24, this terrible "tomorrow" for Ukraine came, which President Kaczynski spoke about.

And today we are fighting for such a bad time for Poland and the Baltic States to never come. We fight together. We have strength.

Remember, there are 90 million of us together! We can do everything together. And this is the historical mission, the historical mission of Poland, the historical mission of Ukraine to be leaders who together will pull Europe out of this abyss, save it from this threat, stop the transformation of Europe into a victim.

Dear Sirs! We can do it.

We saw yesterday what the countries of the European Union talked about and in what manner. We saw who the real leader was and fought for a strong Europe. For common European security. And who tried to stop us, tried to stop you.

We understand why it is so important for Poles to fight with us. Together with all those who are for freedom. For us and for you, for Europe.

We remember the terrible tragedy of 2010 near Smolensk. We remember all the facts of the investigation into the circumstances of this catastrophe. We feel what this means for you. And what does the silence of those who also know all this mean to you, but...

But they still feast their eyes on Russia.

Polish brothers and sisters!

I feel that we have already formed an extremely strong alliance. Even though it is informal. But this is an alliance that grew out of reality, not words on paper. Of the warmth in our hearts, not of the speeches of politicians at summits. Of the way you treated our people. Ukrainians who fled to your country to escape from the evil that came to our land.

More than one and a half million citizens of Ukraine! The vast majority are women and children. They do not feel like they are in a strange land. You met our people in your families. With Polish delicacy. With fraternal kindness.

Although we did not ask for it. And you did not ask anything for it. It's just the way it is between relatives.

That's why I address so simply: friend Andrzej, dear Agata!

That's why I claim that we have already united. We united to constantly gain and create freedom, as a great Pole, a close friend of Ukraine John Paul II said.

Today, I cannot be sure of all the leaders of all European

nations, but I am sure that we will definitely be with you in defending freedom. As much as needed.

I am grateful for all the help we have already received from your state, from your people. I am grateful for your efforts so that we can secure the Ukrainian sky. I believe that we will be able to achieve the result in this, the result that we all desperately need.

If God allows and we win this war, we will share the victory with our brothers and sisters.

This is our greatness. And your greatness.

This is a struggle for our freedom, this is a struggle for your freedom. This is the common history of great nations!

May God help us win!

## Today, everyone is gaining glory for Ukraine in his or her place
## 12 March 2022—00:46

Strong people of the steel country!

This is how the militaries answer the Kremlin command's question about what prevented them from capturing Ukraine in four days. Strong people of the steel country. This information is unverified, but this fact is indisputable.

And if the lost invaders justify their failures with something else, it means that during the 16 days of the war they did not understand anything.

Well, we don't take it so hard. We are ready to explain. Enlighten the invaders until they fully understand who they are and where exactly they should go. Go out of Ukraine.

Today in Melitopol the invaders captured mayor of the city Ivan Fedorov. A mayor who courageously defends Ukraine and the people of his community.

Obviously, this is a sign of the weakness of the invaders.

They did not find any support on our land. Although they counted on it.

Because for years they have been lying to themselves that people in Ukraine were supposedly waiting for Russia to come.

They did not find collaborators who would hand over the city and the power to the invaders.

Therefore, they have switched to a new stage of terror, when they are trying to physically eliminate representatives of the legitimate local Ukrainian authorities.

It is clear to any democratic state in the world that a legitimately elected mayor is a true representative of the people. Usually it's not about ideology, it's not about politics, it's about the lives of people in a particular community.

Probably Russia has become accustomed to this during the years of autocratic rule.

Perhaps they believe that the mayor is just a boss which is easy to remove, and it means nothing.

But it is Ukraine here. It is Europe here. It is a democratic world here.

Therefore, the capture of the mayor of Melitopol is a crime not only against a particular person. Not only against a particular community. And not only against Ukraine.

This is a crime against democracy as such. I assure you that one hundred percent of people in all democracies will know this. The actions of the Russian invaders will be equated with the actions of ISIS terrorists.

The whole country saw that Melitopol did not surrender to the invaders. Just as Kherson, Berdyansk and other cities where Russian troops managed to enter didn't. Temporarily managed to enter.

And this will NOT be changed by putting pressure on mayors or kidnapping mayors. This can only get worse. For the invaders.

Ukraine demands the immediate release of the mayor of Melitopol and guarantees of full security to all heads of communities across the country. If you are becoming an analogue of ISIS terrorists, then what is the point of talking to you about something at all?

We will raise this issue, including in talks with international mediators who communicate with Moscow.

Today, Russian troops also disrupted the work of most humanitarian corridors.

But, despite everything, 7,144 people were saved. From Enerhodar, Bucha, Hostomel and Kozarovychi. And these are 7,144 reasons to try to organize evacuation for Ukrainians from the besieged cities tomorrow and the day after tomorrow.

We will do that. We will do everything to bring humanitarian aid to Ukrainian cities. I have to say this with pain—Mariupol remains blocked by the enemy. Russian troops did not let our aid into the city and continue to torture our people, our Mariupol residents.

Tomorrow we'll try again. Once again send food, water and medicine for our city.

I am confident that the Armed Forces of Ukraine will respond to every minute of our people's suffering.

And it's not pathos. Not a threat. This is a statement of reality.

The number of killed Russian servicemen on the territory of Ukraine already exceeds 12 thousand people. 12 thousand! The number of wounded invaders is many times bigger. We did not invite any of them here.

And we repeat to each of the invaders: you can still save yourself. At any moment. Just lay down your weapons and go home, leave our land.

The number of captured invaders has already reached such a level that this issue cannot be left to the structures that we had before the war.

Therefore, today the Cabinet of Ministers of Ukraine established the Coordination Headquarters for the Treatment of Prisoners of War.

Thousands of enemy soldiers who have been captured or surrendered receive from our state the treatment required by international conventions.

But there are so many of them that a special structure is needed to deal with all related issues.

I want to say it again for Russian mothers. Especially for mothers of conscripts.

Do not send your children to war in a foreign land. Do not believe the promises that they will be sent just somewhere for exercises or just somewhere in non-combat conditions.

Check where your son is.

And if you have even the slightest suspicion that your son may be sent to the war against Ukraine, act immediately. Do not give your son to death or captivity.

Ukraine never wanted this dreadful war. And Ukraine doesn't want it. But it will defend as much as necessary.

Fortunately, we are not alone in this battle. Ukrainians have sincere friends. Good partners.

Speaking in the Polish Parliament today, I paid a lot of attention to the importance of not being alone in today's world. How important it is to protect common values. And as a result—to feel that the borders between nations are blurred.

To make people closer.

Just like our relationship with Polish brothers and sisters. Just like our relationship with all our sincere partners.

Because the one who has friends can do anything. I held talks with US President Biden.

We discussed how else we can put pressure on Russia to end this war and establish

peace.

Russia will be deprived of the opportunity to trade normally with the G7 countries.

The less dollars Russian business earns and the less taxes the Russian state receives, the less opportunity the Russian military will have to kill our people.

Leading international companies are already leaving the Russian market. The Russian government has put its country outside the global world by starting a war against us. By starting this invasion. This is self-closure. Self-humiliation. Self-destruction.

In Moscow currency exchange offices, the dollar has already reached 200 rubles. And this is just the beginning. The beginning of international sanctions.

The next step is the United States' ban on bringing dollars into Russia.

Consequently, there will be a shortage of currency. So, the course will raise even more. Consequently, prices will rise. Consequently, every citizen of Russia will feel that the absence of peace is a threat to him personally.

Not a single country in the world wished harm to ordinary

citizens of Russia. Nobody tried to cause any damage until your government started a war with neighbours, peaceful people. A war of annihilation.

No one wanted to return ordinary Russian life back to the "wicked 1990s". Is that what you call that era? A time of upheaval and poverty. A time of very limited opportunities for ordinary people and very large inequalities.

Perhaps now, due to the efforts of propagandists, most Russians do not yet understand what awaits them. But the Russian authorities ALREADY understand this very well.

Very clear. And they are very afraid.

That is why they are trying to close all free sources of information. Actually, all sources of information. Even Instagram and Facebook.

But the modern world has learned to deal with such censorship.

My advice to thinking Russians is to look for ways to get truthful information.

And try to hide your smartphones and computers from the security forces on the streets. They're getting ready to check what's in people's phones. What do people have in laptops. I specifically warn you: learn to resist the repression that your government plans to increase.

Because thinking people should be in every country. And in Russia, too. And they are in Russia.

And one more thing. Now the good news and the victories of Ukraine for all of us are worth their weight in gold.

Or silver and bronze.

And all this—for Ukraine—is successfully won by our Paralympians in Beijing.

Today, everyone is gaining glory for Ukraine. In his or her place. Shows the world who Ukrainians are and what strength we have.

With a weapon in hands on the battlefield or with a sporting rifle on a biathlon track. Our boys and girls have already won 25 medals at the Winter Paralympics!

And take second place in the overall standings, second only to the hosts of the competition—China.

The Paralympics will end in two days.

I would very much like to say the same about the war. That it will end in two days. Unfortunately, this is still unrealistic. But it will definitely happen.

Both victory for Ukraine and peace for Ukraine are achievable.

And they will be more valuable for us than gold, silver and bronze of the whole world. Well, for now ...

Hold our ground! Hold on! We will win!

Glory to Ukraine

# It is time to be effective in routine affairs and provide everything necessary for the defence
## 12 March 2022—13:46

Brave people of the unconquered country!

From the very morning in the Ukrainian—forever Ukrainian—Melitopol people, our citizens, gathered for the regular protest action against the Russian troops.

Against the attempts to put the city to its knees. More than two thousand people in the square. Do you hear it, Moscow?

If 2,000 people are protesting against the occupation in Melitopol, how many people should be in Moscow against the war? To make it fair. Yesterday the invaders captured the mayor of Melitopol Ivan Fedorov. The city community is demanding his release.

And this is very important.

I am grateful to every Melitopol resident for this resistance, for this position. The invaders must see that they are strangers on our land, on all our land of Ukraine, and they will never be accepted.

Throughout the night and today we constantly talk to our partners about this situation with our mayor. The demand is simple—to release him from captivity immediately.

We appeal to all world leaders who speak to Moscow. France, Germany, Israel and others.

I have personally called German Chancellor Olaf Scholz. I spoke with French President Emmanuel Macron.

I will talk to everyone to free our people.

We expect them, the world leaders, to show how they can influence the situation. How they can do a simple thing—free one person. A person who represents the entire Melitopol community, Ukrainians who do not give up.

Our Armed Forces are doing everything to deprive the enemy of any desire to continue the war against Ukraine. The losses of Russian troops are enormous.

The dynamics of the invaders' losses on the 17th day is such that it is safe to say that this is the biggest blow to the Russian army in decades. They've never lost more than that in such a time period.

Since the beginning of the invasion, 31 battalion tactical groups of the enemy have lost their combat capability. The Russian militaries are being taken prisoners not just alone, but in groups. Groups are trying to leave Ukraine and come back to Russia as well.

The losses of the invaders in technical capabilities are simply astounding. More than 360 tanks. 1205 armoured vehicles. And that's without counting the losses in the battles this night and in the morning.

Already almost 60 planes. More than 80 helicopters. Hundreds and hundreds of units of other equipment, including the most modern models, of which Russia is proud.

Most of the world's armies do not have as much as Russian troops lost during the invasion.

Ukrainians!

I want you to understand me correctly.

We have had extraordinary success. The resistance of the entire Ukrainian people against these invaders has already gone down in history. But we have no right to reduce the intensity of defence. No matter how difficult it is. We have no right to reduce the energy of resistance. The enemy is bringing new and new columns to the territory of Ukraine. They are looking everywhere for fighters. Reservists. Conscripts. Mercenaries.

They are trying to take us with numbers. The number of fighters, the amount of equipment. They use terror to break our faith in victory and in Ukraine.

I'm sure they won't succeed. It will not work for them. But in order for them not to succeed, we still have to fight. We still need to be focused. All of us, all Ukrainians, still need to continue to focus on defence. Work together.

Without internal split. Supporting each other. All over the country. From Uzhhorod to Melitopol. From Chernihiv to Mariupol. From Lviv to Kharkiv.

Just like we all have been doing for 17 days of the war.

Today we again sent humanitarian aid to Mariupol. We will try every day to save our people.

I am grateful to every driver who tries to accomplish this difficult mission.

I am grateful to the representatives of the church who joined the efforts to protect the humanitarian corridor in Mariupol from shelling.

Ukrainian troops, for their part, guarantee complete "silence" along the entire route so that Mariupol receives food, water, and medicine. And so that the civilians of Mariupol can go to a safe area.

Humanitarian corridors from Makariv, Borodyanka, Trostyanets, Sumy, Poltava, Lebedyn, Konotop, Velyka Pysarivka, Krasnopillya, Polohy, Tokmak, Hostomel, Kozarovychi, Mykulychi and Andriivka of the Kyiv region have also been prepared.

The Russian side must ensure "silence" on each of these routes. Otherwise, what can Russia guarantee in any negotiations?

We continue to work with Europeans in two directions. The first is Ukraine's accession

to the European Union. We are working with the European Commission to agree on all procedures for our movement towards the EU as soon as possible. The second direction is sanctions, it is the top priority.

We look forward to a new package of European sanctions against Russia to force it to peace. To make it clear: their economy simply will not survive this war.

The Cabinet of Ministers of Ukraine has made several very important decisions.

The complete abolition of value added tax and excise duty for fuel was approved.

For gasoline, for diesel. This is done not only in the context of the sowing campaign, which should start as usual, but also in the context of the needs of all citizens.

So that there is no shortage of fuel in the country. So that prices are stable. The government has done its part. Now it's up to the deputies.

They must immediately adopt this decision by their vote. Chairman of the Verkhovna Rada Ruslan Stefanchuk is already organizing the relevant sitting.

The second component is to support those Ukrainian communities that receive our migrants from the areas of hostilities.

The government has decided to compensate local budgets for utilities payment when accommodating people.

According to preliminary estimates, communities in at least ten regions of Ukraine will receive concrete money from the central government to ensure that all IDPs are provided with everything necessary.

Ukrainians!

Now all of us have to be efficient in our routine as well.

We must do our job one hundred percent, help colleagues, take care of our loved ones. And at the same time, we must provide everything necessary for our defence. For our defenders.

This is a patriotic war. This is a people's war. This is a war for our independence.

Independence of not just our state.

But of everything Ukrainian that was, is and will be in the world.

Glory to Ukraine!

# Address to Italians and all Europeans
## 12 March 2022—19:21

Greetings to all friends of Ukraine!

Greetings to all friends of Europe, all friends of freedom!

I know that there are over a hundred thousand of you all over the world today. More than a hundred thousand in the squares of different cities. We, Ukrainians, are grateful for this. And now I ask each of you to remember one number in each square... 79.

You will understand what this means. I will tell you now what it means for our lives, for each of us. I will tell all one hundred thousand and millions who will hear us afterwards.

We are experiencing a terrible war in Ukraine. Europe has not seen such a war since World War II. We did not start this war. This is a brutal and cynical Russian invasion of Ukrainian land. This is a war against the Ukrainian people—against peaceful and sincere people, whom I am sure you have known very well during the years of our independence.

And you saw that we are very similar to you. We equally value freedom. We equally value equality. We equally want to live. We just want to live.

We equally want only the best, the brightest for our children, for our families. But now we and you live differently.

Now when the war is going on and thousands of people have died in it! And 79 children have died in it. 79 children!

I'm sure each of you has photos of your loved ones. At home or just on the phone so you can watch when your heart asks for that. Photos of children, photos of parents. Photos of your loved ones.

We don't even realize it, but we always know that these photos are not the last.

Because we believe that we will see how those who are dearest to us will live. We'll see how happy our loved ones are. How our children grow up, how they go to university, how they work. How they have their children. And then we will play with our grandchildren. Meet them after school, have dinner together.

Everyone in the millions lives with that hope. Hope for a truly peaceful life.

For new photos, new memories, new moments of happiness, which our state, Ukraine, is deprived of now.

While the war continues, we are in fundamentally different conditions with you. When you can be sure that you and your loved ones have a long future ahead, a normal future. And we want that. And we are happy for you.

And for us, what we have may be the last time. Just one last time. Today and never again. As for 79 Ukrainian children. 79 Ukrainian families. Destroyed by this shameful war—the invasion of Russia. 79 families who have lost the most valuable, but who are still forced to fight. They are forced to pull themselves up and survive. And fight. Fight for a future that is over for them. In those photos of 79 children killed in the war.

And what should we do... All of us—the Ukrainian people, Europeans—so that this number 79 does not change, does not grow. And so that Europe does not forget Ukraine-79.

Russian troops besiege Ukrainian cities. They are trying to destroy them. Imagine! Entire cities! In 2022! In Europe.

Our Mariupol, the largest Ukrainian city on the coast of the Sea of Azov, is under complete blockade. It is bombed around the clock. Russian troops drop air bombs on it and fire missiles. They even bombed a maternity hospital and a children's hospital in Mariupol...

This is hatred of all mankind. They kill children and destroy maternity hospitals and children's hospitals. Why? So that Ukrainian women don't even give birth?

And this is all over our country, all over Ukraine, which is suffering from the Russian invasion.

They have already destroyed dozens of hospitals, hundreds of schools, and kindergartens. They are destroying universities. Completely destroying residential areas with carpet bombing. Imagine what it is! And how to survive in this? What does it mean for Ukrainians, for our families, for our children? What does it mean when you can't find peace even in church? Because aviation bombs even churches!

Even squares... The same squares as yours... Where you are listening to me now. They bombed the square in our city of Kharkiv—Freedom Square. This is the largest square in Europe, which is no different from your squares. Except that it is destroyed.

Destroyed by a Russian missile strike.

I am constantly asked in interviews: how can Europe help Ukraine?

I formulate the question differently, namely: how can Europe help itself?

Because this is a war not only against our people, not only against Ukrainians. This is a war against the values that unite us. Against our ability to live. Live, not kill like the Russian military on our land.

Do you feel why we are different from them? We live. And they kill. We are 79 lives. And they are 79 deaths.

I am sure that you want to stop the war just like every Ukrainian.

That is why my answer about the help that is needed for Ukraine sounds logical, natural to millions of people in democracies. You need to put pressure.

Such sanctions against Russia are needed so that every Russian soldier knows the price of every shot at civilians. We need such principles of European business that the Russian state does not have the money to ruin lives.

Put pressure on the companies in your countries to leave Russia, so that you are not indirect sponsors of this war and tragedy.

Tell your politicians to close the sky over Ukraine from Russian missiles and planes. From those who killed 79 children and thousands of adults! Thousands in 17 days...

All this will protect us. We are just like you. Absolutely the same! You know that. You feel it. You see me and you understand all this.

And you know that we must be together in the European community. This is extremely important for Ukraine. And this is very important for you, for Europe. Because this will strengthen Europe. This will protect Europe. This will stop the war forever. This will prove that the 79 lives taken in the war for freedom have not been lost in vain. That they are alive. That they live among us. And they are among other children of Ukraine and Europe, who will be able to be free, will be able to dream, will be able to just live as they want. In peace. And not to be afraid that they may be killed. And not to look for the nearest air bomb shelter. Just as you are not looking for it—each of the hundred thousand in the squares of European cities that are listening to me now. And just as millions who, I'm sure, will hear me.

Hear about Ukraine-79. About Ukraine-2022. About Ukraine, which seeks peace. And about Europe, for which it is time to choose.

Choose Ukraine.

For the sake of peace! For the sake of all of us. Glory to Ukraine!

# We still need to fight and inflict maximum damage on the enemy in all areas of defence
## 13 March 2022—01:01

Wise people of a strong country!

The 17th day of the war is over. War for the right to be free. For the right to live on our land the way we, Ukrainians, want it. Not the way someone came up with for us. And against us. Against our nature. Against our character.

The Russian invaders cannot conquer us. They do not have such strength. They do not have such spirit. They are holding only on violence. Only on terror. Only on weapons, which they have a lot. But the invaders have no natural basis for normal life. So that people can feel happy and dream. They are organically incapable of making life normal! Wherever Russia has come to a foreign land, dreams are impossible.

Only a very hard struggle for survival.

As a result of the attack on our land, on Ukraine, the Russian leadership is actually turning its state into an analogue of the so-called "DPR" and "LPR". Into a large area isolated from the rest of the world. Where poverty will reign. Where everything will be determined only by violence. And where people will flee. In any manner they can and whoever can.

Look who is leaving Russia now. Who withdraws business? These are professionals who can be competitive at the global market. These are IT specialists who do not want to live in an area where there is no freedom. These are businessmen who feel that everything will be taken away from them at any moment. These are artists who know that creativity in a territory where human life is worthless is also worthless.

Russia loses its brains. Loses talent. Loses money.

But if this is happening to Russia, then what awaits the so-called "DPR" and "LPR"? Their analogues? Solely complete degradation.

The invaders in the Kherson region are trying to repeat the notorious experience of the formation of pseudo-republics. Blackmail local leaders, put pressure on deputies. Look for someone to bribe. They're trying to organize the so-called "KPR". Stillborn as "DPR" and "LPR". To organize some "committees" against the legitimate government on our land. And against the will of the people who go out to protest every day. And who want Ukraine. I am grateful to them.

I want to tell some figures who lacked the disgust to refuse to talk to the invaders... I want to say—if some of them were suddenly tempted by proposals from the invaders... You sign your sentence.

The sentence is to follow more than 12,000 invaders who failed to understand in time why Ukraine should not be encroached upon.

An emergency meeting of the Kherson Regional Council took place. 44 deputies decided that the Kherson region is Ukraine, and no pseudo-republics have a place there.

Ukraine will stand the test. We need time and strength to break the military machine that came to our land.

I will not underestimate the threat. And I will not exaggerate the achievements. We are honest people, not Russia's Ministry of Defence. Which lies to everyone—millions of its citizens and even the head of the Russian Federation. So, I say frankly: we still need to hold on. We still have to fight. Every day and every night we must look for ways to cause maximum damage to the enemy. In all areas of defence. Near Zhytomyr and Kyiv, near Chernihiv and Sumy, near Kharkiv and Luhansk, near Donetsk and Mariupol, in the south of the country and on the diplomatic frontline.

Having such tactics and having self-confidence, we will regain what's ours.

We will come to Melitopol and Henichesk. We will come wherever our land is. And let the invaders know. Let all the collaborators they find know. That Ukraine will not forgive them. Nobody. Nothing.

Ukraine will not forget. Ukraine will find and prosecute. Every single one. In any possible way.

By the way, all humanitarian corridors, which were agreed upon, worked. 12,729 people were evacuated. The humanitarian cargo for Mariupol is to arrive tomorrow afternoon. Due to the complexity of the route they had to spend the night in Berdyansk.

On every occasion, I constantly repeat to our friends and partners abroad that they should do more for Ukraine, for Ukrainians. Because it is not only for Ukraine. This is for everyone in Europe.

Evil that purposefully bombs peaceful cities... Evil that fires even at ambulances and blows up hospitals will not be able to stop at one country. If it has the strength to go further.

I said this at a very important rally in support of our people, which was organized in Europe. More than a hundred thousand people in the squares of Italy and other countries of the continent gathered for a rally in support of Ukraine and against Russian aggression.

Millions of people heard my appeal later thanks to broadcasts and recordings.


We now enjoy the greatest support in the history of Ukraine for our aspirations and our independence.

You can take a public opinion poll in any country, and you will see that Ukraine is among the leaders of those who are sympathized with and supported.

And Russia is not just among enemies. It is even a bigger enemy, bigger evil than North Korea. That's what Americans think, for example. Ordinary people in all states. As well as ordinary people in all European countries.

And I am grateful to them for this extraordinary support. Grateful for understanding our struggle. Because we are united by one dream—to live freely on our land. And we have the right to what everyone has in the free world. To a safe sky, as well as to our own land.

Dear Ukrainians!

Our heroes!

The world has always loved those who fight against evil.

It was our resistance, the courage of all our people that inspired the world. Millions of people in different countries. Who 17 days ago might not have felt what they all have in common? We all have. And now it's obvious. Peace. Freedom. And love for our children. The children we are fighting for. For them to have a future.

I signed two important decrees.

On awarding 106 servicemen of the Armed Forces of Ukraine who bravely showed themselves in the battles for the independence of Ukraine. 17 of them, unfortunately, posthumously. But they are heroes.

I—the decree on conferring the title of Hero of Ukraine with the award of the Order of the Golden Star to:

Senior Sergeant Vasich Serhiy Viktorovych. Posthumously. He bravely defended our positions in the Kyiv region. Destroyed enemy equipment and a significant amount of enemy manpower.

Senior soldier Parkhomuk Vitaliy Vasyliovych. Posthumously. During the counterattack on the enemy near the city of Makariv, he inflicted significant losses on the enemy and died heroically defending his brothers-in-arms.

Soldier Mrochko Kostiantyn Vasyliovych. Posthumously. He fought bravely against the overwhelming forces of the enemy. Thanks to his effective actions, the invaders suffered painful losses.

Soldier Svynchuk Oleh Anatoliyovych. Posthumously. He heroically performed his duty in the battle against the overwhelming forces of the enemy. He was helping his brothers-in-arms until the last moment.

Sergeant Khanin Andriy Pavlovych. Posthumously. Defending Volnovakha, Donetsk region, he destroyed an enemy tank and about 10 enemies. During the battle, when he was wounded, he helped his wounded brothers-in-arms and performed his duty to the last.

Sergeant Derusova Inna Mykolaivna. Posthumously. Since February 24, the senior combat medic has performed tasks in the city of Okhtyrka, Sumy region. She saved more than 10 servicemen, risking her own life. She died from artillery shelling by Russian troops, helping the wounded. The first woman—hero of Ukraine, who was posthumously awarded this title.

Eternal memory to all who gave their lives for Ukraine!

The title of Hero of Ukraine with the Order of the Golden Star is conferred upon:

Senior Lieutenant Hutsul Volodymyr Oleksandrovych. Thanks to his heroic actions in the Kherson region, 25 units of enemy equipment and about 300 invaders were destroyed.

Senior Lieutenant Chornyi Volodymyr Volodymyrovych. Thanks to his skilful actions during the defence of Volnovakha, Donetsk region, about 50 enemies and a T-72 tank were destroyed, as well as 5 invaders were captured.

Glory to all heroes! Glory to Ukraine!

# We will win thanks to our ability to unite and always care for our people
## 14 March 2022—00:19

Strong people of an unbreakable country!

Today is the 18th day. The 18th day of our war for life, for Ukraine, for independence.

The beginning of this day was black. Russian missiles and air bombs hit our country again. From east to west.

30 missiles for the Lviv region alone. The shelling of the International Centre for Peacekeeping and Security killed 35 people and wounded 134 others.

Nothing was happening there that could threaten the territory of the Russian Federation. And only 20 kilometres away are NATO borders.

Last year, I made a clear warning to NATO leaders that if there were no tough preventive sanctions against Russia, it would start a war. We were right.

I have been saying for a long time that Nord Stream is a weapon that will hit Europe. Now it's obvious.

And now I repeat again—if you do not close our sky, it is only a matter of time before Russian missiles fall on your territory. NATO territory. On the homes of citizens of NATO countries.

An American journalist was killed in the Kyiv region today. Brent Renaud. His colleague was wounded. It was a deliberate attack by the Russian military.

They knew what they were doing. But not everyone in the West seems to know what they are doing.

In the east of our country, the invaders decided to "demilitarize" and "denazify" the Sviatohirsk Lavra of the Ukrainian Orthodox Church, Moscow Patriarchate.

At the time of the attack, only monks and hundreds of refugees were on the territory of the monastery. No military target in or near the monastery. But Russian troops do not stop even before striking at the monastery.

This fact alone demonstrates that the whole ideology of the Russian state is simply a lie.

Today I visited our guys, our defenders who are recovering from wounds at a military hospital.

We talked. I presented awards. Orders and medals—for courage, for glory for Ukraine.

And I really want my greeting "I wish you good health" to work today as powerfully as our Armed Forces have been holding key frontiers. For 18 days already.

By the way, the Russian military from Ryazan is being treated in the same hospital. He is in the same ward with our defenders. Gets the same aid. From the same doctors.

Despite what this guy was doing. Against us, against Ukraine. But Ukrainian doctors saved him. And this is obvious. Because they are people. Not savages. And we have to go through this war so that we all remain human.

I am grateful to all the doctors and nurses who work in Kyiv and Dnipro, in Vinnytsia and Lviv, in Chernihiv and Donbas, in Kharkiv, in Melitopol, in Mariupol...

Everyone!

Mariupol Military Hospital. Pokrovsk Military Mobile Hospital. Chasiv Yar Military Mobile Hospital.

Military Medical Clinical Center of the Eastern Region. Cherkaske Military Hospital.

Military Medical Clinical Center of the Central Region, Vinnytsia.

Military Medical Clinical Center of the Western Region, Lviv.

Military Medical Rehabilitation Center, left Irpin but continues to work. Sincere gratitude!

From all of us. From all Ukrainians.

I also visited checkpoints today. I didn't want it to be very public.

Just to support our guys. To talk. Courageous men, cheerful guys. Who defend Kyiv and know that WE will win. It is felt.

We will win due to our unique ability to unite.

We can always care for our people. Ours in spirit, in heart, in sincerity.

I met an extraordinary person there at the checkpoint who supports our defenders every day and brings them a pot of borscht every day. Really delicious! Truly Ukrainian. Whole-heartedly. And I know that our state has been based on such people for centuries. It is thanks to such people that we will survive any dark days. Because we are together. And we always protect our own people. And our own property. NOT for money. Without coercion. NOT like those who came to us. Just because we are Ukrainians.

Important international negotiations. Bulgaria, Slovakia, Czech Republic, Romania, Poland, Britain.

We feel the support of these countries. We feel the support for our army. It is important.

I also spoke with Charles Michel, President of the European Council. About our European perspective, which is becoming a reality.

Now about the negotiations with the Russian Federation.

Representatives of our countries' delegations speak in video format every day. Our delegation has a clear task—to do everything to ensure a meeting of the presidents. The meeting that I am sure people are waiting for.

Obviously, this is a difficult story. A hard path. But this

path is needed. And our goal is for Ukraine to get the necessary result in this struggle, in this negotiation work.

Necessary for peace. And for security.

So that we have guarantees—normal, effective. NOT like the Budapest ones and not like in our sky. So that Ukrainians could say: this is what works. These are the guarantees.

It is necessary to talk.

More than ten humanitarian corridors worked. Kyiv region, Luhansk region... 5550 people were saved in one day. In six days—more than 130,000. It is necessary to talk.

And this is also due to negotiations. We have to understand that.

Unfortunately, the humanitarian corridor to Mariupol was blocked. Again. We did everything necessary. Ensured "silence". Russian troops disrupted the movement of cargo and buses.

But we will try again. Until we can help our people. Because they are ours. Our Mariupol. Heroic Mariupol.

Ukrainians!

We are going through the worst ordeal in our history. In our lives. We protect the most precious thing we have. We must hold on. We must fight. And we will win. I know that. I believe in that.

Glory to you!

Glory to our people! Glory to our heroes! Glory to Ukraine!

# Today, volunteers are all those who feel a free call to defend Ukraine
## 14 March 2022—14:24

I wish you health, dear Ukrainians!

Good weather, which we now almost do not notice. Clear sky... There is no such thing over Kyiv today. Over Kyiv and other cities of our state. Due to missile strikes, traces of enemy aircraft. The streets are quiet, but I know, I believe it's not for long. Not forever. That's why we work. That is why we fight. That's why we don't give what's ours.

Today we celebrate our purely Ukrainian holiday. Volunteer Day.

It is our ability to instantly unite during ordeals, find common ground and fight together that creates our character, Ukrainian character.

We may not notice each other in everyday life. Agree, this happens to us.

But when we see a threat to our way of life, to our spirit, when we see a threat to Ukraine, our state, we do not hesitate even for a moment. If we are Ukrainians.

We unite. We do everything to protect what's ours.

Ukrainians do not need to be persuaded to become volunteers. Ukrainians do not need to be encouraged to start helping each other.

Strong support for the Armed Forces by all the people of Ukraine, sincere volunteer movement, mass joining the territorial defence, solidarity of all our people—these are the prerequisites for victory. Prerequisites for the liberation of our entire country...

The only and the best.

For us, Ukraine is not just a territory, as for the invaders. They do not distinguish anything here. They do not understand anything. That is why for them everything is just a target.

For us, Ukraine is millions of happy moments, native symbols, memorable places.

We feel this land. For us, Ukraine is our life, and that is why millions of people have come to the defence of our state today. That is why today we are all volunteers. All those who defend Ukraine, our children, those who defend our future.

To all who feel this free call... A call to defend Ukraine... Who are volunteers in battles? Or in the information troops. Who protects roads and cities? All diplomats—official and informal. Everyone who helps with technology. Who keeps the business? Who supplies the necessary goods, products? Who saves and heals under any circumstances? Who works in transport? Who provides communication and repairs networks...? I am grateful to everyone. And I sincerely congratulate you!

Each of the volunteers. Each of the millions working together to win. The 19th day of our resistance.

The Armed Forces of Ukraine are holding on bravely. And creatively. We inflict such losses on the enemy that he no longer knows where else to look for reserves. Where else to look for help.

Help for himself. Help for the invader. This is pathetic.

But we have no right to relax.

The Russian state has been preparing for war for decades. They have accumulated significant military resources. For the evil. For the conquest of neighbours. And for the destruction of Ukraine, Europe, as we know it, as we value it.

That's why we have to hold on. We have to fight. To win. To come to the peace deserved by Ukrainians. Fair peace. With security guarantees for our state. For our people. And to put it on paper. In negotiations. Difficult negotiations.

The video meeting of the delegations has already started today. It continues. Everyone is waiting for the news. We will definitely report in the evening.

As long as the state is at war, as long as the people are defending themselves, the economy must be preserved and restored. As much as possible in the current difficult conditions.

Life must appear on the streets of the cities. Where security allows. Where people can provide it. Pharmacies, trade, any business that can work. For the country to live. For the restoration of Ukraine to already begin. And it depends on each of us, on each of us who is able to work.

Economic suppression of Ukraine is one of the tasks of the war against us. And we have to fight back from that as well. Save our economy. Save our people.

Therefore, the government has received a clear instruction—to return small and medium-sized businesses. Remove any obstacles. Reduce taxes as much as possible, remove all difficulties, absolutely all. So that the system does not press, so that people know that they can work the way they can. Where they can.

A new tax model is needed for the war and for the post-war development. The financial rules also need to be updated. To make people feel that they can be flexible. Feel that all the money and valuables will be saved. And that you shouldn't be afraid of losing something because the state guarantees the security of assets and savings.

The Cabinet of Ministers is already working on how to regulate this. A day or two—and there will be details.

Ukrainians!

Russian troops continue to destroy our infrastructure, continue to destroy our cities. Kyiv region, Chernihiv region, Sumy region, Kharkiv, south, Donbas.

But know—we will rebuild everything. We will restore everything. Every street of every city. Every house, every apartment of every Ukrainian. After the war, I'm sure we can do it quickly. We will direct all our efforts to this. All the help of the world. We are already creating funds for Ukraine to live.

But now that the invaders are still on our land, we must beat them as best as we can. Drive them away in any way we can. Defend the cities. Defend the villages. Defend every meter of our land. And every part of our heart. Ukrainian heart. Ukrainian soul.

Help each other! Support each other! Support the defence! And protect the state! Together we will definitely win.

Glory to Ukraine!

# Responsibility for war crimes of the Russian military is inevitable
## 15 March 2022—01:29

Free people of a free country!

The 19th day of our resistance is over. Historical war. Another difficult day, which is still approaching our victory. Approaching peace for Ukraine.

As before, the enemy is confused. They did not expect such resistance. They believed in their propaganda, which has been lying about us for decades. They still can't recollect themselves. But they have already begun to understand that they will not achieve anything by war.

Their soldiers know this. Their officers are aware of this. They flee the battlefield. They abandon equipment.

We take trophies and use them to protect Ukraine. Today, Russian troops are, in fact, one of the suppliers of equipment to our army. They could not imagine such a thing in a nightmare.

And I want to tell the Russian soldiers. Those who have already entered our land. And who are just about to be sent to fight against us.

Russian conscripts! Listen to me very carefully. Russian officers! You've already understood everything. You will not take anything from Ukraine. You will take lives. There are a lot of you. But your life will also be taken.

But why should you die? What for? I know that you want to survive. We hear your conversations in the intercepts, we hear what you really think about this senseless war, about this disgrace and about your state. Your conversations with each other. Your calls home to your family. We hear it all. We draw conclusions. We know who you are.

Therefore, I offer you a choice. On behalf of the Ukrainian people, I give you a chance. Chance to survive. If you surrender to our forces, we will treat you the way people are supposed to be treated. As people, decently. In a way you were not treated in your army. And in a way your army does not treat ours. Choose!

Our brave defenders continue to inflict devastating losses on Russian troops.

Soon the number of downed helicopters of Russia will reach hundreds of units. They have already lost 80 warplanes. Hundreds of tanks and thousands of other units of equipment.

In 19 days, the Russian army has lost more in Ukraine than in two bloody and years- long wars in Chechnya. For what?

I am grateful to those Russians who do not stop trying to convey the truth. To those who fight disinformation and tell the truth, real facts to their friends and loved ones. And personally, to the woman who entered the studio of Channel One with a poster against the war. To those who are not afraid to protest. As long as your country has not completely closed itself off from the whole world, turning into a very large North Korea, you must fight. You must not lose your chance.

The European Union has approved the fourth package of sanctions against Russia. The fourth—and I'm sure not the last.

We are working with partners on new restrictions that will be applied against the Russian state. Everyone who is responsible for the war. Everyone who is responsible for the destruction of democracy. Everyone who is responsible for repression against people. Everyone will get an answer. The answer of the world. And this is just the beginning.

Responsibility for war crimes of the Russian military is inevitable. Responsibility for a deliberate humanitarian catastrophe in Ukrainian cities is inevitable. The whole world sees what is happening in Mariupol. Kharkiv. Chernihiv. Sumy. Okhtyrka. Hostomel. Irpin. In all our cities.

All our partners are informed of the crimes of the invaders against civilians and local self-government in the Kherson and Zaporizhzhia regions. In the temporarily occupied areas. There will be an answer for that. Necessarily. For the disrupted humanitarian corridors. Necessarily.

During the day of March 14, 3,806 Ukrainians were evacuated from the cities and towns of the Kyiv and Luhansk regions.

Our convoy with one hundred tons of what is most necessary for Mariupol is still kept in Berdyansk. For three days already. But we will try. We will do everything to ensure that Mariupol residents receive food, water, and medicine.

I provided full information about the actions of the invaders on the Ukrainian land in conversations with friends and partners of our state. Every aggressive action of the invaders only pushes the world to new sanctions.

I spoke with President of the European Commission Ursula von der Leyen. With President of Poland Andrzej Duda. Prime Minister of Luxembourg Xavier Bettel. We have 100% mutual understanding.

The conversation with Prime Minister of Israel Bennett was also important. As part of a negotiation effort to end this war as soon as possible. With a fair peace.

Our delegation also worked on this in negotiations with the Russian party. Pretty good, as I was told. But let's see. They will continue tomorrow.

The Cabinet of Ministers of Ukraine has agreed on a package of decisions to support our economy.

So that business works. So that people have jobs. Where security allows. Where people are ready for it.

First, we are starting tax reform. Instead of VAT and income tax we give a rate of 2 percent of turnover and simplified accounting. For small businesses—this is the first and second group of sole proprietors—we set a voluntary payment of a single tax. That is, if you can—pay. You can't—no questions asked.

The second is maximum business deregulation. We cancel all inspections for all businesses. So that everyone works normally. So that the cities come to life. So that life continues wherever there is no hostilities.

The only condition is that you ensure the normal operation of your business in the framework of Ukrainian law.

These are just the first two steps of our tax reform. To be continued. And finally.

I have just signed a decree on awarding state awards of Ukraine to 234 servicemen of the Armed Forces of Ukraine who showed personal courage and heroism in the fight for our land. For our independence. 59 of them posthumously.

May the memory of everyone who gave life for our state live forever! Eternal gratitude to all our heroes!

Glory to Ukraine!

## Every shot of Russia at Ukraine is a step towards its self-destruction
## 15 March 2022—17:29

Strong people of our indomitable country!

Eight years of war against us. The 20th day of full-scale invasion. Attempts to destroy us all, to destroy Ukraine. We are fighting for our lives. We are fighting for our lives against missiles, bombs, artillery, tanks, mortars, and everything else that Russian troops are using to destroy us. Everything else that Russia is destroying itself with now.

Because every shot at Ukraine, every blow at Ukraine are steps towards Russia's self- destruction. Steps to self-isolation, poverty, and degradation.

Everyone who just wants to live and has something to think with is leaving Russia. Scientists, artists, businessmen, IT specialists, etc. The Russian state has not experienced such a blow at human capital for decades. A blow, which it inflicted on itself. We do not care. This is not our problem.

Our problem is to save our people. The strength of our society. Its scientists, its artists, its businessmen, its people, its strong people. All our Ukrainians who defend the state and bring closer the peace that every Ukrainian needs.

Last night there were air alarms almost all over our country. The airport in Dnipro was destroyed by a missile strike. Kharkiv. Russian bombs hit residential areas. Artillery.

Mortars. Fighting continues in the region—Izyum, Chuhuiv.

Disassembly of wreckage in Rivne after the missile strike on the TV tower is ongoing. As of now, 19 casualties are confirmed.

Ancient Chernihiv and Oster are under such a brutal attack

by Russia that it has wiped out any claims to its cultural ties to the times of Rus'. The invaders have no roots, no memory, and no soul.

Russian troops attacked Kyiv, attacked Kyiv residents. Four apartment buildings were destroyed. Disassembly of the debris is still ongoing. As of now, five casualties are confirmed.

I will tell you in Russian: this happened in our capital. In the city that you always called "the mother of Russian cities". That made our nations historical. And that you bombed today. Just people, residential areas. Bombed and bombed again. We don't need such children. No, thanks.

The invaders continue to consider the capture of our capital as their key goal, their political goal. They hope that control over Kyiv will give them control over Ukraine. This is absolute absurdity from all points of view.

To further strengthen the defence of the capital and the Kyiv region, I appointed Hero of Ukraine, Lieutenant General and Commander of the Joint Forces Operation Oleksandr Pavliuk head of the regional military administration.

Dismissed head of the regional administration Oleksiy Kuleba will help the military leadership.

Therefore, the Kyiv direction and the situation in the region will get even more attention.

Major General Eduard Moskaliov became the new commander of the Joint Forces. Professional man, patriotic man. The decree is signed.

Every morning, every evening, I thank the military. I thank all our heroes who bravely defend our state. All who stop the enemy despite the fact that the invaders are many times more. Dozens of times.

And now, today, I want to speak about all peaceful Ukrainians who were taken away by this war.

Eternal memory to everyone who died for Ukraine! Eternal curse to the enemy who took thousands of lives.

Humanitarian corridors have been partially opened today. There is a corridor from Sumy, Trostyanets, Lebedyn, Shostka and Konotop in the direction of Poltava.

The invaders did not stop the shelling and disrupted humanitarian corridors in the Kyiv region.

The convoy with humanitarian cargo for Mariupol also remains blocked. For several days in a row. But still little by little people are leaving the besieged city by private transport.

I want to thank SES officers, police, doctors, and everyone else who saves people for this important work. And of course, I am thankful to our military.

Today I spoke at the summit organized by Great Britain, a friend of Ukraine—Boris Johnson. I addressed the United Kingdom Joint Expeditionary Force. Spoke to the leaders of the Baltic states and the countries of northern Europe.

I said what, of course, all our citizens would like to say.

About NATO. About help. About sincerity and... the fact that not everyone took a moral stance in response to the Russian war.

Each of more than 800 Russian missiles that have hit our country is an answer to a long-standing question about NATO. Whether the doors of the Alliance are really open for Ukraine.

If they were open, if it was fair, we would not have to convince the Alliance for 20 days that the sky over Ukraine should be closed. Closed to the death brought by the Russian Air Force. But... They don't hear or don't want to hear us yet. Some Allies have intimidated themselves. Saying that they allegedly can't answer. They cannot collide with Russian missiles and planes in the sky of Ukraine. Because this, they say, will lead to escalation, will lead to World War III...

And what will they say if Russia goes further into Europe, attacking other countries?

I'm sure it's the same thing they say to Ukraine. Article 5 of the NATO treaty has never been as weak as it is now. This is just our opinion.

When some members of the Alliance are afraid to be truly an alliance capable of protecting everything for which it was created. Freedom and democracy. Humanity and justice. We need to look for effective guarantees. Guarantees for us, for our sky. And we will not give up. We need planes. And I will continue to talk about it, I will continue to pursue it.

We need long-term security guarantees for the state. For all Ukrainians.

Concrete things. Concrete guarantees. Legally enshrined. So that there is no doubt in them. And so that no excuses sound. As they sound now, when we turn to those who signed "Budapest" and who... had the power to stop the Russian invasion even before it began. Using preventive measures. By helping Ukraine, which is convincing. Using sanctions that do not allow war.

Ukrainians!

There are more than 40 million of us in our state. And millions more around the world. This is a great force. Plus, our friends. Plus, many of our partner countries. We all now have a common task, a national task. We must put pressure on Russia so that the price for this war against Ukraine becomes extremely painful. So that everyone in the world takes a moral stance. Not only states, but also companies. I'm talking about business.

Large corporations that still sponsor Russia's military machine and have not left the Russian market, although they should have done so immediately. As soon as the world saw what Russian troops were doing on our Ukrainian land.

You know these brands. They are well known. And there are no secrets here.

Nestle, Mondelez and other giants of the food industry. As well as Raiffeisen, Société Générale and other banks. BASF, Samsung and LG. Bayer, Sanofi, and other pharma companies.

Unilever, Johnson & Johnson... And dozens of other companies. And that's billions of dollars.

We turn to the world. To states and to people. But this is not just the work of politicians.

I appeal to Ukrainians. To everyone and in any country. Where you can influence it. Everything is in your power. All business with Russia must be stopped. All trade operations.

So that they can't sponsor the killings. Killings of us and our children. So that dollars and euros are not paid for blood. Please contact politicians. Put pressure. Talk to reporters. Boycott their products.

They must feel our strength! They must feel your strength! Because we have the strength.

Glory to Ukraine!

## Speech in the Parliament of Canada
## 15 March 2022—19:57

Dear speakers!

Mr. Prime Minister! Dear Justin!

Members of the government and parliament! Dear attendees, Dear friends!

Before I begin, I want you to understand my feelings, the feelings of Ukrainians. As much as possible. Feelings during these 20 days. 20 days of full-scale invasion of the Russian Federation after eight years of war in Donbas.

Just imagine... Imagine that at four in the morning each of you hears explosions. Terrible explosions. Justin, imagine that you hear it. And your children hear it. Hear missile strikes at Ottawa airport. At dozens of other places throughout your beautiful country, Canada. Cruise missiles. Even before dawn. And your children hug you and ask: "what happened, dad?" And you are already receiving the first reports on which facilities in your country have been destroyed by missiles of the Russian Federation. And you know how many people have already died and where.

Imagine you are looking for words to explain this to children. Explain to them that a large-scale war has begun.

The war aimed at the destruction of your state, at the conquest of your people. And you know it.

The second day—and you get a message about the columns of armoured vehicles. Thousands, thousands coming to your land. First—small cities, then larger ones. They want to block them all. And they do so.

They approach Edmonton—imagine—and fire artillery. Fire at residential areas, at people. Schools are being burned down; kindergartens are being blown up. Just as in our cities—in Sumy, in our Okhtyrka. They blockade Vancouver and besiege hundreds of thousands of people who remain in the city. As in our Mariupol. For the second week under fire, without electricity completely, almost without food, definitely without water. In the basements.

Justin! Dear attendees! Gentlemen!

Imagine hearing the report on the dead every day. Yes, you are the president or the head of government, but you just hear about it, about the dead children. And the death toll is growing. 97 children were killed as of this morning.

The famous CN Tower in Toronto... How many Russian missiles will be enough to destroy it? Believe me, I do not wish this to all of you...

But we predict every day how many more missiles can hit our TV towers. And they hit them.

Our Freedom Square in Kharkiv and your Churchill Square in Edmonton. Imagine Russian missiles hitting its heart.

Our Babyn Yar is the burial place of the Holocaust victims... The Russians did not stop before bombing even this land. And what about the National Holocaust Monument in Ottawa? Will it withstand the impact of three or five missiles? It happened to us. Air bombs. A minute ago, there were people alive. There was a family that just came there. They were alive. And now... You understand.

And then a terrible night... each of these 20, when the Russian militaries fire from tanks at housing estates.

From tanks—at the Zaporizhzhia nuclear power plant. Direct guidance. When the fire started there. Can you imagine that happening to your Bruce Station in Ontario?

And what would you feel if you saw your flag in every city where they pass, how your flag in Montreal is removed... Removed to be thrown away and replaced with a Russian one.

I know that you support Ukraine, sincerely, effectively. We are friends with Justin. But I want you to understand me, and to feel it.

Feel what we feel. Feel how we want to live. And how we want to win. Win for life.

I want you to feel what it's like when you call your friends and say: close the sky, stop the shelling. No matter which way, just do it. Stop the bombing. How many more missiles must fall on our cities?

And in response you hear that someone does not want to do it ... But they are deeply concerned!

Then give us planes, we tell our partners.

They answer: Soon. Be patient a little. Everyone is deeply

concerned. They just don't want to. And someone is looking for reasons. The main thing is the result.

They talk about escalation. How can it get worse? They say Ukraine is not in NATO now. Although "the door is open". But for whom are these doors and where do they lead, if we are told that we will not be admitted.

War always shows everything people are capable of. Who is strong? And who is weak. Who is wise? Who does not see the obvious? Who is honest and who is a hypocrite?

And we saw it all. And we understood all this. In 20 days and eight years. I'm sure you've seen it all.

Dear speakers!

Mr. Prime Minister!

Members of the government. Members of parliament! Dear friends!

Canada has always been, is and, I am sure, will be a reliable partner in Ukraine.

Partner of our land, our people of Ukraine, each of our families.

You came to our aid as soon as we asked for it. You are giving us the weapons and other support we so desperately need now. You have imposed sanctions against Russia
- truly moral. Really substantial. However, we see that the war, unfortunately, continues. That Russian troops are not leaving our territory. You see that our cities: Kharkiv, Mariupol are not as protected as your Edmonton and Vancouver. That Kyiv is under missile strikes. Like Chernihiv, Zhytomyr, Ivano-Frankivsk and dozens, dozens of our Ukrainian cities that yesterday were peaceful and quiet.

That means more needs to be done. Much more! For peace. We all have to do more to stop Russia. To protect Ukraine and protect Europe from this total evil that is destroying everything: memorials, churches, schools, hospitals, neighbourhoods and all our businesses.

They have already killed 97 Ukrainian children!

We do not ask for much. We ask for justice. We ask for real support that will help us endure and defend our life. Life of the whole world.

Canada is already showing the necessary leadership! It is already the first to do what other countries come to later. But we need more leadership, and we ask for more participation from you.

Justin! All friends of our country Ukraine! All friends of the truth!

You understand how important it is for us to protect our skies from Russian missiles and planes. You can influence this. It seems so to me.

You can force even more companies to leave the Russian market. So that there is not a single dollar for the war. If they stay in Russia and sponsor the war, they are not allowed to work in Canada. Let it be so—and it will give us peace.

You know, perhaps better than many in the world, that this attack by Russia is an attempt to destroy us, to destroy the Ukrainian people. Nothing else. This is their main goal.

This is a war against the people. Against our people. This is a war to destroy everything that makes Ukrainians. Against our future. Against our character. Against our will. Everything that you, Canadians, know very well, feel very well.

So I ask you: do not stop. Do not stop helping Ukraine. Do not stop in leadership and in efforts to bring peace back to our peaceful land.

I believe, I know you can handle it. I know that with Canada, our anti-war coalition, which we are reinforcing, will definitely yield the result.

I want to address our Ukrainian diaspora, all Ukrainians in Canada.

It is at this historic moment that we need your effective help. And you must prove with your steps that you are a part of the history of Ukraine, the living history of Ukraine.

Remember this—living. Because we want to live. And we strive for peace.

I thank you for your support. I am thankful to everyone present in this hall of parliament. To every citizen of Canada. I'm grateful to you, Justin. Grateful on behalf of the entire Ukrainian nation.

I am sure that together—and only together—we will defeat all enemies.

Glory to Ukraine! Thank you, Canada!

## For every act of terrorism by Russian troops on the territory of Ukraine there will be an international tribunal
## 16 March 2022—13:38

Ukrainians!

Our defenders!

We are stepping up work to bring the invaders to justice. There must be an international tribunal. And it will be. For everything they did against Ukraine. Against our people. For every act of terrorism of Russian troops on the territory of our state.

The Prosecutor's Office of Ukraine and law enforcement agencies have already started this work. The launch of the activity of the investigative group of the International Criminal Court in Ukraine is also important, which together with our law enforcement officers is already collecting all the evidence, collecting the facts of war crimes of the invaders on the territory of our state. So that they receive the legal answer—legal and concrete.

I spoke with Karim Khan, the Prosecutor of the International Criminal Court in The Hague. He is already in Ukraine; he has already started working. Therefore, the invaders will be responsible for all war crimes against Ukrainians.

Last night, Russian troops continued shelling Ukrainian territory, our peaceful cities, our citizens. Kharkiv and the region... They bombed the coast of the Odesa region.

They fired missiles at Kyiv. Hit civilian infrastructure of Zaporizhzhia. As of this morning, 103 children have been killed.

Russian troops have now inflicted hundreds of times more damage on Ukraine than on Donbas in eight years of war. And the territories of Donbas, border regions in the Russian direction, Kyiv region and the south of Ukraine suffered the most. The most affected areas are those Russian propagandists have always spoken of as the place of residence of people especially close to Russia.

Apparently, there are no non-nuclear weapons that the invaders have not yet used against our civilians. That's their closeness. That's their friendship. That's, as they said in Moscow, "a divided nation."

A total of 400 educational institutions have been destroyed in Ukraine to date, the largest number is in the Donetsk region—119. In Mariupol, the invaders seized a hospital, a regional intensive care hospital. Already damaged by Russian bombs.

Patients and doctors are in captivity. Residents of neighbouring houses were forced to go inside the hospital as well.

More than 400 people are hostages!

And the invaders are using the hospital as a firing position to shell the city. This regular crime of the Russian military against Mariupol is no different from

Basayev's seizure of the hospital in Budyonnovsk. Although... It is different. Now it's even more treacherous.

Last night, the invaders took hostage six people in the Bucha City Council.

A Ukrainian rescuer who was captured in an agreed humanitarian corridor is being held hostage! The mayors of several of our cities, activists, a journalist are being held hostage... The Russian state has become an outspoken terrorist. And it is not ashamed. But it will be responsible for everything.

The world is already beginning to understand that without the recognition of Russia as a terrorist state, it will be impossible to restore justice for Ukraine, it will be impossible to restore international order.

Today I signed an important decree on a nationwide minute of silence to honour the memory of all Ukrainians who died in our patriotic war. All those we lost because of the Russian invasion. Because of the terror committed by the invaders.

Every morning at 9 am in the whole territory of our state we will remember the Ukrainians who gave their lives. All who fought. All military and all civilians. Adults and children... Everyone! All those who could still be alive if Russia had not started this war.

May the memory of everyone who died for Ukraine live forever! The losses of the invaders continue to grow.

The number of killed enemy soldiers is already approaching 14,000. Tens of thousands

of Russian servicemen were wounded. They have already lost more than a hundred helicopters. Soon there will be hundreds of lost planes.

More than 400 Russian tanks were destroyed, plus several thousand units of other equipment.

We take abandoned enemy equipment from the battlefield and use it to protect our state and our people.

Ukrainians!

If you know where the enemy is and where he abandoned his tanks or other armoured vehicles, ordnance, inform the Ukrainian forces. Let's use everything for our victory! And for the sake of victory be wise.

Don't publish details of our air defence work when you hear the guy's work. Do not publish maps that you find in abandoned Russian vehicles and in the broken command posts of the invaders. Please give them to our military. Let them use it to make the enemy suffer!

Today at 3 pm Kyiv time I will address the Congress of the United States of America.

This will be an important speech. A speech from all of us, from each of our defenders, from each of our citizens. Addressed to the most powerful democracy in the world. To the state and the people who can do a lot to stop Russian aggression, to restore peace on our land.

Eight years ago, on this day, the Russian state organized a fake "referendum" on the territory of our Ukrainian Crimea. Which it later used to justify the seizure of our territory. It was illegal. This was the destruction of the entire security architecture in Europe, which was created after World War II. But Russia went for it.

If then there had been at least a hint of such resistance, which we are showing now, which you are showing now... If then the world had reacted at least half as it should react now and reacts... I'm sure we would have had neither this invasion, nor eight years of war in Donbas. All this evil was born from the occupation of Crimea. From our weakness, the brutal actions of Russia, for which it should have been punished already in 2014.

We are much stronger now, we are united. Now we are a great nation.

But... We don't have a time machine and we can't go back to the moment when everything was decided.

We can and must fight today, now. We can and must protect our state, our Ukrainian life. We can and must negotiate on a just and fair peace for Ukraine. On the real security guarantees that will work.

This is an ambitious task. A difficult one. This is a long way. But I am sure that we, Ukrainians, can do all this. We, Ukrainians, can win. And return to peace.

To the peace we all so strive for.

Glory to our heroes! Glory to Ukraine!


## Address to the US Congress
## 16 March 2022—17:27


Mrs. Speaker, Members of Congress, Ladies and Gentlemen, Americans! Friends!

I am proud to greet you from Ukraine, from our capital—Kyiv. From a city that is under missile and air strikes by Russian troops. Daily. But it does not give up. And it didn't even think to give up for a single minute! Just as dozens of other cities and communities in our country, which found themselves in the worst war since World War II.

I have the honour to greet you on behalf of the Ukrainian people, brave and freedom- loving people. For eight years they have been resisting the aggression of the Russian Federation. They sacrifice the best children—sons and daughters to stop the full-scale Russian invasion.

Now the fate of our state is being decided. The fate of our people. It is being decided whether Ukrainians will be free. Whether they will preserve their democracy.

Russia has attacked more than just our land and our cities. It went on a brutal offensive against our values. Basic human values. It threw tanks and planes against our freedom. Against our right to live freely in our country, choosing our own future.

Against our desire for happiness. Against our national dreams. Just like yours, ordinary people of America. Just like those of everyone in the United States.

I remember your Rushmore National Memorial. The faces of your prominent presidents. Those who laid the foundations of America. As it is today. Democracy, independence, freedom, and care for everyone. Everyone who works diligently. Who lives honestly? Who respects the law?

We in Ukraine want the same for ourselves. All that is a normal part of life for you. Ladies and Gentlemen!

Americans!

In your great history you have pages that will allow you to understand Ukrainians. Understand us now. When it is needed most.

Remember Pearl Harbour. Terrible morning of December 7, 1941. When your sky was black from the planes attacking you. Just remember that.

Remember September 11th. A terrible day in 2001, when evil tried to turn your cities into a battlefield. When innocent people were attacked. Attacked from the air. In a way no one expected.

In a way you could not stop it. Our state experiences this every day! Every night! For three weeks now! Different

Ukrainian cities... Odesa and Kharkiv, Chernihiv and Sumy, Zhytomyr and Lviv, Mariupol and Dnipro. Russia has turned the Ukrainian sky into a source of death. For thousands of people.

Russian troops have already fired nearly a thousand missiles at Ukraine. Countless bombs. They use drones to kill more precisely. This is a terror Europe has not seen for 80 years!

And we ask for a response. For the response from the world. For the response to terror. Is this too much of a request?

To establish a no-fly zone over Ukraine is to save people. Humanitarian no-fly zone. Conditions under which Russia will no longer be able to terrorize our peaceful cities every day and night. If that's too much, we offer an alternative.

You know what defence systems we need. C-300 and other similar systems.

You know how much depends on the battlefield on the ability to use aircraft. Powerful, strong aircraft. To protect your people. Your freedom. Your land. Aircraft that can help Ukraine. That can help Europe.

And you also know that they are available. But on land. Not in the Ukrainian sky. They do not protect our people.

"I have a dream"—these words are known to each of you. Today I can say: I have a necessity. The necessity to protect our sky. The necessity for your decision. Your help. And it will mean exactly the same thing. The same thing you feel. When you hear: I have a dream.

Ladies and Gentlemen! Friends!

Ukraine is grateful to the United States for its overwhelming support. For all that your state and your people have already done for our freedom. For weapons and ammunition, for training and funding, for leadership in the free world, which helps put pressure on the aggressor economically.

I am grateful to President Biden for his personal involvement, for his sincere commitment to the defence of Ukraine and democracy around the world.

I am grateful to you for the resolution, which recognizes all those who commit crimes against the Ukrainian people as war criminals.

However, now, in the darkest time for our country, for the whole of Europe, I urge you to do more! New packages of sanctions are needed every week. Until the Russian military machine stops. Restrictions are needed as regards everyone on whom this unjust regime is based.

We offer the United States to impose sanctions against all politicians in the Russian Federation who remain in office and do not sever ties with those responsible for the aggression against Ukraine. From State Duma deputies to the last official who lacks the morale to sever ties with state terror. All American companies must leave Russia, their market. Leave this market flooded with our blood.

Ladies and Gentlemen. Members of Congress!

Take the lead! If you have companies in the constituencies that sponsor the Russian military machine, keeping their business in Russia... You have to put pressure. So that the Russian state does not receive a single dollar, which it spends on the destruction of Ukraine. On the destruction of Europe.

All American ports must be closed to Russian goods and ships. Peace is more important than profit. And we must defend this principle throughout the world together.

We have already become part of the anti-war coalition. The great anti-war coalition, which unites many states, dozens of states. Those who reacted in a principled manner to President Putin's decision—to Russia's invasion of our state.

But we have to move on. We have to create new tools. To respond quickly! And stop the war. The full-scale Russian invasion of Ukraine began on February 24. And it would be fair if it ended in a day. In 24 hours. So that evil is punished immediately. Today the world does not have such tools.

The wars of the past have prompted our predecessors to create institutions that were supposed to protect us from war. But... They don't work. We see it. You see it. So, we need new ones. New institutions. New alliances.

And we offer them.

We offer to create an association—U-24. United for peace. A union of responsible states that have the strength and conscience to stop conflicts. Immediately. Provide all necessary assistance in 24 hours. If necessary—weapons. If necessary—sanctions.

Humanitarian support. Political support. Funding. Everything necessary to preserve peace quickly. To save lives.

In addition, such an association could provide assistance to those who are experiencing natural disasters, man-made disasters. Who fell victim to a humanitarian crisis or epidemic?

Remember how difficult it was for the world to do the simplest thing—to give everyone vaccines. Vaccines against Covid. To save lives. To prevent new strains. The world spent months and years doing things that could have been done much faster. So that there were no human losses.

Ladies and Gentlemen! Americans!

If such an alliance, the U-24, had already been formed, I believe it would have saved thousands of lives. In our country, many other countries that need peace so crucially, that suffered inhuman destruction... I ask you to watch one video now. Video of what Russian troops did on our land. We have to stop this. We must prevent such things. Preventively destroy every aggressor who seeks to conquer another nation.

Please watch...

And in the end to sum it up.

Today it is not enough to be the leader of the nation.

Today it takes to be the Leader of the world. Being the Leader of the world means to be the Leader of Peace.

Peace in your country does not depend anymore only on you and your people. It depends on those next to you, on those who are strong.

Strong does not mean big. Strong is brave and ready to fight for the life of his citizens and citizens of the world.

For human rights, for freedom, for the right to live decently and to die when your time comes, not when it is wanted by someone else, by your neighbor.

Today the Ukrainian people are defending not only Ukraine, but we are also fighting for the values of Europe and the world, sacrificing our lives in the name of the Future.

That's why today the American people are helping not just Ukraine, but Europe and the world to keep the planet alive, to keep justice in history.

Now I am almost 45 years old. Today my age stopped when the hearts of more than 100 children stopped beating. I see no sense in life if it cannot stop death. And this is my main mission as the Leader of my people — great Ukrainians.

And as the Leader of my nation, I am addressing President Biden. You are the Leader of the nation, of your great nation.

I wish you to be the Leader of the world. Being the Leader of the world means to be the Leader of Peace.

Thank you.

Glory to Ukraine!

# The world must officially recognize that Russia has become a terrorist state
## 17 March 2022—01:05

Wise people of a strong country!

We have finally managed to release the mayor of Melitopol from captivity. Our Ukrainian Melitopol, which did not submit and will not submit to the occupiers. Ivan Fedorov is free. I talked to him today. The Russian military abducted him on March 11, trying to persuade him to collaborate. But our man withstood. He did not give up. Just as we all endure. You all. Just as we all do not give up. Because we are Ukrainians. And we always protect our own.

Today a protest action took place in Berdyansk again. Protest against the occupiers from the Russian Federation. Thousands of brave civilians came out against the armed Russian military. And they told them everything, everything they deserve. It is very important.

I know it's hard. But it is also important that what they heard from our people, including in Russian, is clear and unambiguous: occupiers, go home.

There is still such an opportunity. Every soldier thrown into the territory of our country has such an opportunity. Everyone who has not yet been killed, wounded, or taken prisoner.

Russian troops suffer such losses in Ukraine, which were inflicted neither in Syria, nor in Chechnya. Neither did the Soviet troops suffer such losses in Afghanistan. If your war, the war against the Ukrainian people, continues, the mothers of Russia will lose more children than in the Afghan and Chechen wars combined. What's the point of it?

Every Russian soldier who lays down weapons will get a

chance, a chance to survive. I appeal specifically to the conscripts who were thrown into the furnace of this war.

Not your war. And to the rest of the Russian soldiers who still have the instinct of self- preservation.

Lay down your weapons. It's better than dying on the battlefield, on our land.


Unfortunately, the humanitarian corridors did not work on Wednesday. The Russian military did not stop shelling, did not guarantee security.

We are ready to ensure silence. We are ready to take people out and send humanitarian aid. But we can't expose people to shelling on the road. Understand us. Expose to the fact that for the Russian military there is no such war crime, which they would not commit.

We are taking away Mariupol residents who managed to escape to Berdyansk... We are taking them to Zaporizhzhia. In total, more than 6,000 Mariupol residents were transported in one day, more than 2,000 of them are children.

The Russian military tried to disrupt this movement as well. They opened mortar fire on the section of the road between Vasylivka and Kamyanske in the Zaporizhzhia region. Only by a miracle there were no casualties. Five Ukrainians were wounded, including two children.

In Chernihiv, the occupiers fired at civilians who were simply standing in line for bread. Imagine. Ten dead people.

In Mariupol, in besieged Mariupol, Russian aircraft purposefully dropped a huge bomb on the Drama Theater in the city centre. Hundreds of people were hiding from the shelling there... The building was destroyed. The death toll is still unknown. Our hearts are broken by what Russia is doing to our people. To our Mariupol. To the Donetsk region...

Citizens of Russia! How is your blockade of Mariupol different from the blockade of Leningrad during World War II? Who do you inherit?

We will not forget anyone whose lives were taken by the occupiers. We will not forgive any murdered soul. Eternal memory to all victims of this terror! To all the victims of the war unleashed by the Russian state.

What else do the occupiers have to do, how many more people do they have to kill in order for Western leaders, NATO leaders to respond positively to Ukraine's request for a no-fly zone or for providing our country with the aircraft we so desperately need?

I spoke about this today in a speech to the United States Congress.

Ukraine has received strong support from our American friends. And I'm grateful to President Biden for that. I am grateful for the leadership that has united the democratic world.

But the war does not end. Russia's war crimes do not stop. The Russian economy is still able to maintain their military machine. That is why new packages of sanctions against Russia are needed. The world must finally officially recognize that Russia has become a terrorist state.

And most importantly, Ukraine needs to get more support. Even more than we get now. Air defence systems. Aircraft. Enough lethal weapons and ammunition to stop the Russian occupiers.

It was in this speech in Congress that I addressed both the United States and all the relevant states as regards creating a new U-24 union.

A new alliance that will ensure that each aggressor receives a coordinated response from the world. Fast and efficient. Immediately. Not in weeks, months, years, but in the first 24 hours after the attack.

We can no longer trust the existing institutions. We cannot expect bureaucrats in international organizations to change so quickly. Therefore, we must look for new guarantees. Create new tools. Take those who have courage and do what justice requires. We have already proved that we can do historical things. This is not just our resistance. Not just defence.

Even at this time—the biggest test for Ukraine—we managed to join the European energy network. Now Ukraine can use electricity flows from the European Union. We have been moving towards this for decades. It finally happened! I am grateful to all the power engineers of our country, to all those who worked for this result.

We are already working on programs to restore our country after the war.

I promise everyone, every Ukrainian who has lost home, who has lost an apartment because of hostilities or shelling that the state will restore everything. Restore independently.

I am confident that we will be able to rebuild our state quickly. Whatever the damage may be... It will be a historic reconstruction. A project that will inspire the world just as our struggle for our freedom. Just as our struggle for our Ukraine.

During the day I spoke with friends of Ukraine—President of Turkey Erdogan and Prime Minister of Canada Trudeau. I thanked them for their support. We agreed on new steps for the sake of peace for our country.

In a conversation with the Prime Minister of Ireland, I expressed condolences over the murder by the Russian military of an Irish citizen—journalist Pierre Zakrzewski.

I also spoke with European Commission President Ursula von der Leyen. We agreed on the support for our citizens—temporary displaced persons.

I will address the German Parliament on Thursday morning. I will continue to fight for even greater support for Ukraine, for even greater pressure on Russia. For the sake of our common victory, for the sake of peace for us.

For the sake of peace for us, the Ukrainian delegation speaks with the Russian delegation. And I want all our citizens, citizens of Ukraine, to hear me now.

Negotiations are ongoing. Negotiations for the sake of Ukraine.

My priorities in the negotiations are absolutely clear: the end of the war, security guarantees, sovereignty, restoration of territorial integrity, real guarantees for our country, real protection for our country.

Glory to all our heroes! Glory to Ukraine!

# Address to the Bundestag
## 17 March 2022—12:02

Dear President, Göring-Eckardt. Dear Mr. Scholz.

Dear ladies and gentlemen, deputies, guests, journalists. German people!

I am addressing you after three weeks of full-scale Russian invasion of Ukraine, after

eight years of war in the east of my country, in Donbas.

I appeal to you when Russia is bombing our cities, destroying everything in Ukraine. Everything—houses, hospitals, schools, churches. Using missiles, air bombs, rocket artillery.

Thousands of Ukrainians died in three weeks. The occupiers killed 108 children. In the middle of Europe, in our country, in 2022.

I am addressing you after numerous meetings, negotiations, statements, and requests. After steps in support, some of which are overdue. After sanctions, which are obviously not enough to stop this war. And after we saw how many ties your companies still have with Russia. With a state that just uses you and some other countries to finance the war.

During the three weeks of war for our lives, for our freedom, we became convinced of what we had felt before. And what you probably do not all notice yet.

You are like behind the wall again. Not the Berlin Wall. But in the middle of Europe. Between freedom and slavery. And this wall grows stronger with each bomb that falls on our land, on Ukraine. With every decision that is not made for the sake of peace.

Not approved by you, although it may help. When did it happen?

Dear politicians.

Dear German people.

Why is this possible? When we told you that Nord Stream was a weapon and a preparation for a great war, we heard in response that it was an economy after all. Economy. Economy. But it was cement for a new wall.

When we asked you, what Ukraine needs to do to become a member of NATO, to be safe, to receive security guarantees, we heard the answer: such a decision is not on the table yet and will not be in the near future. Just as the chair for us at this table. Just as you are still delaying the issue of Ukraine's accession to the European Union. Frankly, for some it is politics. The truth is that it is stones. Stones for a new wall.

When we asked for preventive sanctions, we appealed to Europe, we appealed to many countries. We turned to you. Sanctions for the aggressor to feel that you are a force.

We saw delays. We felt resistance. We understood that you want to continue the economy. Economy. Economy.

And now the trade routes between you and the country that has once again brought a brutal war to Europe are barbed wire over the wall. Over the new wall that divides Europe.

And you don't see what's behind this wall, and it's between us, between people in Europe. And because of this, not everyone is fully aware of what we are going through today.

I am addressing you on behalf of Ukrainians, I am addressing you on behalf of Mariupol residents—civilians of a city that Russian troops have blocked and razed to the ground. They just destroy everything there. Everything and everyone who is there. Hundreds of thousands of people are under shelling around the clock. No food, 24 hours a day without water, no electricity, 24 hours a day without communication. For weeks.

Russian troops do not distinguish between civilians and military. They don't care where civilian objects are, everything is considered a target.

A theatre that was a shelter for hundreds of people and was blown up yesterday, a maternity hospital, a children's hospital, residential areas without any military facilities—they are destroying everything. Round the clock. And they do not let any humanitarian cargo into our blocked city. For five days, Russian troops have not stopped the shelling specifically to prevent the rescue of our people.

You can see it all. If you climb over this Wall.

If you remember what the Berlin Airlift meant to you. Which could be realized because the sky was safe. You were not killed from the sky as now in our country when we cannot even make an airlift! When the sky gives only Russian missiles and air bombs.

I am addressing you on behalf of older Ukrainians. Many survivors of World War II. Those who escaped during the occupation 80 years ago. Those who survived Babyn Yar.

Babyn Yar that President Steinmeier visited last year. On the 80th anniversary of the tragedy. And that was hit by Russian missiles now. It is exactly this place that was hit. And the missile strike killed the family that went to Babyn Yar, to the monument.

Killed again, 80 years after.

I appeal to you on behalf of everyone who has heard politicians say: "Never again." And who saw that these words are worthless. Because again in Europe they are trying to destroy the whole nation. Destroy everything we live by and live for.

I am addressing you on behalf of our military. Those who defend our state, and therefore the values that are often talked about everywhere in Europe, everywhere—and in Germany as well.

Freedom and equality. Opportunity to live freely, not to submit to another state, which considers a foreign land its "living space". Why are they defending all this without your leadership? Without your strength? Why are overseas states closer to us than you are?

Because this is the Wall. The wall that someone doesn't notice and that we are hammering on while fighting to save our people.

Ladies and Gentlemen! German people!

I am grateful to everyone who supports us. I am grateful to you. Ordinary Germans who sincerely help Ukrainians on your land. To journalists who do their job honestly, showing all the evil that Russia has brought to us. I am grateful to the German businessmen who put morality and humanity above accounting. Above the economy. Economy. Economy. And I am grateful to the politicians who are still trying... Trying to break this Wall. Who choose life between Russian money and the deaths of Ukrainian children? Who support the strengthening of sanctions against Russia that can guarantee peace? Peace to Ukraine. Peace to Europe. Who do not hesitate to disconnect Russia from SWIFT?

Who know that an embargo on trade with Russia is needed? On imports of everything that sponsors this war. Who know that Ukraine will be in the European Union?

Because Ukraine is already more Europe than many others.

I am grateful to everyone who is taller than any wall. And

who knows that the stronger one bears more responsibility when it comes to saving people.

It is difficult for us to endure without the help of the world, without your help. It is difficult to defend Ukraine, Europe without what you can do. So that you don't look over your shoulder even after this war. After the destruction of Kharkiv... For the second time in 80 years. After the bombing of Chernihiv, Sumy and Donbas. For the second time in 80 years. After thousands of people tortured and killed. For the second time in 80 years. Otherwise, what is the historical responsibility to the Ukrainian people still not redeemed for what happened 80 years ago?

And now—so that a new one does not appear, behind the new Wall, which will again demand redemption.

I appeal to you and remind you of what is needed. The things without which Europe will not survive and will not preserve its values.

Former actor, President of the United States Ronald Reagan once said in Berlin: Tear down this wall!

And I want to tell you now.

Chancellor Scholz! Tear down this wall.

Give Germany the leadership you deserve. And what your descendants will be proud of.

Support us.

Support peace.

Support every Ukrainian.

Stop the war.

Help us stop it.

Glory to Ukraine!

## Our tactics is when the enemy does not know what to expect from us
### 18 March 2022—00:52

Great people of a great country!

The 22nd day of our struggle, our defence against one of the world's largest armies is over. Which we make smaller every day. Every day. But it still has numbers, equipment, and reserves.

We have information that the Russian military is recruiting mercenaries from other countries, trying to deceive as many young people as possible into military service.

We know that this will not help them.

So now I warn everyone who will try to join the occupiers on our Ukrainian land. This will be the worst decision of your life.

Long life is better than the money you are offered for a short one.

Our courageous defenders continue to hold all the key areas that the enemy is pressing. And respond to every attack. To every blow of the occupiers to our peaceful cities, to our people. New Russian conscripts have been taken prisoner.

Among them are those who refuse to return to Russia. And there are many who are not even mentioned in Russia. They don't even try to take them back.

Their death notifications have been sent to their families although they are in captivity and alive.

All Russians who can hear me now, speak about it. Tell it in Russia.

Every mother who knows that her son was sent to war against Ukraine must check where her son is. And especially those who cannot contact their children, who have been told that their children had been killed. And who didn't receive the bodies. There are phone numbers on the Internet that you can call and find out what is really happening to your children.

We did not plan to take thousands of prisoners. We do not need 13 or any number of thousands of dead Russian soldiers. We do not need it. We didn't want this war. We only want peace. And we want you to love your children more than you fear your authorities.

I addressed the parliament of Germany today. One of the most influential countries in the world. In Europe. One of the natural leaders of the European continent.

I spoke not just as President, but as a Ukrainian citizen. As a European. As someone who has felt for many years that the German state seems to have fenced itself off us with a wall. Invisible yet solid wall.

We have seen Germany fight for the economy for decades. For new Russian gas pipelines and old European dreams. Dreams of some kind of cooperation that Russia has not taken seriously for a long time.

We see that the views of the Germans are changing. And this is very important. We see Germany looking for a new path. We see how sincerely the majority of Germans stand in favour of revising the old policy.

We see that Chancellor Olaf Scholz has a great chance, a great mission—to give Germany a renewed leadership. Give Europe peace. Long-lasting and most importantly—fair. One that guarantees security to every state in Europe and Ukraine in the first place. And I sincerely wish Chancellor Scholz from all Ukrainians, from all Europeans that Germany and its partners succeed in carrying out this mission.

I will continue such speeches in the parliaments and squares of the partner states. Necessarily. As much as it takes to stop the war. To restore our territorial integrity. To return to all of us, Ukrainians and all Europeans, the long-awaited peace.

I feel that we are being increasingly understood. In Europe, in the world, in different countries. And it gives us more and more support. The one we have been asking for so long.

I spoke with French President Macron. We are strengthening the defence of Ukraine. We coordinated our joint steps towards peace. I'm grateful for that.

I am also grateful to President Biden for his new and effective support for our country. Please, understand I can't reveal all the details of this support package and others to you. Because this is our tactic. Our defence. When the enemy does not know what to expect from us. Just as they did not know what would await them after February 24.

Didn't know what we had for the defence and how we were preparing to face the attack.

The occupiers thought they were going to Ukraine, which they had seen before, in 2014-2015. Which they constantly corrupted and which they were not afraid of. But we are different.

And this allows us to defend ourselves against a full-scale strike for 22 days already. Everything we have done in a few years. For our defence. For our tactics. For defence tactics, which is not the time to reveal while the war is going on.

It is not the time to reveal our tactics of negotiations as well. Negotiations for peace, sovereignty, territorial integrity of our state, our freedom. Working more in silence than on television, radio or Facebook. I think this is right.

Today I visited the wonderful Vlasenko family from Vorzel, Kyiv region, at the hospital.

Escaping, they got under Russian shelling. The eldest daughter, Katya, who is only 16 years old, covered her brother Ihor, who is 8. The brother got out of the car and cursed the occupiers. Tetiana, mother, received shrapnel wounds. The father carried his daughter in his arms.

Thank God they all survived. Because they stayed together, as a family, and defended each other. I was really moved to talk to them. Probably the most during this war. I sincerely wish health and happiness to this family, the Vlasenko family. Like all other families. I wish you peace and work for it.

Also today, I awarded five employees of the State Emergency Service with the Order of Courage. Everyone is a hero. Everyone was awarded for selfless actions, for dedication with which they save all of us, save Ukrainians.

And some more news, very important and, of course, positive. About our economy. About how we bring our country back to life. Right now, wherever security allows. Wherever business can run.

Our government has already prepared a decision to expand the lending program for entrepreneurs on the basis of the program "5-7-9%" creating a new opportunity. Any business will be able to get a loan at 0%. For the time of martial law plus 1 month after the war.

Then there will be a minimum rate of 5%. And the total loan amount can be up to 60 million hryvnias. So that a wider range of businesses can take advantage of our program.

The second news is that the Cabinet of Ministers will vote tomorrow for a large-scale reduction of regulations.

There were more than 600 permits and licenses for business, and about 20 remain mandatory. Only those that simply cannot be revoked. For example, radioactive waste management.

So, for the vast majority of businesses in Ukraine, the declarative principle will work you have announced the start of business and you work freely.

And the third news, which concerns millions of Ukrainians. This is a special task for the National Bank of Ukraine, for people's deputies and our government officials.

I instructed to find such a legislative opportunity for the

state to guarantee 100% of deposits in Ukrainian banks. 100%. Not part, as now, as always, but 100%.

The whole deposit. In any bank of our state. So that people do not lose money and are not afraid of it under any circumstances.

So I'm waiting for specifics. Draft decision. And I hope that the Verkhovna Rada will not delay the support.

Because Ukrainians need it. Ukraine needs this. And finally.

Our Mariupol, our Kharkiv, our Chernihiv, Kyiv region, Izyum and all our hero cities.

Which are in a very difficult situation. Extremely difficult. We are doing everything. All of us. Absolutely.

Our army, police, SES, humanitarian convoys, church... All our people. We will not leave you. And we will not forgive them.

You will be free. Definitely. I know it. Like all of us on our land.

Glory to all our heroes! Glory to Ukraine!

## By attacking Ukraine, Russia will destroy everything it has achieved over the past 25 years
18 March 2022—15:35

Strong people of the indomitable country!

The 23rd day of our patriotic war continues. After eight years of war in the east. The occupiers do not stop burning their national wealth in the war against Ukraine.

I am confident that by attacking us, they will destroy everything that Russian society has achieved over the past 25 years. And they will return to where they once began to

rise from, as they say, to the "the wicked 90's". But without freedom, without the creative desire of millions of people to work for the development of their state.

This will be the price of war against Ukraine for Russia.

It will be a fall for them, a painful fall. And they will feel it even despite the "opium for the people" from television propagandists.

Unjust and aggressive war always has a high price for the aggressor.

But no matter what happens to them, it cannot comfort us. It will not resurrect our dead people. It will not restore our cities. It will not heal the emotional wound that will stay with us forever.

We will rebuild everything—I have no doubt about that. We will become a full member of the EU—each representative of our state works for this 24/7.

But life will be different, and for many—without the thousands of hearts stopped by this war.

May the memory of everyone who gave life for Ukraine live forever!

Russian troops have continued treacherous shelling of our peaceful cities and our communities. Lviv, Kyiv and the region, Zhytomyr region, Sumy region, Kharkiv and the region, Chernihiv, cities of Donbas—Severodonetsk, Kramatorsk, our Mariupol... Missile strikes, air bombs, "Grads".

We are shooting down Russian missiles as much as we can. We are destroying their planes and helicopters. And this even though we do not yet have adequate anti- missile weapons. Advanced weapons. We do not have enough combat aircraft.

But we have a goal, pure and fair—to protect our people, our state.

Undoubtedly, we will continue to do everything we can. We will remind some Western leaders even louder that this will be a moral defeat for them, it will destroy their prestige if Ukraine does not receive advanced weapons that will really save the lives of thousands of our people.

Russian missiles will not fall from shotguns, which some are trying to replace really useful supplies with.

Today is a busy day of negotiations for me. Ursula von der Leyen, President of the European Commission. Charles Michel, President of the European Council. Ukraine's great friend, Prime Minister of the United Kingdom Johnson.

The subject is clear. First, these are concrete steps that will give Ukraine even more strength, not only directly for the defence, but also for the economy. For our people, for Ukrainians who really defend Europe. Here and now. On our land.


President Ursula von der Leyen has promised to do everything possible to speed up Ukraine's accession to the EU. We reduce bureaucratic processes for our state, which usually take years, to weeks, to months. It's not easy, but we do it. I am sure.

We also agreed on the EU's support for Ukrainians who were forced to flee their homes due to the war. For those who are abroad and within our state.

We agreed on a new macro-financial aid—another 300 million euros for Ukraine. In addition to those on which a decision has already been made.

Secondly, we are discussing the next package of sanctions against Russia. Significant enough. To make them feel that every missile against our state, every bomb, every shot has its price. For the Russian budget, for Russian companies, for Russian ambitions and for specific people who represent the Russian government.

And until there is peace for Ukraine, sanctions against Russia must grow steadily.

I am grateful to all public initiatives from around the world that offer restrictions for Russia not only at the state level, but also at the level of societies. In particular, I am grateful to the Swedish Port Workers' Union, which promises not to service vessels connected with Russia. This is right. This is a good example for all public structures, all trade unions and business associations to follow.

If Russia is not stopped now, if Russia is not punished now, other aggressors in the world will start other wars. In different regions of the world. On different continents. Wherever a state dreams of conquering its neighbours.

We need to act now so that all other potential aggressors see that war is only a loss and no benefit.

That is why it is necessary for all Europeans to block ports for all Russian ships. So that all Russian commercial vessels follow the Russian warship.

It is necessary that all Western companies leave the Russian market and not cover with cheap PR their thirst for profit despite blood, despite war crimes. Like Nestle or Auchan for example.

To date, humanitarian corridors in the Sumy, Donetsk and Kharkiv regions have been agreed upon. Sumy, Konotop, Trostyanets, Lebedyn, Krasnopillya, Velyka Pysarivka. It is especially difficult from the besieged Mariupol to Zaporizhzhia. The occupiers are doing everything to complicate the movement of people and prevent Ukrainian humanitarian cargo from entering the city. This is outright terror. But we try, we do our best. More than 35,000 people have already been rescued from Mariupol.

Rescue work is underway at the site of the bombing by the occupiers of the theatre where Mariupol residents hid from shelling, used it as a shelter.

It is known that as of now, more than 130 people were rescued. But hundreds of Mariupol residents are still under the debris. Despite the shelling, despite all the difficulties, we will continue rescue work.

The situation in the Kharkiv region is very difficult. The occupiers do not stop trying to destroy our city of Izyum. People in Balakliya are being tortured. Our team is doing everything to organize a working humanitarian corridor to these cities and deliver food, water, and medicine.

I instructed the Cabinet of Ministers, the Secretary of the National Security and defence Council and the Speaker of the Verkhovna Rada to develop a format of decisions that will speed up the supply of all necessary goods from abroad.

This is especially topical for food, fuel and other goods that meet the basic needs of society.

War is not a time for bureaucrats and careerists from different departments to complicate the provision of goods for people. We want to simplify the passage of goods that Ukrainians need now through customs as much as possible.

If this requires the removal of taxes and excises during martial law, we are ready to do so. If it is necessary to remove customs officers who do not understand the tasks of wartime to act quickly, we will do so.

Our borders must be open to everything Ukrainians need. I am waiting for the appropriate decisions by the end of the day. And then—the support from people's deputies.

Because now everyone has to work only for Ukrainians, only for our state, for defence. Not for ambitions. Not for fear. Not for bureaucracy.

Everything is for the protection of Ukraine!


Today I signed a decree on the awarding of state awards to 138 servicemen of the Armed Forces. In particular, the Order of Bohdan Khmelnytsky of the II degree is awarded to:

Syrskyi Oleksandr Stanislavovych, Commander of the

Land Forces. Since the beginning of the full-scale Russian invasion, he has been leading the defence of Kyiv. Thanks to his professional and courageous actions, the enemy suffered significant losses and was driven away from the capital. During the defence of Kyiv, more than 30 settlements in the Kyiv region, which were temporarily occupied by the enemy, were liberated.

Major Mazurok Taras Leonidovych, commander of the tank battalion. Defending the Donetsk region, he inflicted significant losses on the enemy and significantly stopped his advance.

Sergeant Nutsa Ruslana Vasylivna was awarded the Order of Courage of the III degree. Senior combat medic. She personally took part in the evacuation of the wounded from Vodyane, Shyrokyne and Mariupol. Thanks to her actions, 31 of our defenders were saved. She continues to perform tasks in Mariupol.

Glory to all our heroes! Glory to Ukraine!

# Meaningful talks on peace and security for Ukraine are the only chance for Russia to reduce the damage from its own mistakes
## 19 March 2022—01:13

Good evening to everyone.

Usually on such days we used to say: "Spring has come". But now we are saying: "War has come".

But we will definitely defeat everyone no matter what. Because we are free people of a free country.

Today, government officials have elaborated the decision to fully reboot the customs service.

Cargo for our defence, for our people will be brought into Ukraine as easily as the physics laws allow that.

We eliminate the whole bureaucracy, all paperwork, VAT, all customs duties.


The goal is clear—to prevent the human factor from hindering the speedy supply of goods, which are really needed now.

Chairman of the Verkhovna Rada of Ukraine Ruslan Stefanchuk and profile committees are working to ensure the support of people's deputies for the innovations. I emphasize: this decision is necessary for the defence of the state, for ensuring normal life during martial law.

I urge certain MPs not to speculate on this issue, as it is for the benefit of our state, not the government or the opposition. We must all work jointly for the sake of our Ukraine, our people. Let's think about PR after the victory.

Another important area of government work is helping Ukrainians who have been forced to flee their homes due to hostilities.

I commissioned the Cabinet of Ministers to develop a comprehensive program to support such people, our citizens. Everyone who was deprived of home because of the war. We already have the outlines of this program. The first component is financial.

State support for all displaced persons. Adults and children. Government support for jobs for such people—where they are temporarily staying. So that every person, every family has a basis for life.

The second component is housing. The government is preparing concrete proposals for housing for IDPs right now. And also organizes the reconstruction of destroyed housing after the war.

The third component is no less important. This is the support for the families who have housed people from areas of hostilities or temporary occupation. At a minimum, they will be reimbursed for the cost of utilities related to the stay of IDPs.

Prime Minister of Ukraine Denys Shmyhal will soon explain all the details of such a comprehensive program to support our citizens.

A coordination headquarters has been set up to regulate all issues related to the delivery of humanitarian aid to Ukraine. Under the chairmanship of Head of the Office of the President Andriy Yermak, a meeting was held with Ukrainian ambassadors to intensify the supply of humanitarian goods to Ukraine, primarily to help internally displaced persons.

I also commissioned the government to provide assistance together with the International Committee of the Red Cross to those of our citizens who found themselves abroad after February 24 and need the attention of our state and international organizations.

Today there were seven humanitarian corridors in Ukraine. Six—in the Sumy region, one—in the Donetsk region. More than 9,000 people were evacuated from the besieged Mariupol. In total, more than 180,000 Ukrainians have been rescued by the humanitarian corridors. Hundreds of tons of essential products were delivered.

But the occupiers continue to block the supply of humanitarian aid to the besieged cities in most areas. This is a totally deliberate tactic. They have a clear order to do absolutely everything to make the humanitarian catastrophe in Ukrainian cities an "argument" for Ukrainians to cooperate with the occupiers.

This is a war crime. They will be held accountable for this. 100%. Every Russian figure who gives such orders and every Russian soldier who carries out such orders will be identified. And will receive a compulsory one-way ticket to The Hague.

To the city where the International Criminal Court is located.

People are being rescued from the rubble of the drama theatre destroyed by the occupiers in Mariupol, where civilians had been hiding from Russian shelling and bombs. More than 130 people are already on the surface. Some of them are seriously wounded. But at the moment there is no information about the dead.

Thanks to the courage and professional training of the Ukrainian Armed Forces, the occupation forces were stopped in almost all directions.

Heavy fighting in the Kharkiv region—especially heavy near Izyum. Russian troops have already thrown people from training centres there. Absolutely unprepared contingent. People who can't endure half an hour in battle.

Kyiv region, Sumy region, Chernihiv region, the south of our state—the army stopped the occupiers. The initial plan of the Russian military to seize our state failed. And it seems that they do not know what else can be done to us. It seems that their military commanders are not able to offer their political leadership anything but cruel and erroneous tactics to exhaust us, to exhaust Ukraine. Nothing but constant strikes at the civilian population, peaceful cities, people, children, missiles, air bombs, shelling from "Grads", "Uragans". Nothing but the destruction of non-military infrastructure—residential buildings, hospitals, schools, churches.

But this tactic of their military only worsens the situation for the Russian state. Leads to new and new destructive sanctions. Encourages new members to join our anti-war coalition. It allows us to unite even those states that have always tried to remain neutral to put pressure on Russia.

Therefore, negotiations on peace, on security for us, for Ukraine—meaningful, fair and without delay—are the only chance for Russia to reduce the damage from its own mistakes.

We have always insisted on negotiations. We have always

offered dialogue, offered solutions for peace. Not only during 23 days of invasion.

And I want everyone to hear me now, especially in Moscow. It's time to meet. Time to talk. It is time to restore territorial integrity and justice for Ukraine. Otherwise, Russia's losses will be so huge that several generations will not be enough to rebound.

Many words were heard in Moscow today in connection with the anniversary of the seizure of Crimea. A big rally took place. And I want to pay attention to one detail. It is reported that a total of about 200,000 people were involved in the rally in the Russian capital. 100,000 on the streets, about 95,000 at the stadium.

Approximately the same number of Russian troops were involved in the invasion of Ukraine.

Just imagine 14 thousand corpses and tens of thousands of wounded and maimed people at that stadium in Moscow. There are already so many Russian losses as a result of this invasion.

This is the price of war. In a little more than three weeks. The war must end. Ukraine's proposals are on the table.

In the coming days, I will continue to appeal to the nations of the world to call for peace for Ukraine. My appeal to the Swiss people is ahead, to the people and to the state.

Appeals to Israel, Italy and Japan are also planned. The world hears Ukraine's position. The world supports our defenders, defenders of Ukraine.

Today I want to express my sincere gratitude to each defender of our strong Mariupol. Our heroic city, which is experiencing the greatest ordeal in its history, in the history of Ukraine.

36th Separate Marine Brigade. 501st Separate Marine Battalion. 1st Separate Marine Battalion.

12th Brigade of the National Guard.

And a separate detachment of special purpose "Azov".

I am grateful to each and every one of our defenders of Mariupol. I am grateful to everyone who defends Ukraine.

Also, at the request of the Commander-in-Chief of the Armed Forces of Ukraine I decided to confer the title of Hero of Ukraine upon:

Colonel Baranyuk Volodymyr Anatoliyovych, Commander of the 36th Separate Marine Brigade.

And Major Prokopenko Denys Hennadiyovych, Commander of a separate detachment of special purpose "Azov". For courage, for effective actions to repel enemy attacks, for the defence of the hero city of Mariupol.

Glory to all our heroes! Glory to Ukraine!

## Address to the people of Switzerland
## 19 March 2022—18:29

Dear Mr. President, dear Ignazio!

My greetings to all Swiss friends of Ukraine! To all your beautiful people, the people of Switzerland!

I am grateful to you for supporting our people.

Thank you for defending freedom together with all those who value it. This is very important now. Nowadays. At a special time period.

And especially important—from you.

When terror became the national idea of one of the largest nations in the world. The basis of their foreign policy.

When the crimes of terrorism are committed not by some outcast or group of persons and not by an organization, but by the state. Which has a nuclear arsenal.

When a permanent member of the UN Security Council deliberately destroys everything for which the UN was built. Having unleashed a cruel, bloody, senseless war against us.

But we now have a chance. A chance to show not only to Russia, but also to any aggressor in the world, any terrorist state, that war will destroy not the victim, but the one who came with it.

And, perhaps, this is the last chance for humanity—to stop the wars. Stop the state terror.

And I'm telling you now. Switzerland. A state that has a very long history of peace. And an even longer history of influence. In many areas—a decisive influence on the world.

Even before I became President, I was thinking what life of our beloved Ukrainians I would like to see.

I have often been to your country. And I know very well how you live. And one day, standing near Chillon Castle, I asked my friends—we were one company—why can't we live like this?

To have such a standard of living. A high level. And with the same freedom. In such friendly communities. And with such confidence in our own strength.

And I sincerely wanted the Ukrainians to live like the Swiss. So that we can jointly decide everything about our own lives. About our land. Not expecting anything from politicians, unnecessary words, but voting in a referendum.

So that we can be sure, despite all the financial crises in the world, that our state will withstand and remain a leader. A leader of trust, a leader of stability. A dream for all people. Successful, not very successful—no matter what level, just for all people.

So that the Ukrainians, like the Swiss, can feel that they live in real communities that care about what is common to all—for the good of all.

Maybe these are all ordinary things to you. For us, these are reforms. And this is the path we are taking, and we wanted to take.

And we passed the relevant laws. For all this to work. We gave opportunities. Opportunities for our people.

So that we gradually reach your standard of living.

And we did it until the black day. February 24. The day of the beginning of the full- scale Russian invasion of our land, Ukraine.

And then everything changed.

It has changed for each of us, Ukrainians. I'm sure it has changed for all Europeans. And it has changed for all world democracies.

It has changed for you, too.

I am grateful to you and your state for supporting us in such a difficult time. I am thankful that you did not stay away, didn't say that it wasn't related to you at all.

Because, in fact, it is impossible to stay away from the fact that in the 21st century, in the heart of Europe, hundreds of rockets and bombs are flying at peaceful cities.

It is impossible to stay away when the army of the world's largest state, albeit only in size, directs all its deadly potential to destroy us, to destroy hospitals, ordinary schools, churches, universities, maternity hospitals, residential areas.

It is impossible to be indifferent when children are killed. As of this morning, the Russian army has killed 112 Ukrainian children.

And just as I wanted the Ukrainians to live like the Swiss... I also want you to be and become like the Ukrainians. In the fight against evil.

So that there is no question about banks. About your banks.

Where the money of all those who started this war is kept.

It's painful and it's hard. But it is also a struggle against evil.

It is necessary to completely freeze all the assets of these people and their accounts. It's a big fight, and you can do it.

I want you to become Ukrainians who feel what it is like when whole cities are destroyed, peaceful cities. Destroyed on the orders of those who like to live in communities—different, European, in your communities, in beautiful Swiss communities.

Who enjoys real estate in your country?

And it would be fair to deprive them of this privilege. To deprive of what they are taking from us.

And I want you to be as Ukrainians in the issue of business. Business that works in Russia in spite of everything. Despite this war.

Despite all our murdered children. Despite the people killed. Despite the destroyed cities. Like our city of Mariupol, heroic Mariupol, which has been under complete blockade for weeks. Imagine—no food, no water, no electricity. Just under the bombs.

"Good food. Good life." This is the slogan of Nestlé. Your company that refuses to leave Russia. Even now—when there are threats from Russia to other European countries.

Not only to us. When there is even nuclear blackmail from Russia.

And I want all of you, Swiss people, to become like all of us, Ukrainians. I want us not to lose our common chance now.

A chance to restore peace, a chance to stop any wars in the world. Because when Switzerland is with you, you are definitely successful. Because when Ukraine is with you, you are definitely strong.

Last year we agreed on a big conference with the President of your country. Conference in Lugano. For the sake of economic transformation, for the sake of Ukraine's reforms.

It was to take place this July. As well as the next summit of the first ladies and gentlemen.

And I believe, I know we can hold them. This year. On your land.

For the restoration and development of Ukraine. So that you have the opportunity to show again and again all the best that is in your hearts. In our hearts.

In the hearts of all those people who are fighting for freedom and fighting for life. I am grateful to you. I am grateful to Switzerland!

Glory to Ukraine!

## It was another day that brought us all closer to victory
22 March 2022—00:39

Free people of a free country!

Our 26th day of full-scale war is over. After 8 years of aggression in the east of our state.

The enemy is slowly trying to move. To go on the offensive somewhere. To capture our road somewhere. To cross the river somewhere. The Ukrainian army—well done—repels these attempts. And holds back the occupiers.

Today, Russian troops hit the Zhytomyr region with Grads. They got a decent answer.

Another enemy aircraft was shot down in the Kharkiv region near Chuhuiv. Our military has already shot down so many Russian planes and helicopters that one can only wonder: what do their pilots have instead of mind? Is it also emptiness?

I said "also" not by accident, because they definitely have emptiness instead of heart. Instead of soul. Instead of everything that makes a human human.

Borys Romanchenko, a former prisoner of Nazi concentration camps, was killed in Kharkiv. He was 96 years old. Think about it—he went through so much! He survived in Buchenwald, Dora-Mittelbau, Peenemünde and Bergen-Belsen—the death conveyors created by the Nazis.

And he was killed by a Russian projectile that hit an ordinary Kharkiv high-rise building...

Each passing day of this war makes it increasingly clear what their "denazification" is.


In Kherson, the occupiers shot at people who peacefully took to the streets without weapons at a rally for their freedom. For our freedom.

The Russian soldiers do not even know what it is like to be free. They were driven here, to be honest, as if sentenced. Sentenced to death, sentenced to disgrace.

A column of civilians came under fire in the Zaporizhzhia region. There were many children.

Four children were hospitalized. Two are in grave condition.


During the day 8 humanitarian corridors worked. Kyiv, Donetsk and Luhansk regions. Vorzel, Bucha, Velyka Dymerka, Mariupol, Lysychansk, Severodonetsk, Popasna and Kreminna. 8 thousand 57 people were rescued. Thank you to everyone who did it, who worked for the people.

We also managed to deliver 200 tons of humanitarian aid.

I spoke today with Prime Minister of the Netherlands Rutte and President of France Emanuel Macron.

We are coordinating our positions on the eve of important summits in Europe. Meetings of the G7, leaders of NATO and the European Union will take place on March 24. Our position will definitely sound. It will sound, believe me, firmly.

I signed a decree on awarding orders and medals to 105 of our warriors. I am grateful to each of them. 7 of them are, unfortunately, awarded posthumously.

It was a day of difficult events. Difficult conclusions.

But it was another day that brought us all closer to our victory. To peace for our state.

Glory to Ukraine!

## Address to the Italian Chamber of Deputies
## 22 March 2022—13:35

Dear speakers!

Dear Mr., Prime Minister Draghi!

Dear ladies and gentlemen, senators, and deputies! Dear Italian people!

This morning I spoke with His Holiness Pope Francis, and he said very important words: "I understand that you want peace. I understand that you have to protect yourself. Both the servicemen and civilians courageously defend the homeland. Everyone is defending the homeland."

And I replied: "Our people have become this army."

They became this army when they saw the trouble the enemy was causing. The devastation it leaves behind. And the huge amount of blood it wants to shed.

When I addressed a rally in Florence and dozens of other European cities a little over a week ago, I asked all Italians, all Europeans to remember the number 79. The number of children killed in Ukraine at that time.

Now it's 117.

38 children more during these days. This is the price of the delay.

Delay with pressure on Russia. So that it ends this brutal war. 117 children, thousands of adults. Thousands wounded. Tens of thousands of destroyed families. Hundreds of thousands of ruined destinies. Millions, already millions of abandoned homes. And it all started with one person.

In the occupied areas, murdered families are buried right in the yards of high-rise buildings. In the parks. In mass graves. This is happening today. In 2022. And we know that every next day of the war will take the lives of our children. 117 is not a final number. The Russian invasion will destroy more families and destinies. Unfortunately, the full-scale war continues. Russian missiles, aircraft and artillery do not stop killing. Ukrainian cities are being ruined. Some are almost completely destroyed.

Like Mariupol. You heard of it. Our city on the shore of the Sea of Azov. Where about half a million people lived. Just as in your city of Genoa. I was there. And now there is nothing in Mariupol. Only ruins.

Imagine completely burned Genoa. After three weeks of total blockade. Bombing, shelling, which did not stop for a moment. Ruined Genoa, from which people are being evacuated, your wonderful people. On foot, by cars, by buses... Just to get to where it is safe.

I am addressing you from Kyiv, our capital. From a city that is as important to our region as Rome is to the whole world. The origin of the great culture of a great nation is in Kyiv. And now we are on the verge of survival. Kyiv has gone through brutal wars throughout its history. And it deserves, after all the losses and tragedies, to live in peace. In eternal peace.

As Rome and any other city in our world deserves. But, unfortunately, there is an air alarm in Kyiv every day. Bombs and rockets fall every day.

Near Kyiv, in neighbouring towns and districts, there are several groups of Russian troops. Those who kill and torture, rape and kidnap children, destroy and rob. The occupiers take our property to Russia by trucks. The last one who did something like this in Europe were the Nazis. When they invaded other countries.

Russian troops have even mined the sea near our ports. And now it threatens neighbouring shores and neighboring countries, because mines can drift by sea to them.

Ladies and Gentlemen! Italian people!

It's time to do everything possible to ensure peace!

This is a war that Russia has been preparing for a long time. Which one person has been preparing for a long time? One! For decades. Earning crazy money on oil and gas exports and directing them to prepare for war. And not only against Ukraine. Their goal is Europe. Decisive influence on your life, control over your policy, destruction of your values. Not only ours. Democracy, human rights, equality, freedom... The same values as ours.

Ukraine is the gateway to Europe for Russian troops. They want to break in. But barbarism must not pass. Ukrainians were one of the first to come to your aid when you needed it during the COVID pandemic. We sent our doctors. Italians were among the first to come to our aid when our people were affected by the terrible floods.

You supported us—sincerely, quickly. Without asking for anything in return. You are helping us now—we really appreciate it. But still...

The invasion has not stopped in 27 days. Almost a month. So more sanctions are needed, even more pressure, so that Russia is looking not for military reserves or mercenaries somewhere in Libya or Syria, but for peace. So that the same one person is looking for peace. The consequences of this war are already felt in many parts of the world. Not only in Europe. And the worst thing will be famine. Approaching different countries.

Ukraine has always been one of the largest exporters of food. But how can we sow under the blows of Russian artillery? How can we sow when the enemy deliberately mines the fields, destroys fuel bases? We do not know what harvest we will have and whether we'll be able to export. When our ports are blocked and seized. Corn, vegetable oil, wheat and many other products. Vital goods. For your neighbours as well. Across the sea.

Prices are already rising. So how many tens of millions of people will need help? In front of your shores...

Ladies and Gentlemen! Italian people!

You know Ukrainians well. Our people who never wanted to fight. Who are Europeans just like you? You know those who brought war to Ukraine. You know for sure. Those who order to fight. And those who promote it. Almost all of them use Italy. As a place for vacation. So don't be a resort for murderers. Block all their real estate, accounts, and yachts—from "Scheherazade" to the smallest ones. Block the assets of all those who have influence in Russia. Let them apply their influence for peace. To be able to come back to you someday. Support greater sanctions against Russia. A complete embargo on trade, starting with oil. Support a ban on entering your ports for Russian ships. So that they feel the price for their aggression and for mining the sea.

There should be no exceptions to the sanction's regime for any Russian bank. Do not allow the food crisis in your neighbouring regions. Help us. Stop the killings. Save Ukrainian families.

This war must end as soon as possible. Peace must be restored. Enemy troops must be withdrawn from Ukraine. Demining must be carried out. And reconstruction.

Reconstruction of Ukraine after this war. Together with you, together with Italy. Together with Europe. Together—in the European Union.

Before the war, I often visited your country. I appreciate your hospitality, sincerity and sometimes loudness. I saw what family and children mean to you. You have wonderful families; you have wonderful children. What life means to you. I want to thank you for helping the Ukrainians who found a shelter from this war in your country.

Today, there are more than 70,000 of our people in Italy who, unfortunately, had to hide from the war. More than 25 thousand children. And many of them have received warmth in your Italian families. Including in the families present in this hall. The first Ukrainian was born in Italy, whose mother found refuge on your land. Dozens of Ukrainian children with severe shell shock and injuries are being treated by you.

We are grateful to you for that, very grateful! And we are waiting for them to return home. To Ukraine—already peaceful. And you can definitely help us with that.

From the first day of this war, you have shared our pain and are helping sincerely—from the heart. Ukrainians will always remember this. Your warmth, your care and your strength that must stop one person. Just one person for millions to survive.

Glory to Ukraine! Grazie Italia!

# The more Russia uses terror against Ukraine, the worse the consequences will be for it—
## 20 March 2022—02:33

Our strong people of our indomitable country!

The 24th day of Russia's full-scale invasion of Ukraine is over. After eight years of aggression. Ukrainians have proved that they know how to fight more professionally than an army that has been fighting for decades in different regions and under different conditions. We respond with wisdom and courage to the huge number of their equipment and soldiers sent to Ukraine.

That is why, for example, the Ukrainian Chornobaivka will go down in war history. This is a place where the Russian military and their commanders have shown themselves completely as they are: incompetent, capable of simply driving their people to slaughter. Six times our military destroyed the occupiers near Chornobaivka. Six times! And they still come there.

The besieged Mariupol will go down in history of responsibility for war crimes. The terror the occupiers did to the peaceful city will be remembered for centuries to come. And the more Ukrainians tell the world about it, the more support we find. The more Russia uses terror against Ukraine, the worse the consequences will be for it.

Today I addressed the people of Switzerland.

This is a special state. It does not elbow its way on the international stage. But when it speaks its word, it is heard by absolutely everyone. Switzerland has backed European Union sanctions against Russia. This means a lot for the Russian state machine. For people who are used to the fact that power is money. Hence, banks. Hence, Switzerland and other countries that help save capital. I am grateful to the President and to the people of Switzerland and to their country for their sincere support in our struggle for life and liberty. For not staying away. And I urged them to take a few more steps.

So that all Swiss companies that have not yet left the Russian market do so immediately in order not to give a single dollar, franc or euro to a Russian military machine to kill our people.

So that all those responsible for the war against our state cannot enjoy life in Switzerland, real estate in Switzerland, banks in Switzerland.

Our Armed Forces continue to deter the enemy in all major areas. Inflict unprecedented losses on Russian troops. Some units of the occupiers were destroyed by 80-90%.

In places of especially fierce battles, the frontline of our defence is simply piled with the corpses of Russian soldiers. And these corpses, these bodies, are not taken away. New units are driven on the offensive through these bodies. Some reserves that the command of the Russian troops collect wherever they can.

We are well aware that Russia has just a bottomless human resource and a lot of equipment, missiles and bombs.

But I want to ask the citizens of Russia. What have they done to you over the years that you stopped noticing your losses?

Do the words "son", "mother", "father" mean nothing to you anymore?

Already more than 14 thousand of your soldiers have been killed. This is 14 thousand mothers. This is 14 thousand fathers. These are wives, these are children, relatives, and friends. And you don't notice it? But there will only be more victims. As long as this war continues. Your war against us, Russia against Ukraine. On our land.

Eight humanitarian corridors worked on Saturday. 6623 people were rescued.

Due to the shelling of the occupiers, we were unable to rescue people from Borodyanka, Kyiv region. But we will not abandon these attempts.

Ukrainians were evacuated from Bervytsya, Bucha, and Bohdanivka to Brovary.

People were taken to Bakhmut from Lysychansk, Popasna, Severodonetsk, and Rubizhne in the Luhansk region.

More than 4000 Mariupol residents managed to leave for Zaporizhzhia.

Unfortunately, it was not possible to deliver the humanitarian cargo to the cities of the Kherson region. Russian troops blocked the movement of our convoy. Why? Their goal has not changed—in the same way they try to portray in their propaganda that Ukraine has left its citizens without the essentials. As if Russia is constantly saving them from something.

Although on February 23 our Kherson residents had more than the regions of Russia itself.

I spoke today with French President Macron. About our interaction. About finding a solution for peace, for the liberation of our territories. To save our people.

I am sure you understand that negotiations are not easy and pleasant. But they are needed. Because it's about life.

Ukraine has always sought a peaceful solution. The more we are interested in peace now.

Because we count everyone killed. Because every ruined family, every ruined house matters to us. Because we are Ukrainians, and for us a person is priceless.

Today I signed a decree on awarding 161 of our defenders with state awards of Ukraine. 40 of them posthumously.

And the decree on awarding the title of Hero of Ukraine to 12 servicemen. 8 of them posthumously.

I also met with warriors of the special unit of the National Police of Ukraine KORD to award them. I thanked them for their service, for the protection of our peaceful cities and for their help to the army.

In total, during the days of the full-scale war, 70 of our defenders have already been awarded the title of Hero of Ukraine. 2180 Ukrainians were awarded orders and medals for courage, for saving brothers-in-arms and civilians, for effective actions in defence of the state.

I am sure I can say on behalf of all our Ukrainian people: we are sincerely grateful to each of you. To each and every one who defends our state and stops the army of occupiers, which was called one of the few most powerful in the world.

Ukrainian poet Lina Kostenko celebrates her birthday on March 19. I sincerely congratulate you. On behalf of all Ukrainians.

And let me remind you today her words:

[Quotes Lina Kostenko's poem]

In fact, each of us has a nation. And we should not think meanly. Especially those whom Ukrainians have given the right to be politicians.

I want to remind all politicians from any camp: wartime shows very well the meanness of personal ambitions of those who try to put their own ambitions, their own party or career above the interests of the state, the interests of the people.

Those who hide somewhere in the rear but pretend to be the only one who cares about defence.

Any activity of politicians aimed at splitting or collaborating will not succeed. But it will get a tough response.

That is why the National Security and Defence Council

of Ukraine decided... Given the full-scale war waged by the Russian Federation and the ties of some political structures with this state, any activity of a number of political parties during the martial law is suspended. Namely: "Opposition Platform—For Life", "Shariy Party", "Nashi", "Opposition Bloc", "Left Opposition", "Union of Left Forces", "State", "Progressive Socialist Party of Ukraine", "Socialist Party of Ukraine", "Socialists" Party, "Volodymyr Saldo Bloc".

The Ministry of Justice is instructed to immediately take comprehensive measures to ban the activities of these political parties in the prescribed manner.

Everyone must now take care of the interests of our state, the interests of Ukraine. Because it's for us.

Because it is for the sake of life.

Glory to all our heroes!

Glory to Ukraine

# Speech in the Knesset
## 20 March 2022—20:17

Dear Mr. Speaker, members of the Knesset.

Dear Prime Minister Bennett, thank you very much for your support.

Dear members of the Government of the State of Israel, all attendees, guests, people of Israel!
The Ukrainian and Jewish communities have always been and, I am sure, will be very intertwined, very close. They

will always live side by side. And they will feel both joy and pain together.

That is why I want to remind you of the words of a great woman from Kyiv, whom you know very well. The words of Golda Meir. They are very famous; everyone has heard of them. Apparently, every Jew. Many, many Ukrainians as well. And certainly, no less Russians. "We intend to remain alive. Our neighbours want to see us dead. This is not a question that leaves much room for compromise."

I don't need to convince you how intertwined our stories are. Stories of Ukrainians and Jews. In the past, and now, in this terrible time. We are in different countries and in completely different conditions. But the threat is the same: for both us and you—the total destruction of the people, state, culture. And even of the names: Ukraine, Israel.

I want you to feel it all. I want you to think about this date. About February 24. About the beginning of this invasion. Russia's invasion of Ukraine. February 24—this day has twice gone down in history. And both times—as a tragedy. A tragedy for Ukrainians, for Jews, for Europe, for the world.

On February 24, 1920, the National Socialist Workers' Party of Germany (NSDAP) was founded. A party that took millions of lives. Destroyed entire countries. Tried to kill nations.

102 years later, on February 24, a criminal order was issued to launch a full-scale Russian invasion of Ukraine. The invasion, which has claimed thousands of lives, has left millions homeless. Made them exiles. On their land and in neighbouring countries. In Poland, Slovakia, Romania, Germany, the Czech Republic, the Baltic States and dozens of different countries.

Our people are now scattered around the world. They are looking for security. They are looking for a way to stay in peace. As you once searched.

This Russian invasion of Ukraine is not just a military operation, as Moscow claims. This is a large-scale and treacherous war aimed at destroying our people. Destroying our children, our families. Our state. Our cities. Our communities. Our culture. And everything that makes Ukrainians. Everything that Russian troops are now destroying. Deliberately. In front of the whole world.

That is why I have the right to this parallel and to this comparison. Our history and your history. Our war for our survival and World War II.

Listen to what the Kremlin says. Just listen! There are even terms that sounded then. And this is a tragedy. When the Nazi party raided Europe and wanted to destroy everything. Destroy everyone. Wanted to conquer the nations. And leave nothing from us, nothing from you. Even the name and the trace. They called it "the final solution to the Jewish issue". You remember that. And I'm sure you will never forget!

But listen to what is sounding now in Moscow. Hear how these words are said again: "Final solution". But already in relation, so to speak, to us, to the "Ukrainian issue".

It sounded openly. This is a tragedy. Once again, it was said at a meeting in Moscow. It is available on official websites. This was quoted in the state media of Russia. Moscow says so: without the war against us, they would not be able to ensure a "final solution" allegedly for their own security. Just like it was said 80 years ago.

People of Israel!

You saw Russian missiles hit Kyiv, Babyn Yar. You know what kind of land it is. More than 100,000 Holocaust victims are buried there. There are ancient Kyiv cemeteries. There is a Jewish cemetery. Russian missiles hit there.

People of Israel!

On the first day of this war, Russian projectiles hit our city of Uman. A city visited by tens of thousands of Israelis every year. For a pilgrimage to the tomb of Nachman of Breslov. What will be left of all such places in Ukraine after this terrible war?

I am sure that every word of my address echoes with pain in your hearts. Because you feel what I'm talking about. But can you explain why we still turn to the whole world, to many countries for help? We ask you for help... Even for basic visas...

What is it? Indifference? Premeditation? Or mediation without choosing a party? I will leave you a choice of answer to this question. And I will note only one thing—indifference kills. Premeditation is often erroneous. And mediation can be between states, not between good and evil.

Everyone in Israel knows that your missile defence is the best. It is powerful. Everyone knows that your weapon is strong. Everyone knows you're doing great. You know how to defend your state interests, the interests of your people. And you can definitely help us protect our lives, the lives of Ukrainians, the lives of Ukrainian Jews.

One can keep asking why we can't get weapons from you. Or why Israel has not imposed strong sanctions against Russia. Why it doesn't put pressure on Russian business. But it is up to you, dear brothers and sisters, to choose the answer. And you will have to live with this answer, people of Israel.

Ukrainians have made their choice. 80 years ago. They rescued Jews. That is why the Righteous Among the Nations are among us.

People of Israel, now you have such a choice.

Thank you!

Thank you for everything.

# We are working to make the whole world friends of Ukraine
## 21 March 2022—00:49

Free people of a free country!

The 25th day has come to an end since the Russian military has gone to the exercise and found themselves on our land. They all say so when taken captive.

It is already the 25th day since the Russian military has been vainly trying to find imaginary "Nazis" from whom they allegedly wanted to defend our people. Just as they are vainly trying to find Ukrainians who would meet them with flowers. At least in one city of our state. At least in one village.

And most importantly—the Russian military cannot find a way home. That is why our soldiers help them with the path to God's judgment.

To God's judgment where I am sure they receive only one punishment, one for all: the eternal cellar. Forever under the bombs. Forever without food, water and heat. For everything they did to our people, ordinary Ukrainians. To peaceful people. In Okhtyrka and Kharkiv, in Borodyanka and Chernihiv. In Volnovakha and Mariupol.

And many of our other courageous cities.

In besieged Mariupol, Russian aircraft dropped a bomb on an art school. People were hiding there. Hiding from shelling, from bombing. There were no military positions. There were about four hundred civilians. Mostly women and children, the elderly.

They are under the debris. We do not know how many are alive at the moment.

But we know that we will definitely shoot down the pilot who dropped that bomb. As we already did to almost a hundred other similar mass murderers.

Today, in the Knesset, I addressed all deputies and government officials. But first of all, I spoke on your behalf, on behalf of all Ukrainians with the people of Israel, who, I am sure, understand us. As free people understand free people.

Of course, Israel has its own interests, a strategy to protect its citizens. We understand that. Israeli Prime Minister Bennett is trying to find a way to negotiate with Russia.

And we are grateful for that. For every effort. So that sooner or later we start talking to Russia, perhaps in Jerusalem. This is the right place to find peace. If it is possible.

Well, Russian propagandists today have a rather difficult task.

After all, for the first time in history, the president of a foreign state spoke in the Knesset via video call. And spoke to the people of Israel. The President of Ukraine accused in Moscow of "Nazism" spoke in the Knesset to the people of Israel.

This fact alone confirms how wrong things are in Moscow.

During the day on March 20, only 4 humanitarian corridors worked. A total of 7,295 people were evacuated. Almost 4,000 Mariupol residents arrived in Zaporizhzhia in one day.

Tomorrow morning, we are preparing to send new buses to Mariupol to continue this important mission. More than 3,000 people were rescued in the Kyiv region. But in the Kharkiv region... Russian troops captured our convoy, our humanitarian cargo for the city of Vovchansk. There is no connection now with six people. Five drivers and one doctor. We will release them. We will try again and again to deliver to our people what they need.

The Kherson region fought again today. I am grateful to

them. Again, on the streets. And as always—for all of us, for Ukraine. With national flags. And with our Ukrainian courage. Unarmed against the occupiers. Against shots and military vehicles. This is a feat that inspires us all. This is Ukraine we are proud of. These are Ukrainians to whom I am immensely grateful. Just as all our people are.

In the afternoon I spoke with Prime Minister of the United Kingdom Boris Johnson. A true friend of Ukraine who does not hesitate and does not seek excuses.

We agreed on concrete support for our country at next week's G7 and NATO summits. Although we are not members of these organizations, I see that Ukraine has at least one vote there.

I also spoke with Ashton Kutcher and Mila Kunis. A star couple who sincerely believe in us, in our victory, in our future. They help Ukrainian IDPs by raising funds. And the two of them have already raised $ 35 million. I thanked them on behalf of our people, on behalf of all of us. Agree, this is a good result for one couple of our friends in America.

And we are working to make the whole world our friends.


I personally presented state awards to Ukrainian intelligence officers. Please understand—I can't say their names publicly.

But believe me, the contribution of these people to our defence is so significant that the orders and the title of Hero of Ukraine for them is the minimum we can give. Just to express gratitude. To them and to all our heroes. Thanks to which we are holding on.

And we're doing it pretty well. And Ukraine lives.

Glory to Ukraine!

# Drive the occupiers out, drive these slaves out: address to the residents of Ukrainian cities

21 March 2022—21:17

Great people of great Ukraine!

In this video, I want to appeal separately to the Ukrainian cities and the brave inhabitants of these cities. To the free south of Ukraine, where the sun shines only to welcome guests, not to random "tourists" on tanks. To Berdyansk, Kakhovka, Enerhodar, Melitopol and, of course, Kherson.

To Kherson, where today we saw slaves shooting at free people. Slaves of propaganda that replaces their consciousness. Slaves who used to pack everyone in paddy wagons.

Even an old woman with a clean white poster. Even a girl with an A4 sheet on which only one word is written—"peace".

These slaves sent by Russia have never seen so many free people in the squares and streets. They have never seen thousands of people who are not afraid of them, of slaves with weapons in their hands. Slaves perceive freedom as savagery, as danger. They are scared. The fear that propagandists know how to turn into hatred. And then—shots at peaceful free people.

Kherson, hold on! We will never forget these shots. Shots from your city. We were all with you in your square and streets. 40 million Ukrainians of our state. Millions and millions of Ukrainians in the world. We've all seen you stand. We've seen who you are. We have all felt how you want to regain your freedom. On land, where, watching the Milky Way, the Chumaks went for salt, the enemies felt terrible.

And as soon as we can break through to you, every occupier who shot at peaceful Kherson residents just for the blue-yellow colour will have a black stripe.

And the same awaits the Russian military pale from the fright who were driven out today in Enerhodar. Peaceful Ukrainians drove them out with bare hands.

The occupiers in Berdyansk, Melitopol and Kakhovka will have a black stripe. Wherever the occupiers kidnap our people. Those who they think are organizing the resistance. But we are not Russia. Remember. And there is no need to organize resistance here. Resistance for Ukrainians is a feature of the soul. And I really want you, all our Ukrainians in the south, to never think even for a moment that Ukraine does not remember you.

Whenever you are in pain, when you resist in spite of everything, please know that our hearts are broken at this time, because we are not with you.

And we ask God to support you until we can drive strangers out. This is a feat that you are protesting. This is happiness that we have such people. That we are all Ukraine.

During this invasion, heroes have constantly declared themselves among millions of our people. Once—ordinary Ukrainians, and now—fighters. Men and women who stand up for our state. Everywhere: in the south, in the east, in the north, in the centre, in the west and abroad. Stand up so that the enemy does not believe that this is a reality.

But we will make them believe. And we will make them remember that they are not welcome.

And they will never be. In Kyiv, which stands bravely and majestically above the Dnieper. In Kharkiv... Proud, tidy, educated Kharkiv. Which they beat, and it does not obey. Chernihiv. Ancient! Chernihiv, which since the time of the Horde has not faced such atrocities committed by the Russian military now.

Sumy, Okhtyrka and Lebedyn... Izyum, Derhachi ... Volnovakha, Popasna... Borodyanka, Hostomel, Makariv... Mykolaiv...

Mariupol! Hardworking and honest city! Mariupol. Which

the occupiers are simply destroying. Destroying to ashes. But it will survive them all. Worthless slaves who do not know how to take care of their own country. Of their own people. And they go to someone else's.

We are fighting for every Ukrainian! And we remember everyone! We are grateful to everyone. Both to the people and to these beautiful cities.

As well as to Lviv, as well as to Ivano-Frankivsk, Khmelnytskyi, Chernivtsi, Ternopil, Lutsk, our Uzhhorod... Kropyvnytskyi, Zaporizhzhia, Dnipro, Kryvyi Rih... Vinnytsia, Rivne... Cherkasy, Poltava... Odesa!

Those who may be infrequently mentioned in speeches. But who care about our common future? About Ukraine. And about freedom—for each of us. Who shelter people who have been forced to leave their home? Who work for defence? Who send humanitarian goods? Who deploy the evacuated businesses? Who heal, who help. Help all of us, and therefore themselves.

Great people of great Ukraine!

And I say this not accidentally—great Ukraine. Because I appeal to everyone in our country and to those abroad. In cities and villages. Those who are free and who are temporarily under occupation. In Crimea, in Donetsk, in Luhansk. Where they must also fight for freedom, not sit and wait.

I appeal to all Ukrainians. Wherever we are. Do everything to protect our state.

To save our people. Fight. Fight and help. Drive these slaves out! Drive the occupiers out! So that Ukraine lives. So that all of us live with it.

Free and peaceful. Which we love so much.

Glory to Ukraine!

## Speech by Head of the Office of the President Andriy Yermak at Chatham House
## 22 March 2022—22:17

The hardest part of any speech is the beginning. You all probably know that. In other circumstances, I would have spent a lot of time on it. On the right, most appropriate beginning. But I don't have time. So, I'll start with the simple.

We have been told for years that Ukraine is not reforming properly. But let's look at the results. The modernized Armed Forces have been holding back the aggression of one of the world's most powerful armies for almost a month already. Logistics chains are functioning. The courts are working. Trains run and transport millions of people. Utilities are doing their job even under shelling and bombing.

The test of war is perhaps the most severe. We are successfully reforming even now. And our sustainability turned out to be absolutely real.

But sustainability is not an absolute category. It's not about availability, it's about measure. How much is left? Depends on many factors:

On our determination—here there are no changes. We are on our land. We defend our values. Our way of life. Our freedom. You can be sure of us.

On external support—everything is ambiguous here.

We now enjoy serious support. The West has finally become collective. This is evidenced by sanctions against Russia and support for Ukraine—humanitarian, economic, political, military, and technical. But is that enough? And for how long will the West keep it? For how long are those states that have sought to maintain economic ties with Russia at all costs, even in the face of Russia's invasion of Ukraine willing to suffer losses from disruption of these ties?

Given the experience of the previous eight years, we cannot be too optimistic here. However, now the risks for the whole world have grown so much that they will simply not be allowed to do business as usual.

The next factor is the factor of Russia itself. What is its margin of safety? What are its goals?

The West is constantly talking about increasing the price that Russia will have to pay for aggression. But can we imagine the limit beyond which the Russian leadership will say: it is too expensive? It should be understood that the narrative of "victory at any cost" is not just a propaganda cliche. Moscow has repeatedly instrumentalized it, beating the stake of those it considered enemies. In the number of victims. In the violation of international law. In resorting to blackmail, including threats of man- made disasters and unconventional weapons. In everything. This must be understood.

At the same time, it should be understood that "small victorious wars" that do not achieve their goal always increase Russia's risk of a social explosion and coup. Success in war, on the other hand, stabilizes and preserves the regime. Nourishes its desire for further conquests.

You may ask, what is the conclusion?

And the conclusion is that Ukraine must win the war that Russia has started against us.

We must work only for such a result. All of us.

What is happening in Ukraine now concerns everyone. Everyone in this room. Every government. Everyone in the world. The war in Ukraine is not just another local conflict. This is a world war that is so far going on in our country.

I would like to emphasize once again that Russia's encroachments go far beyond Ukraine. It claims to restore the Soviet sphere of influence in both Europe and Asia. It claims to break the entire system of international relations and discredit all security institutions.

Therefore, Kazakhstan, Poland, the Baltic States, Slovakia, Moldova, and Georgia may be next... Yes, Moldova and Georgia again. Georgia, which after Saakashvili is again afraid to say the wrong word to Moscow. Well, apparently, this is such a non-trivial course of Tbilisi's European integration.

On the Russian military equipment, they write "To Berlin!" once again. Do you know what that means? We know. The Israelis know. Believe those who promise to kill you.

In the case of Ukraine, the goal of Russia is one—to destroy. To deprive of agency. To stop nation building. According to the program thesis about one nation, which we have been hearing for two decades. Therefore, one may say that this war has no rational basis. It is a war of will, not of necessity. But this is probably the first historiosophical war in history.

Therefore, we must assume that the current leadership of Russia will not abandon this goal. And it is ready to pay. The question of whether its entourage is willing to pay can now be omitted.

So, let's focus on this—the intention to destroy Ukraine.

This was not achieved by rapid operation. None of the strategic tasks of the invading force were fulfilled.

Therefore, the aggressor is trying to provoke a humanitarian catastrophe, destroy critical civilian infrastructure and industrial potential.

We must take into account that the war is taking place on our territory. That our people are dying, that our cities are being destroyed. Our Armed Forces and citizens are holding on with superhuman courage, but we cannot win the war without offensive weapons, without medium-range missiles that can be a means of deterrence (I emphasize in our case—deterrence, not aggression) threatening Russian territory with comparative destruction.

Without a full Lend-Lease, we can only defend ourselves. But it is impossible to defend effectively for a long time without a reliable echelon of air defence systems that shoot down enemy ballistic missiles at a long distance.

However, we are not given it. Just as we are not given fighter jets. Just as we are not welcome in NATO.

This fear of escalation is understandable. But this fear will not save you.

Winston Churchill explained everything: he who chooses shame between shame and war, gets both shame and war.

I once produced "Forebodings" movie directed by the talented Vyacheslav Kristofovich. So, the protagonist has such a remarkable phrase: "Everything must happen on time." Today I feel the power of this phrase more than ever. Everything must happen on time. Now it is high time.

An extraordinary meeting of the Allies is scheduled to take place in Brussels this Thursday, March 24. There is still time to take concrete steps towards Ukraine. Or to say honestly and publicly that there will be no such steps. That NATO is refusing to allow Ukraine to join, not Ukraine is refusing to join, as many have been trying to pretend lately. To say—and together start building a new security system.

The Russian leadership understands only the language of power and always confuses peacefulness with weakness. I want to ask our European partners: what are you really like? Are you peaceful or weak?

Will you finally give us the weapons that will allow Ukraine to remain an independent sovereign state within internationally recognized borders? Will you finally launch a

full-fledged Lend-Lease for us? Or will you continue to watch with concern as our cities turn into ruins?

I'll just say simply: close our skies or at least give us long-range air defence systems. Your fear of escalation nurtures aggression. Your determination holds it back.

Clearly articulated position "We will shoot down planes that are instruments of terror. We will destroy the Russian air defence systems that will attack our air police," is what we need.

Tomorrow. Now. Yesterday. Otherwise, Ukraine will bleed out. Become depopulated. We will not surrender; it is already clear to everyone. But let me remind you what I said at the beginning: sustainability is not about availability, but about measure.

After the Russian occupation of Crimea and the invasion of Donbas, foreign experts began to talk about the "Finlandization" of Ukraine. They meant only one thing: neutral status and "special" relations with Russia. But for some reason none of them said that "Finlandization" is the preservation of the state, its agency, and the freedom of the people at the cost of the forced loss of certain territories as a result of aggression.

But we will not give up our sovereignty or territorial integrity. And when we return our territories at the cost of incredible efforts and sacrifices, it will be our victory, but not Russia's defeat.

Because without decisive actions of the world community, nothing will prevent the aggressor from continuing to strike at any place of our state.

And every such blow to Ukraine will be a blow to international law. The intensification of the refugee crisis in the EU. The collapse of the world security system and the institutions that guarantee it. After all, it is a blow to global food security.

In fact, all this is a key sign of a world order crisis. An order where the readiness of the international community to punish acts of aggression, punish genocide remains largely declarative. Profit over justice—was that why the UN was created? Has Europe united around this?

If so, none of the existing security systems is suitable for Ukraine. We need a new one. Fair. This system will have to be built from scratch. We are ready. And we paid for it. Paid the highest price—pain, sweat, blood, lives. This fee gives us the moral right to demand act! Right now!

To put it simply, the "Finlandization" of Ukraine or any other model of neutralization on Russian terms, which does not involve building a new security system, will only guarantee that these challenges and threats will last forever.

So I will ask: European countries, where will your refugees flee to?


Ukraine remains Europe's only shield. But what happens if this shield is critically damaged?

The half-hearted position of the world community, unfortunately, makes this scenario possible. In this case, reliable guarantees of our security become fundamentally important for us. Multilateral legally binding guarantees. But is there anything as reliable in the West as the NATO umbrella? Sorry, we are not aware of that.

And the world needs the same credible assurances that Russia will no longer be able to successfully pursue its military ambitions in the international arena. We demand such guarantees from our partners. Citizens of other states, demand such guarantees from your government officials. Demand now, because tomorrow will be late.

Without such guarantees, any of our agreements will be fragile and temporary. And they will hold until the moment when Russia regains its strength and tries to attack again. The timing of this will depend directly on the pace of easing of sanctions pressure on Russia and its ability to circumvent restrictive measures. We therefore call for steady and unwavering strengthening of these sanctions. International businesses should not think about how to bypass them for the sake of profits. They must not become an accomplice in crimes against humanity. Such complicity should not only be a burden on the conscience. We call on foreign governments to prosecute such collaborations. Up to the criminal liability.

President Zelenskyy said this very clearly: "Do not sponsor Russia's military machine. No euro for the occupiers. Close all your ports to them, do not supply goods, give up Russian energy resources, force Russia to leave Ukraine. I believe that peace is possible, but you must act to come to peace."

Governments are hesitant. But ordinary people have already made a choice. They are convinced that Ukraine has a place in the EU. This is the average opinion of 71% of respondents. 79% of Europeans believe that sanctions against Russia are the right thing to do. 67% of EU citizens believe that Ukraine needs to be provided with weapons. These are the results of a poll published by the French Institute of Public Opinion (IFOP).

These figures are more than eloquent. So, I will tell governments to finally listen to your voters.

We call on the international community—not only the collective West, but also China and India—to put aside discord among themselves. The war in Ukraine affects all of you. You are the leaders of this world. Someone will talk about the two poles. I'm talking about two parts of the whole. The Russian issue should not prevent you from reaching an agreement. The interpenetration of economies and integration is a much more powerful guarantee of global peace than the threat of mutual destruction.

You can reach an agreement. Russia's aggression against Ukraine may seem to some a good opportunity to fulfil their own ambitions. However, in reality this is a false impression: hopes that the war will be "localized" in Ukraine are in vain. Without proper rebuff, Moscow will not stop, and each of its subsequent ventures will inevitably bring the world closer to the hot global conflict.

The dramatic events in Ukraine, the heroic struggle of our country for freedom and democracy have shown the whole world: our east and west are together. Now we call on the world to become a little bit like Ukraine.

East and West, stand together to protect the planet from those who seek to replace the force of law with the law of force.

## Address to the G7, NATO and EU summits, new sanctions packages and new assistance take place this week
### 23 March 2022—00:02

Free people of a free country!

Today was one of those days that allows us to say with confidence that the whole world is with us.

In the morning I spoke with His Holiness Pope Francis about the search for peace for Ukraine, for our state, about the atrocities of the occupiers, about the humanitarian corridors to the besieged cities. I thanked His Holiness for a clear and strong position against the war and for his prayers for Ukraine. I invited him to visit our country at this crucial time. I believe that we will be able to organize this important visit, which will unequivocally support each of us, each of the Ukrainians.

I addressed both chambers of the Italian parliament today. I felt maximum support. Sincere warmth in words. I called on Italy to strengthen sanctions against Russia and its regime. And strike hard at all Russian figures responsible for this war. For the war against us. Strike at their real estate, accounts, and yachts. Strike at their habit to earn money by war and to live and have a rest far away, in Europe, where it is peaceful and cosy.

I am sure that new sanctions will be introduced this week.

And I am grateful to Italy for supporting Ukraine's membership in the EU.

I spoke with President of Slovakia Zuzana ?aputová. About our cooperation and our security. About the development of Ukraine—with all together, in the European Union.

An important conversation also took place with the Prime Minister of Canada. We continue to coordinate our positions on the eve of this week's NATO and G7 summits. Justin Trudeau will support us.

A special aspect is security guarantees for Ukraine. They are vital not only for us, but also for all neighbouring countries. Because of our security, which will cement peace in Eastern Europe.

I am grateful to the Minister of Foreign Affairs of Greece who was the first European official to decide to support the work of our humanitarian corridors in Mariupol. To evacuate our people from the city and bring in humanitarian aid, which is crucially important for everyone.

As of today, there are about a hundred thousand people in the city. In inhumane conditions. In a complete blockade. No food, no water, no medicine. Under constant shelling, under constant bombing.

For more than a week now we have been trying to organize stable humanitarian corridors for Mariupol residents. And almost all our attempts, unfortunately, are disrupted by the Russian occupiers. By shelling or deliberate terror.

Today, one of the humanitarian columns was simply captured by the occupiers. On the agreed route near Manhush. SES employees and bus drivers were taken prisoner.

We are doing everything we can to free our people and unblock the movement of humanitarian aid. That is why I am grateful when a high-level representative of a European state agrees to personally join the humanitarian mission.

We expect the implementation of this plan by the Greek Foreign Minister in the coming days.

Despite all the difficulties, 7,026 Mariupol residents were rescued today. Tomorrow we will continue this important work.

Our representatives are trying to agree on humanitarian corridors in the Kyiv, Kharkiv, Zaporizhzhia and Luhansk regions.

Another important news is that an online tool has been created for everyone who can and wants to help with humanitarian goods for Ukraine.

In the last two weeks alone, our country has received more than 100,000 tons of humanitarian aid.

These cargoes are quickly distributed through special hubs for the regions. But there are even more appeals. Even more opportunities. Even more work.

Therefore, to simplify the process as much as possible, the website help.gov.ua was created.

On the website you can learn how to buy, how to send and whom to address humanitarian aid. This is for everyone who wants to join. For anyone who can help. In Ukraine and in the world. So that the aid is sent constantly, 24/7.

Our Armed Forces pleased us today. Chornobaivka again—the defeat of the occupiers again. Russian planes were shot down again. Especially important—the bomber was shot down over Mariupol. And so it will be with everyone who kills our people, peaceful people on our peaceful land.

I want to repeat once again to all Russian pilots who do not think about the order, they fulfil. Killing civilians is a crime. And you will be responsible anyway. Today or tomorrow—this is less important. The main thing is that it is inevitable.

We continue to work at various levels to force Russia to peace. To the end of this brutal war. Ukrainian representatives are working on the negotiations, which continue virtually every day. It's very difficult. Sometimes scandalous. But step by step we are moving forward.

I am also grateful to all the international mediators who are fighting for Ukraine, for Europe, for the truth. Who bring to Moscow the real picture? Honest. And encourage to look realistically. At what happens in battles. And at the fact that the world will not stop defending the truth. Our truth.

Three important summits this week: the G7, NATO and the EU. New sanctions packages, new aid. We will work, we will fight in any way we can. Till the end. Bravely and openly. At all these sites. With full energy.

For the result. With all our strength. And we will not get tired. Let's rest when we win. And it definitely will happen.

Glory to all our heroes! Glory to Ukraine!


## Speech in the Parliament of Japan
## 23 March 2022—12:37

Dear Mr., Hosoda!

Dear Mrs. Santo!

Mr. Prime Minister Kishida!

Distinguished Members of the Japanese Parliament! Dear Japanese people!

It is a great honour for me, the President of Ukraine, to address you for the first time in the history of the Japanese Parliament.

Our capitals are separated by a distance of 8 thousand 193 kilometres. On average, it's 15 hours on a plane. Depending on the route. But what is the distance between our feelings of freedom? Between our desires to live? Between our aspirations for peace?

On February 24, I did not see any distance. Even a millimetre between our capitals. Even a second between our feelings. Because you immediately came to our aid. And I'm grateful to you for that.

When Russia destroyed peace for the entire Ukraine, we immediately saw that the world is truly against the war. Truly for freedom. Truly for global security. Truly for the harmonious development of every society. Japan has become the leader of this position in Asia. You immediately started working to stop this brutal war started by the Russian Federation. You immediately started working for peace in Ukraine. Hence, in Europe. And this is really very important. It is important for everyone on Earth.

Because without peace for Ukraine, no person in the world will be able to look to the future with confidence.

Each of you knows what Chornobyl is. Nuclear power plant in Ukraine, where a powerful explosion occurred in 1986. Radiation release. The consequences of which have been recorded in different parts of the planet. The 30-kilometer zone around the Chornobyl station is still closed. It is hazardous. During the elimination of the consequences of the explosion at the station, thousands of tons of contaminated materials, debris and cars were disposed of in the forests in the closed area. Just in the ground.

On February 24, Russian armoured vehicles passed through this land. Lifting radioactive dust into the air. The Chornobyl station was captured. By force, by weapon. Imagine a nuclear power plant where a disaster happened. Confinement that closes the destroyed reactor. Operating nuclear waste storage facility. Russia has turned this facility into an arena of war as well. And Russia is using this 30-kilometer territory, this closed zone, to prepare new attacks against our defence forces.

It will take years after Russian troops leave Ukraine to investigate the damage, they have done to Chornobyl. What sites of radioactive materials disposal were damaged? And how radioactive dust spread on the planet.

Ladies and Gentlemen!

There are four operating nuclear power plants on our land! These are 15 nuclear units. And they are all under threat. Russian troops have already fired from tanks at the Zaporizhzhia nuclear power plant, the largest in Europe. The fighting has damaged hundreds of plants, many of them particularly dangerous. The shelling threatens gas and oil pipelines. Coal mines.

The other day, Russian troops also fired at a chemical plant in the Sumy region of Ukraine. There was a leak of ammonia. We are warned about possible chemical attacks, in particular with the use of sarin. As it was in Syria.

And one of the main topics for discussion of world politicians is the question: how to react if Russia also uses nuclear weapons. Any confidence of any person in the world, any country is completely destroyed.

Our servicemen have been heroically defending Ukraine for 28 days already. 28 days of full-scale invasion of the largest state in the world. But not the greatest in potential. Not the most influential. And the smallest from a moral point of view.

Russia has used more than a thousand missiles against peaceful cities in Ukraine. Countless bombs. Russian troops destroyed dozens of our cities. Some were burned to the ground. In many towns and villages that have come under Russian occupation, our people cannot even bury their murdered relatives, friends and neighbours with dignity. They have to bury them right in the yards of broken houses, near roads, anywhere where it is possible...

Thousands were killed, including 121 children.

About 9 million Ukrainians were forced to leave their home, their native places, fleeing from Russian troops. Our northern territories, eastern, southern are becoming empty, because people are fleeing from this deadly threat.

Russia has even blocked the sea for us. Usual trade routes. Showing some other—potential—aggressors of the world how to put pressure on free nations by blocking sea navigation.

Ladies and Gentlemen!

Today, it is Ukraine, the partner states and our anti-war coalition that can guarantee that world security will not be completely destroyed. That in the world there will be a foothold for the freedom of nations. For people and for the preservation of diversity in societies. For security of borders. To make sure that we, our children, our grandchildren still have peace.

You see that international institutions have not worked. Even the UN and the Security Council... What can they do? They need reform. They need an injection of honesty. To become effective. To really decide and really influence, not just discuss.

Due to Russia's war against Ukraine, the world is destabilized. The world is on the verge of many new crises. And who is now sure what tomorrow will be like?

Turbulence in world markets is a problem for all countries that depend on imports of raw materials. Environmental and food challenges are unprecedented. And most importantly, it is now being decided whether all the aggressors on the planet—explicit and potential—will be convinced that the war they have waged will lead to a punishment so powerful that they should not start a war. That they should not destroy the world. And it is absolutely logical and correct that the responsible states unite to protect peace.

I am grateful to your state for its principled position at such a historic moment. For real help to Ukraine. You were the first in Asia to put real pressure on Russia to restore peace.

Who supported the sanctions against Russia. And I urge you to continue to do so.

I call for the united efforts of the Asian countries, your partners, to stabilize the situation. So that Russia seeks peace. And stops the tsunami of its brutal invasion of our state, Ukraine. It is necessary to impose an embargo on trade with Russia. It is necessary to withdraw companies from the Russian market so that the money does not go to the Russian army. It is necessary to help our state, our defenders, our soldiers who are holding back Russian troops even more. It is necessary to start thinking about rebuilding Ukraine already now. About the return of life to the cities destroyed by Russia and the territories devastated by it.

People need to go back to where they lived. Where they grew up. Where they feel is their home. Their small homeland. I'm sure you understand this feeling. This need. The need to return to your land.

We need to develop new security guarantees. So that it is possible to act preventively and strongly every time there is a threat to peace.

Is it possible to do this on the basis of existing international structures? After such a war—definitely not. We need to create new tools. New guarantees. Which will work preventively and strongly against any aggression. Which will really help. Japan's leadership can be indispensable in their development. For Ukraine, for the world. I offer it to you.

So that the world can feel confident again. Confident about what tomorrow will be like. Confident that tomorrow will come and will be stable and peaceful. For us, for future generations.

Ladies and Gentlemen! Japanese people!

We can do a lot together with you. Even more than we can imagine.

I know what a brilliant history of development you have. How

235

you can build and defend harmony. Follow the principles and value life. Protect the environment. The roots of this are in your culture. Which Ukrainians really love. My words are not unsubstantiated. This is actually true.

Back in 2019, literally six months after I became President of Ukraine, my wife Olena took part in a project for children with visual impairments. In the project to create audiobooks. And she voiced Japanese fairy tales. In Ukrainian. Because they are understandable for us, for children. And it was only a drop in the huge sea of our attention, the Ukrainian attention, to your attainment.

We have similar values with you despite the huge distance between our countries. A distance that doesn't really exist. Because we have equally warm hearts. Thanks to joint efforts, thanks to even greater pressure on Russia, we will come to peace. And we will be able to rebuild our country. Reform international institutions.

I am sure that Japan will be with us then—just as it is now. In our anti-war coalition. At this crucial time for all of us.

Thank you!

Arigato gozaimasu! Glory to Ukraine!
Glory to Japan!

# Speech at a joint meeting of the Senate, the National Assembly of the French Republic and the Council of Paris
## 23 March 2022—18:00

Ladies and gentlemen senators! Ladies and gentlemen deputies! Councillors of Paris!

French people!

Thank you for the honour of speaking to you today.

I am sure that you are well aware of what is happening in Ukraine. You know why this is happening. And you know who is to blame. Even those who hide their heads in the sand know. And whose hands are still trying to get money from Russia.

So today I am addressing you. Honest, brave, rational and freedom loving. I am addressing you with questions: how to stop the war? How to return peace to our state? Because most of the puzzles that make up the answer are in your hands.

On March 9, Russian bombs were dropped on a children's hospital and a maternity hospital in our city of Mariupol. It was a peaceful city in the south of Ukraine.

Absolutely peaceful—until Russian troops approached and besieged it, as in the Middle Ages. Until they began to torture people with famine, thirst, kill with fire.

There were people in the maternity hospital on which the Russians dropped bombs. There were women in labour. Most of them were saved. Some were seriously injured. One woman had to have her foot amputated, as it was completely shattered.

And another woman... She had a shattered pelvis. Her child died before birth. Doctors tried to save the woman. Fought for her life! But she begged the doctors for her death. She begged to leave her, not to help her. Because she didn't know what to live for. They fought. She died. In Ukraine. In Europe. In 2022. When hundreds of millions of people could not even think that it could be so, that the world could be so ruined.

I ask you now to honour the memory of thousands of Ukrainian men and women, all those who were killed as a result of Russia's invasion of the territory of our peaceful Ukraine with a moment of silence.

After weeks of Russian invasion, Mariupol and other Ukrainian cities hit by the occupiers resemble the ruins of Verdun. As in the photos of the First World War, which, I'm sure, each and every one of you saw. The Russian militaries do not care which targets to hit. They destroy everything: residential neighbourhoods, hospitals, schools, universities. Warehouses with food and medicine are being burned. They burn everything.

They do not take into account concepts such as "war crime" and "binding conventions". They brought terror to Ukraine, state terror. Each and every one of you is aware of this. All information is available. All the facts are there.

About women raped by the Russian military in the temporarily occupied areas. About refugees shot on the roads. About journalists they kill knowing for sure that they are journalists. About old people who survived the Holocaust and are now forced to save themselves from Russian attacks on peaceful cities in bomb shelters.

For 80 years, Europe has not seen the things that are happening in Ukraine now. Because of Russia's actions. When there are people so desperate that they beg for death! Like this woman.

In 2019, when I became President, there was already a format for negotiations with Russia. It was the Normandy format. The format of negotiations that were to end the war in Donbas. The war in eastern Ukraine, which has been going on for 8 years, unfortunately.

Four countries took part in the Normandy format— Ukraine, Russia, Germany, and France. Four, but through them the whole world, all positions were represented.

Someone supported. Someone was trying to delay the process. Someone wanted to ruin everything. But it seemed important that the world was always present at that Normandy table, the table of peace.

And when the negotiations yielded the result, when we managed to free people from captivity, when we were able to agree on some decisions in December 2019, it was like a breath of fresh air. Like a glimmer of hope. Hope that talks with Russia can help.

That the Russian leadership can be convinced in words so that Moscow chooses peace.

But February 24 came. A day that ruined all those efforts. All of us. Ruined the old meaning of the word "dialogue". Ruined the European experience of relations with Russia. Ruined decades of European history.

All this was bombed by Russian troops. Destroyed by Russian artillery. Burned after Russian missile strikes.

The truth was not found in the offices. So now we have to look for it and gain it on the battlefield.

So what now? What do we have left? Our values. Unity. And the determination to defend our freedom. Common freedom! One for Paris and Kyiv. For Berlin and Warsaw. For Madrid and Rome. For Brussels and Bratislava.

Sips of fresh air will definitely not help anymore. It makes sense to act together. To put pressure together. To force Russia to seek peace.

Ladies and Gentlemen! French people!

On February 24, the Ukrainian people united. Today we have no right or left. We do not look at who is in power and who is in opposition. The usual policy ended on the day of Russia's invasion and will resume only when there is peace.

And this is right—to fight for life. To protect our state.

We are grateful to you; we are grateful that France helps. We are grateful for the efforts of President Macron. Who showed true leadership? We are constantly communicating with him, it is true, we are coordinating some of our steps.

Ukrainians see that France values freedom as much as it

has always been. And you protect it. You remember what it is. Freedom, equality, brotherhood. Each of these words is full of power for you! I feel it. Ukrainians feel it.

That is why we expect from you, we expect from France, from your leadership, that you will be able to make Russia seek peace. To make it end this war against freedom.

Against equality. Against brotherhood. Against everything that made Europe united and full of free diverse life.

We expect from France, from your leadership, that Ukraine's territorial integrity will be restored. And together we can do it.

If among the attendees there are those who doubt it, your people are already sure. Like other nations of Europe.

And that during France's presidency in the European Union the long overdue historical decision will be made—on Ukraine's full membership in Europe and the EU. Historical decision in historical time. As has always been the case in the history of the French people.

Ladies and Gentlemen! French people!

Tomorrow will be a month since Ukrainians have been fighting for their own lives, for

their own freedom, since our army has been heroically opposing the overwhelming forces of Russia.

We need more help! We need more support!

In order for freedom not to lose, it must be well-armed. Tanks and anti-tank weapons, aviation and air defence. We need all this! You can help us. I know. You can!

In order for freedom not to lose, the world must support it with sanctions against the aggressor. A new sanctions package every week. Every week!

French companies must leave the Russian market. Renault, Auchan, Leroy Merlin and others. They must cease to be sponsors of Russia's military machine, sponsors of the killing of children and women, sponsors of rape, robbery and looting by the Russian army.

All companies must remember once and for all that values are worth more than profit. Especially profit on blood. And we must already think about the future. About how we will live after this war.

Guarantees are needed. Strong guarantees. Guarantees that security will be unshakable, that there will be no war, and that war in general will be impossible.

We are creating such a system of guarantees. A new security system. In which France, I believe, will play a leading role. So that no one will ever have to beg for death again! So that people live their life. Full life. And so that we say goodbye to people not under bombs, not in war, but when the time comes.

Only in peace. Only in dignity. Because you have to live so that you are respected. So that you are remembered. And so that people say goodbye to you in a way France said goodbye to the great Belmondo.

Thank you, France! Glory to Ukraine!

# Address to Ukrainians and the nations of the world
## 24 March 2022—00:18

Free people of the free world!

Ukrainians and citizens of all countries who value freedom! Friends!

On March 24 it will be the month of our resistance. Heroic resistance of the Ukrainian state, the Ukrainian people to the ruthless invasion of Russia. It's already a month of our defence against the attempt to destroy us. Wipe off the face of the earth.

The original plan of the Russian troops failed already in the first days of the invasion. They thought Ukrainians would be frightened. They thought Ukrainians would not fight. They were wrong.

They know nothing about us, about Ukrainians. They know nothing at all about freedom. About how valuable it is. They do not know how freedom enriches life. Gives meaning to life.

But there are many of them! There are still many invaders. Russia is getting manpower from everywhere. Equipment. Air bombs, missiles. Looking for mercenaries around the world. Any scum capable of shooting at civilians.

Russian troops destroy our cities. Kill civilians indiscriminately. Rape women. Abduct children. Shoot at refugees. Capture humanitarian convoys. They are engaged in looting.

They burn museums, blow up schools and hospitals. The target for them is universities, residential neighbourhoods... Anything! Russian troops do not know the limits of evil.

But...

The war of Russia is not only the war against Ukraine. Its meaning is much wider. Russia started the war against freedom as it is.

This is only the beginning for Russia on the Ukrainian land. Russia is trying to defeat

the freedom of all people in Europe. Of all the people in the world. It tries to show that only crude and cruel force matters.

It tries to show that people do not matter, as well as everything else that makes us people.

That's the reason we all must stop Russia. The world must stop the war.

I thank everyone who acts in support of Ukraine. In support of freedom. But the war continues. The acts of terror against peaceful people go on. One month already! That long!

It breaks my heart, hearts of all Ukrainians and every free person on the planet.

That's why I ask you to stand against the war! Starting from March 24 — exactly one month after the Russian invasion... From this day and after then.

Show your standing! Come from your offices, your homes, your schools, and universities. Come in the name of peace. Come with Ukrainian symbols to support Ukraine, to support freedom, to support life.

Come to your squares, your streets. Make yourselves visible and heard. Say that people matter. Freedom matters. Peace matters. Ukraine matters.

From March 24.

In downtowns of your cities.

All as one together who want to stop the war.

I want to address the citizens of Russia separately.

I am sure that there are many of you who are disgusted by the policy of your state. Who are already just sick of what you see on TV? Of the lies of your propagandists on the Internet. Propagandists who are paid by your taxes. And they lie about the war, which is paid for by your taxes. And which makes all the citizens of Russia poorer.

Poorer every day.

Isn't that stupid? Your state collects taxes from you to make you poorer. To isolate you from the world. To make it easier for them to control you. And easier to send you to the war to die.

Ukraine has never threatened the security of Russia.

Even now, we are doing everything just to bring peace back to our land. Not to yours—to our land. To our people.

243

We are doing everything to end this war. And when we succeed—it will certainly happen—you will be sure of at least one thing: your children will no longer be sent to die on our land, on our territory.

Therefore, you, the citizens of Russia, are also interested in peace. Save your sons from the war. Tell the truth about the war. And if you can leave Russia so as not to give your taxes to the war, do it.

All polls show that the people of Europe and America support us.

I am grateful to all of you for that. Grateful on behalf of Ukraine. To everyone in the European Union, the United States, Canada, Britain and other countries for supporting us. For supporting freedom. For supporting Ukraine.

On March 24, three important summits will take place in Brussels, Europe. Important for the security of each of us. NATO Summit. EU Summit. G7 Summit.

I'm sure people will show how they support us. But politicians must also support freedom. All of them. They must support the struggle for life.

We are waiting for meaningful steps. From NATO, the EU and the G7.

We know that the Russians have already begun to lobby their interests. These are the interests of war. We know that they are working with some partners. We know that they want to put this issue out. The struggle against war. But this is the war that needs to be put out.

Our firm position will be represented at these three summits. At these three summits we will see: Who is a friend, who is a partner, and who betrayed us for money.

Life can be defended only when united. Freedom must be armed.

Ukrainian sky has not been made safe from Russian missiles and bombs. We have not received aircraft and modern anti-missile weapons. We have not received tanks, anti-ship equipment. Russian forces can keep killing thousands of our citizens, destroying our cities. Just because there are too many invaders. Just because Russia has been preparing for such a war for decades.

We asked to close our sky. And we asked for assistance from NATO to be effective and without limits. Any support in weapons that we need. We asked the Alliance to say it will fully help Ukraine win this war, clear our territories of the invaders and restore peace in Ukraine.

Free people of the free world!

Together we must prevent Russia from breaking someone in NATO, EU or G7. From breaking and taking it to the war side. We will see on March 24.

Ukrainians! All our heroes!

A month has passed. We withstood six times longer than the enemy had planned, than the Russian command had reported to the Russian president.

They were convinced that Ukraine is not a state. They were convinced that Ukrainians are not a nation. They deceived themselves. But we don't care about them. This is their state suicide. And we are just protecting our lives. Our freedom. Our own state. Our children. Hence, our future.

This is a war for independence. And we must win.

We will rebuild every city that heroically resists. We will bring the invaders to justice for every crime. Zhytomyr and Sumy, Kyiv and Chernihiv, Kharkiv and Mariupol, Volnovakha and Mykolaiv, Okhtyrka and Hostomel, Kherson and Odesa, Izyum and Donetsk, Luhansk and Chornobaivka... All our people will live! In a free Ukraine. After our victory.

Which will come sooner, the more we will all be united.

We are all Ukrainians. We are all Europeans. We are all free people of the free world.

In unity! On the battlefield and in political positions, at rallies and summits, at work and in communication with people. By all our actions, we must force Russia to seek peace. By all our actions, we must bring the victory of freedom closer.

May the memory of all who died for Ukraine live forever!

Eternal glory to all our heroes! Glory to Ukraine!

## Speech at the NATO Summit
24 March 2022—12:49

Dear attendees!

I am addressing you from Kyiv, our capital, which has been fighting for a month already, just as our entire state.

Yes, it is true—we are not in the Alliance. Not in the most powerful defence union in the world. Not one of the 30 states under the umbrella of joint protection. Under the umbrella of Article 5. It feels like we are in the "gray zone". Between the West and Russia. But we defend all our common values. And we are bright people! And we have been defending all these values for a month now!

A month of heroic resistance. A month of the darkest suffering.

A month of unpunished destruction of the peaceful state, and with it—the whole architecture of global security. All this is before the eyes of the whole world.

Over the decades, Russia has accumulated considerable resources, military resources, manpower and equipment, air bombs, missiles.

They invested crazy money in death while the world invested in life. But Ukraine is holding on bravely! At the cost of thousands of lives. At the cost of destroyed cities. At the cost of almost ten million migrants. Three and a half of them are already in your territories, in the territories of NATO countries. I am grateful for the support of these people. And people, unfortunately, continue to leave their homes. They are fleeing the terror that the occupiers brought with them.

The very first hours of the invasion meant brutal missile strikes for us. During the month of the war, Russia fired more than a thousand different missiles at our cities. Made hundreds of air raids.

On February 24, I addressed you with a perfectly clear, logical request to help close our skies. In any format. Protect our people from Russian bombs and missiles. We did not hear a clear answer. Ukraine does not have powerful anti-missile weapons and has a much smaller aircraft fleet than Russia. Therefore, their advantage in the sky is like the use of weapons of mass destruction.

And you see the consequences today—how many people were killed; how many peaceful cities were destroyed.

The Ukrainian army has been resisting for a month in unequal conditions! And I have been repeating the same thing for a month now. To save people and our cities, Ukraine needs military assistance—without restrictions. As Russia uses without restrictions its entire arsenal against us. Destroys all living things. Any objects—from houses to churches, from food warehouses to universities, from bridges to hospitals.

Ukraine asked for your planes. So that we do not lose so many people. And you have thousands of fighter jets! But we haven't been given any yet.

We asked for tanks. So that we can unblock our cities that are now dying—Mariupol, Berdyansk, Melitopol, others. Cities where Russia is keeping hundreds of thousands of people hostage and artificially creating famine—no water, no food, nothing there.

You have at least 20,000 tanks! Ukraine asked for a percent, one percent of all your tanks to be given or sold to us! But we do not have a clear answer yet... The worst thing during the war is not having clear answers to requests for help.

Ukraine never wanted this war. And does not want to fight for years. We just want to save our people. We want to survive! Just survive! Like any nation, we have the right to it. The right to life. The right to this one percent.

And I do not blame NATO—I want to be clear. You are not guilty. It's not your missiles, it's not your bombs that are destroying our cities. This morning, by the way, there were phosphorus bombs. Phosphorus Russian bombs. Adults were killed again, and children were killed again. I just want you to know that the Alliance can still prevent the deaths of Ukrainians from Russian strikes, from Russian occupation, by providing us with all the weapons we need.

Yes, we are not in the Alliance. And I do not make these claims. But Ukrainians never thought that the Alliance and the Allies were different.

That in matters of life and death you can be a force separately, but together—no. That NATO may be afraid of Russia's actions. I am sure you already understand that Russia does not intend to stop in Ukraine. Does not intend and will not. It wants to go further.

Against the eastern members of NATO. The Baltic states, Poland—that's for sure. Will NATO then stop thinking about it, worrying about how Russia will react? Who can be sure of that? And do you have confidence that Article 5 can work?

"Budapest" hasn't worked for us already. Our Budapest Memorandum. Has not worked for peace in Ukraine.

And I will tell you honestly—today Budapest is not working for peace in Ukraine as well. Yes, we receive help from individual members of the Alliance. I am very grateful. Ukrainians are sincerely grateful for this. To each of you who gives what you have, supporting us.

But what about the Alliance? The question of Article 5 is fundamental. I just want you to know what we think about it. And I sincerely wish you that we are wrong in our assessments and in our doubts. I sincerely wish that you actually have a very strong Alliance. Because if we are wrong, the world is safe. But if we are at least one percent right, I ask you to reconsider your attitude. Your own estimates. And really take care of security, security in Europe and, consequently, in the world.

You can give us one percent of all your aircraft. One percent of all your tanks. One percent! We can't just buy it. Such a supply directly depends only on NATO's decisions, on political decisions, by the way.

MLRS systems. Anti-ship weapons. Means of air defence. Is it possible to survive such a war without it?

So when it's finally available, it will give us and you as well, one hundred percent security. And we need one. And the only thing I demand from you… After such a month of war. This is a request for the sake of our military. After such a war against Russia … Never, please, never tell us again that our army does not meet NATO standards.

We have shown what our standards are capable of. And how much we can give to the common security in Europe and the world. How much we can do to protect against aggression against everything we value, everything you value. But NATO has yet to show what the Alliance can do to save people. To show that this is truly the most powerful defence union in the world. And the world is waiting. And Ukraine is very much waiting. Waiting for real actions. Real security guarantees. From those whose word is trustworthy. And whose actions can keep the peace.

Truly. All offers are on the table. Our needs are on the table. We need peace immediately. The answers are up to you.

I am thankful to those who help us! Thank you!

Glory to Ukraine!

# Speech by the President of Ukraine at the Riksdag in Sweden
## 24 March 2022—14:18

Greetings, Mr. Speaker!

It is a great honour and opportunity to address you today. Greetings also to the Prime Minister!
To the Swedish Riksdag MPs and members of the Government! Swedish people!

Now the blue and yellow flag in the world is probably the most popular. These colours are associated with freedom. This is true for different people on different continents.

And of course, in Europe.

The blue and yellow colours of the national flag are not just about Ukraine. This is about you as well, about Sweden. And obviously this is not a coincidence. This is fate.

Because we are equally for freedom. We are equally for a peaceful life. We are equally for respect for everyone. We are equally for justice and equally for caring for the natural world in which we live. Therefore, it is logical that Sweden is now among those who support Ukraine the most.

And I am sincerely grateful to each of you for this.

Today is exactly the month of the worst ordeal—the full-scale war waged by Russia against our state.

Europe has never known such a dark month since World War II. It has not seen such destruction and such war crimes. The list of those killed already reaches thousands. Dozens of our cities and communities were destroyed. Russian troops do not distinguish between civilian and military targets. They destroy everything. They burn residential neighbourhoods and houses. They blow up hospitals. They even fire at kindergartens with rocket artillery! Hundreds of educational facilities and more than 200 schools were destroyed. Russian troops bombed universities.

Imagine—they destroy any infrastructure that simply serves life. Warehouses with food and medicine. They seized two nuclear power plants. Yesterday they hit the second chemical production already. Phosphorus bombs were used today! Both adults and children were killed.

What is the purpose of such actions of Russia? What is the reason of such terror against us?

This is an attempt to conquer the whole nation. An attempt to make the neighbouring state a slave.

Ladies and Gentlemen! Swedish people!

Modern Europe, which has finally become peaceful, is built on clear principles.

Namely: there can be no forced border revision. And every nation has the right to choose its own future—without dictatorship, without coercion, without occupation. Thanks to these two principles, we in Europe have had an unprecedented era of cooperation. Peace. Confidence.

We had it until the Russian leadership decided that it could travel in time. That it allegedly could cancel the 21st century. Allegedly could act as in the old days of totalitarian ideologies.

If Ukraine failed to endure, defend itself, it would mean that everything we, living and modern people, value was lost.

Everything you value. Everything that is valued by any free people of any state. This would mean that all of Russia's neighbours are in danger. This would mean that you are in danger, because only the sea separates you from this aggressive policy of this state.

And Russian propagandists are already discussing on state television how Russia is occupying your Gotland Island in particular. And how to keep it under control for decades. They show it to the Russians on the map, show the directions of the offensive... You may ask for what purpose? They say it will be beneficial for Russia to deploy air defence systems and a military base in Gotland. To cover the capture of the Baltic states.

Russia went to war against Ukraine because it expects to go further to Europe. Expects to destroy freedom further in Europe. This is a fundamental challenge for the European security system.

Please take a look at what the Russian military has already done in our country. 8 years of war in the east. Occupation of Crimea. This is repression. Torture of people, suppression of all manifestations of freedom and diversity.

A month of full-scale war. Total cruelty. The bombing of peaceful cities is as terrible as it was in Syria. Abduction of children. Forced transportation of children and adults to Russia. Rape in the occupied areas. Large-scale looting by the Russian military. Now tens of thousands of houses and tens of thousands of apartments have been destroyed. And there are already almost ten million migrants, three and a half million of them in the European Union.

I deliberately do not want to call these Ukrainians refugees. Because I know that they will return to Ukraine. As soon as Russia leaves our land, as soon as peace is established.

Ladies and Gentlemen! Swedish people!

Sweden was one of the first to come to our aid. I am grateful to you! Your support is

absolutely sincere. It is based on values. On our love for

freedom. On what our blue- yellow national colours symbolize.

The whole world knows what Sweden wants. The whole world has seen in a month of this shameful war what Ukraine wants. We are together in our anti-war coalition. And we must do everything to make Russia seek peace.

Sweden has made a historic decision to provide Ukraine with the necessary weapons. We thank you for that! For your prudence. For your foresight.

Sweden supports the sanctions policy. A policy without which there will be no peace. Because the Russian leadership will not understand any language other than effective sanctions.

But for peace to come faster, sanctions packages against Russia must be applied on a weekly basis. Not a single barrel of Russian oil! No Russian ships at your ports! Not a single euro of taxes of your companies in Russia! Their military machine must be left without means of subsistence.

Deliberate actions of Russian troops to destroy civilians in Ukraine, to destroy our peaceful cities must receive an inevitable and principled response from all European countries. From the free world.

This has already become the typical feature of Russian troops... Syria, Ukraine... Massacres. Cities destroyed to the ground. Phosphorus and other prohibited munitions. To prevent this from becoming a victorious strategy, all war crimes must be punished. Those who gave the order to kill and those who killed must face the Tribunal. So that no other country in the world thinks that it can kill people with impunity just like that, that it can destroy neighbouring countries.

I am confident that together we will be able to ensure peace, and that is why we must now think about rebuilding Ukraine after this war. And it will happen!

I invite Swedish architects, Swedish companies, the Swedish state, your people to take part in this historic project.

Ukraine was beautiful. But now it will be great because this is our nation. Great Ukraine. Great recovery project. For the sake of the people. For the development of our country and the whole of Europe.

I invite you to show to the world, to all present and future generations that war does not bring the result. And peace does. And it gives life.

Sweden is the first country we offer this project to. You can take patronage over any city, region or industry to restore them. I am confident that your leadership will be indispensable. Your technology, business, and your love of life. Your ability to organize space in people's best interest.

Ukraine—all our heroic defenders, all our citizens—has already done a lot to protect our common European values, our common European home.

We are fighting not only for Ukraine, but also for the security of the European Union! And we have proved that we deserve to be a full member of the European Union. The decision is already being elaborated. It's time to adopt it!

I believe that you will support us in this as well.

Thank you, thank you Sweden! Glory to Ukraine!


## Address to the participants of the Group of Seven summit
24 March 2022—17:21


Ladies and Gentlemen!

The world's greatest democracies represented by you!

First of all, I would like to thank Chancellor Scholz and the German presidency for the opportunity to address you today. At this urgent summit.

Today is exactly one month since the beginning of the full-scale invasion of Ukraine by the Russian Federation. Russia, which was present at this format together with advanced democracies. Then the G7 was the G8. And there were a lot of hopes for its participation, for a dialogue with Russia. I want to emphasize that most of those hopes, as well as the place next to the Group of Seven, Russia received in advance. And it still hasn't deserved this advance.

But this and other similar advances gave the Russian leadership the impression that they would get away with anything.

In recent years, the Russian state has created so many crises and such instability that it has now become a major problem for the world. A problem that is only growing.

And you and I still have no idea how many more such urgent summits will have to be held before the problems created by Russia are resolved.

Europe is going through a war, every day of which is full of war crimes of Russian troops.

This morning I received information that Russian troops had used phosphorus bombs against civilians in Ukraine.

The threat of large-scale use of chemical weapons by Russia on the territory of Ukraine is quite real.

We are trying to find out the exact number of deported Ukrainians. People who are forcibly deported to Russia on a daily basis are deprived of documents, means of communication—everything is taken away—and distributed among their regions. And even then, Russia tries to mobilize them into its army!

It illegally abducts children. According to our data, more than two thousand already!

Ukrainian cities—Mariupol, Kharkiv, Chernihiv, Okhtyrka

and other cities—look like a global catastrophe. They are ruined. The roads from these cities, which people used to escape, resemble the set of a post-apocalyptic movie with hundreds of burned and shot cars.

But it is true: there is a global catastrophe! Russia has destroyed the global security architecture and dealt a powerful blow to international relations.

But this is just the beginning. This war may be followed by a global food crisis. The longer there is no peace on Ukrainian land, the less food the world market will receive from Ukraine. Consequently, many countries in Asia, Africa, and even Europe, may have extraordinary problems with access to basic products, with food prices. This will definitely result in political destabilization. Maybe this is also the goal of the Russian leadership? I do not know.

We must all act immediately! Immediately stop Russian troops, remove them from the territory of Ukraine.

Peace is needed immediately before the world faces an even greater level of problems.


It is better now to tighten sanctions against Russia as much as necessary to stop its military machine than to deal with the consequences of the food and political security global crisis. Unprecedented challenges!

If so, a full embargo on trade with Russia is needed. It is necessary to deprive Russia of the opportunity to use GPS in war. It is very important. So that this system does not help Russian missiles and bombs destroy peaceful cities.

Russian banks and, most importantly, the Central Bank of Russia must get a complete blockade from the global financial system. War criminals should be left without money at all! And their frozen assets should turn, inter alia, into reparations for the reconstruction of Ukraine.

It is better to give Ukraine the kind of weaponry support we really need now than to look for weapons for other countries later. We mean Georgia, Moldova, the Baltic States, Poland, and Central Asia.

The sooner this happens as we ask, the sooner there will be peace in Eastern Europe. This is in our best interest. This is in your best interest. This is in the interests of all democracies. Because democracies must be able to defend themselves. Freedom must be armed. Life must overcome death.

And I emphasize this: no advances to such a Russian state! Never again. Any steps towards it or towards any other violator of international law should take place only after their steps towards peace, towards universally recognized rules. And on the basis of a system of preventive deterrence.

I am grateful to you for the unprecedented unity. For your resolute support for peace for our country, for our people. I am grateful to those of you who are trying one hundred percent to stop this war.

I believe we can do it. We will be able to make your Group of Seven not just the Great Seven, but the Great Seven of Peacekeepers.

What do we need for this? Ukraine is very specific in answering this question.

First—to intensify sanctions against Russian aggression on a weekly basis until it stops and restores peace for us.

Second—to take part in the creation of a new system of security guarantees for Ukraine, for our region. Real guarantees. Effective. Those that can stop any aggressor in 24 hours.

We offered to create an association—U-24. This is what the world really needs. Not just to preventively stop the war or hostilities that have already begun. But also, to provide assistance to the states that were affected by the natural disaster, that need to be supported during a pandemic, that are facing migration or food crises.

The world needs new effective alliances! New effective guarantees! This can support developing democracies. This can support the economies of countries where there are no stable institutions yet.

And third—which directly concerns our state and Eastern Europe. We must rebuild our state together as soon as possible after the war. Rebuild cities. Restore economic life. Bring people back.

I offer you to participate in such a project. Recovery project. I am sure it will be in our common interest.

But first—weapons for Ukraine. First—increase sanctions against Russia every week. That is, peace comes first. We have the strength to do it. You have the strength to do it. So, may there be peace!

I am grateful to everyone who supports us.

Thank you.

Glory to Ukraine!

## Speech at a meeting of the European Council
### 25 March 2022—01:03

Greetings to all of you, greetings to all our friends, friends of Ukraine! Greetings to all who support freedom!

Mr. President of the European Council, my friend Charles, I congratulate you and congratulate all of us on your re-election. I think this is very important and this is right.

I am grateful for the opportunity to address you and the nations of Europe.

Today it's already been a month since the Russian invasion.

After 8 years of aggression in Donbas. The month of the great war.

In short, about its chronicle. Because everything is in my head, and everything is fragments. Unfortunately, tragic ones.

It all started on February 24. From Russia. When the missiles flew. Early in the morning. Against our peaceful cities. People have still been sleeping. Death has already come.

Russia sent armoured vehicles against us. Brought several thousand tanks to Ukraine.

It's hard to count how many of them have already been burned. How many can still kill us.

Bombs fell on our people. From planes that took off from Belarus. And they didn't even admit that they did it.

Russia captured the Chornobyl NPP. Staff have not been released for 24 days there. Imagine, people lived 24 days at such a facility, worked at such a facility. These are our people.

So that nothing terrible happens in Chornobyl again. To prevent the catastrophe. And the Russian military held them hostage.

Russian tanks fired at the Zaporizhzhia nuclear power plant. Russia fired missiles at Babyn Yar.

It has already destroyed more than 230 schools and 155 kindergartens. Killed 128 children. Fired missiles at universities. Burns residential neighbourhoods with rocket artillery.

Whole cities, villages. Just to ashes. Nothing remains. The Russian military killed journalists. Although they saw the inscription "Press" on them. They may not have been taught to read. Only to kill.

Russia has blocked Mariupol. This is a blockade that no one could have imagined in our time. Hundreds of thousands of people without water, without food. Under constant shelling, under constant bombing.

The Russian militaries deliberately blow-up hospitals, maternity hospitals, shelters. They even blow-up shelters, imagine! Knowing for sure that people are hiding there.

They killed 96-year-old Borys Romanchenko in Kharkiv. A Russian projectile flew into his apartment. Into the apartment of a man who survived the Nazi concentration camps but could not survive Russia that went to our Ukrainian Kharkiv. Thank God, our military stopped Russia there.

Russian troops are using phosphorus bombs—it was this morning. Rape women. Loot houses. Destroy churches! All churches. Even those of the Moscow Patriarchate.

Abducted more than 2,000 children from Ukraine. We don't know where our children are, where our 2,000 children are. Fire at humanitarian convoys. They don't care who's there. Children, women, church representatives who accompany the humanitarian cargo.

They kill people in Donetsk and say it's us. They say it's us, the "nationalists". Russia is doing all this. For a month already. On our land.

And Ukraine? What is Ukraine doing?

It did not go to a foreign land. Never dreamed of any war. Shoots down missiles. Urges strangers to lay down their arms and return home. For the sake of life.

Do you understand? For the sake of life. Not death.

Heals and feeds war prisoners. Allows them to contact their relatives by phone. Collects the corpses of Russian soldiers from the fields, which they simply leave, abandon. Hundreds and hundreds.

Ukraine has united for peace. And for the sake of peace, it unites the world. Tries to unblock the besieged cities.

Maintains the safe operation of nuclear power plants. Even in the presence of the occupiers.

Calls on the IAEA to intervene and patiently explains to the international bureaucracy what is happening. Evacuates people from dangerous areas. Does not stop trying to deliver humanitarian aid. Records Russian war crimes. Gathers evidence.

Invites journalists. Maintains the functioning of all institutions of a normal state. Defends its own country!

And every morning... Do you hear me? Every morning, the whole state, the whole of Ukraine—children, grandparents—everyone honours the memory of all those who died for our state with a moment of silence.

Have you heard anything like this on Russian television? Have you seen this in their schools?

They are even ashamed of the word "war". They call it a "special operation".

Although they organized a massacre here, as the Nazis did. These are different worlds. We and they.

These are different values. This is a different attitude to life. The Russian military does not see what dignity is. They do not know what conscience is. They do not understand why we value our freedom so much. This is what determines how the country will live.

And who should be in Europe.

And what about the European Union?

I want to thank you—you are united, united around us. But I want to say that it was done in one way or another. But once again, the main thing is that you have united.

And we really appreciate that. You have applied sanctions. We are grateful. These are powerful steps.

But it was a little late. Because if it had been preventive, Russia would not have gone to war. At least no one knows for sure. There was a chance.

You blocked Nord Stream 2. We are grateful to you. And rightly so. But it was also a little late. Because if it had been in time, Russia would not have created a gas crisis. At least there was a chance.

And now you and I are preparing Ukraine's membership in the European Union. Finally.

Here I ask you—do not be late. Please. Because during this month you have compared these worlds, and you see everything. You saw who is worth what. And you saw that Ukraine should be in the EU in the near future.

At least you have everything for that. And we have this chance.

Lithuania stands for us. Latvia stands for us. Estonia stands for us. Poland stands for us. France—Emanuel, I really believe that you will stand for us. Slovenia stands for us. Slovakia stands for us. The Czech Republic stands for us. Romania knows what dignity is, so it will stand for us at the crucial moment. Bulgaria stands for us. Greece, I believe, stands with us. Germany... A little later. Portugal—well, almost... Croatia stands for us. Sweden—yellow and blue should always stand together. Finland—I know you are with us. The Netherlands stands for the rational, so we'll find common ground. Malta—I believe we will succeed. Denmark—I believe we will succeed.

Luxembourg—we understand each other. Cyprus—I really believe you are with us.

Italy—thank you for your support! Spain—we'll find common ground. Belgium—we will find arguments. Austria, together with Ukrainians, it is an opportunity for you. I'm sure of it. Ireland—well, almost.

Hungary... I want to stop here and be honest. Once and for all.

You have to decide for yourself who you are with. You are a sovereign state. I've been to Budapest. I adore your city. I have been many times—very beautiful, very hospitable city. And people, too. You have had tragic moments in your life. I visited your waterfront. I saw this memorial... Shoes on the Danube Bank. About mass killings. I was there with my family.

Listen, Viktor, do you know what's going on in Mariupol? Please, if you can, go to your waterfront.

Look at those shoes. And you will see how mass killings can happen again in today's

world. And that's what Russia is doing today. The same shoes. In Mariupol, there are the same people. Adults and children. Grandparents. And there are thousands of them. And these thousands are gone.

And you hesitate whether to impose sanctions or not? And you hesitate whether to let weapons through or not?

And you hesitate whether to trade with Russia or not? There is no time to hesitate. It's time to decide already.

We believe in you. We need your support. We believe in your people. We believe in the European Union.

And we believe that Germany will also be with us at the crucial moment.

Thank you!

Glory to Ukraine!

# If Russia had known what it would face in Ukraine, it would have definitely been afraid to come here
## 25 March 2022—01:11

Free people of our free country!

It's already night, but we're working. The country must move towards peace, move forward.

With each day of our defence, we are bringing the peace

we need so much closer. We are bringing victory closer. Because in this war it is simply impossible for us not to win. And it will be so. And we can't stop even for a minute. Because every minute is about our destiny, about our future. About whether we live or not.

The 30th day. It's been a month! If Russia had known it would face that, I'm sure they would have definitely been afraid to come here.

During this month, we've withstood all the main directions of Russian strikes. The world has applied destructive sanctions. And we are reaching an agreement on new ones.

Today I have delivered some important speeches. To the participants of the NATO summit, the G7 summit, to the summit of the leaders of the European Union. To the Swedish Parliament. All this is for the sake of support for our state. We need it for our protection.

I spoke with the President of Lithuania, Mr. Nauseda, Prime Minister of Israel Bennett and Prime Minister of the United Kingdom Johnson. All this is for Russia to understand one thing: it is necessary to seek peace. Russia also needs to seek peace.

I informed the President of Egypt about the current situation. And today I signed some very important decrees.

On awarding the title of Hero of Ukraine to seven servicemen of the National Guard, to

five of them, unfortunately, posthumously.

Also, on state awards to 240 servicemen of the National Guard of Ukraine and 119 servicemen of the Armed Forces.

On state awards to 14 heads of local communities, local authorities. On state awards to 31 medical workers.

And on awarding the honorary title "The Hero City of Ukraine" to four more cities: Bucha, Irpin, Okhtyrka, Mykolaiv.

You know, after signing these decrees, I felt that it would really be worthwhile to award and confer the title of hero to millions and millions of our people. To you, to all Ukrainians who are doing everything they can for the sake of victory. For peace. In a place where they are.

And I am grateful to each and every one of you. To each and every one for this month of great struggle. And, of course, to our Armed Forces, of course, the National Guard, our border guards, doctors, rescuers, territorial defence, reconnaissance officers, special services and many, many people, representatives of other professions who save our lives. Who protects our free Ukraine?

Glory to all our heroes! Glory to all our people! Glory to us all!

Glory to Ukraine!

# By restraining Russian actions, our defenders are leading the Russian leadership to the idea: talk is necessary
## 25 March 2022—22:18

Strong people of the best country in the world!

I want to begin this address with words of congratulations. On my own behalf and on your behalf, on behalf of all our citizens of Ukraine to the employees of the Security Service of Ukraine. Today is their day.

30 years ago, on March 25, the Security Service of our state was founded.

The Service has come a long way. And we all know that. But we also know that during the eight years of the war in Donbas and during the 30 days of Russia's full-scale invasion of Ukraine, many members of the Security Service have shown themselves from the best—heroic—side.

They have shown themselves principled, courageous and able to inflict losses on the enemy that the enemy does not expect. This is exactly what Ukraine needs now.

I am grateful to all our heroes from the Security Service of Ukraine. I am grateful to everyone in the Service who during 30 years of our common history broke the plans of enemies and worked in the interests of the Ukrainian people only.

Congratulations on the holiday! Respect to everyone!

And we will always remember all the employees of the Service who died for Ukraine while performing tasks to counter Russian aggression.

During this month of hostilities, 77 employees of the Security Service were awarded state awards. Two of them were posthumously awarded the title of Hero of Ukraine. Both distinguished themselves in the battles near Makariv, Kyiv region. Thanks to their courageous actions, the enemy headquarters and more than 20 occupiers were destroyed.

I can't tell you the names of our heroes. This is the specifics of the service. But I can say with confidence: the memory of them will truly be eternal!

Today I signed a decree on state awards to 63 law enforcement officers of Ukraine. Seven of them were awarded posthumously.

Police, rescuers, border guards, special service officials of the State Bureau of Investigation and employees of the Court Protection Service. Thank you to everyone!

Over the past week, our heroic Armed Forces have dealt powerful blows to the enemy, significant losses. They say that the Minister of Defence of Russia has disappeared somewhere... I wonder if he personally wanted to visit Chornobaivka?

I am grateful to our defenders who showed the occupiers that the sea will not be calm for them even when there is no storm. Because there will be fire. As on those Russian ships that departed this week on the famous route from the port of Berdyansk.

I want to warn all traitors of Ukraine who sided with the enemy in Crimea years ago. You switched sides because you thought you would live better, right? Not because you want to repeat the tragic fate of your colleagues who died on those ships or somewhere else on land or at sea in Ukraine. Well, live. Stay as far away from our cities and our army as possible.

The number of Russian casualties in this war has already exceeded 16,000 killed. Among them are senior commanders. There have not been reports about killed Russian colonels-general or admirals yet. But the commander of one of the occupying armies and deputy commander of the Black Sea Fleet are already there.

The Armed Forces continue to repel enemy attacks in the south of the country, in Donbas, in the Kharkiv direction and in the Kyiv region.

By restraining Russia's actions, our defenders are leading the Russian leadership to a simple and logical idea: talk is necessary. Meaningful. Urgent. Fair. For the sake of the result, not for the sake of the delay.

16,000 Russian servicemen have already died. For what? What does it give and to whom?

The conversation must be meaningful. Ukrainian sovereignty must be guaranteed. Ukraine's territorial integrity must be ensured. That is, the conditions must be fair. And the Ukrainian people will not accept others.

During the week we managed to establish 18 humanitarian corridors. A total of 37,606 people were rescued from the blocked cities.

In particular, 26,477 Mariupol residents were evacuated from Mariupol to Zaporizhzhia via the humanitarian corridor. The situation in the city remains absolutely tragic. The Russian military does not allow any humanitarian aid into the city. They only use Mariupol residents in fakes for their propagandists. Pretending to start giving something to people.

I will continue to inform the nations of other countries in great detail about such disgusting cynicism of the occupiers, about all the war crimes of Russia against the civilians of our heroic Mariupol and other cities of Ukraine. It is very important. I want to emphasize not only politicians and government officials, but nations. Everyone on the planet needs to know what Russia is doing. So that the responsibility for crimes against the Ukrainian people becomes inevitable and as severe as possible for the Russian military.

During the week alone, I addressed the parliaments of Italy, Japan, France and Sweden. I spoke at the summits of NATO, the G7 and the leaders of the European Union.

Each of these speeches attracted maximum attention in the respective countries and in the world as a whole. The reviews show that the Ukrainian position was heard. And this is my main goal in such speeches.

You know perfectly well what a powerful system of state propaganda Russia has built. They have spent and are spending tens of billions of dollars on it. Probably no one in the world has ever spent such crazy money on lies. But they did not take into account one thing. Where the path of lies needs to be paved with money and the result is not guaranteed, the path of truth is difficult, but the path of truth paves itself. The main thing is to be honest.

Next week I will continue this important work for our interests. Interests of Ukraine. Interests of freedom and independence.

I had a conversation today with Turkish President Erdogan.

The results of the NATO summit were discussed. Of course, we also talked about the efforts that could bring peace closer to Ukraine and end this senseless Russian invasion of a foreign land.

There is important news from our government officials.

First. They have already started paying pensions for April. In particular, the Pension Fund has transferred to Oschadbank the entire number of pensions for the Chernihiv and Luhansk regions. Tomorrow people will have money on their bank cards and Ukrposhta will deliver cash.

Tomorrow or the day after tomorrow, the payment of April pensions will continue in other regions of Eastern and Central Ukraine. The other day a wave of payments will cover the entire state.

This is one of our priorities: the Ukrainian state has fulfilled and will fulfil all obligations to our citizens, to our pensioners.

Second. Under the support program, more than 20 billion hryvnias have already been paid to people who have lost their jobs or the opportunity to have business. The amount of payment is 6,500 hryvnias.

Third. Officials are preparing a new support program for our IDPs from the war zones.

Regional administrations have been given a clear task to quickly allocate land for the construction of temporary housing for displaced persons. I want to emphasize once again—this is temporary housing. Once we establish peace, we will begin the immediate, large-scale reconstruction of our state. But now people need a temporary home. Their home.

And it is better to have a home in Ukraine than somewhere abroad. We pay aid, we give a job. Native people. Native country. All the details of this support program will be presented by Prime Minister Denys Shmyhal.

And a few more words about the path of truth. About those

who bring you and us true information about everything that is happening in our country.

I would like to express special gratitude to our journalists today. To all those who ensure the work of the national telethon "United News", to all our media people. Correspondents, presenters, editors, media managers, cameramen, directors, video editors, make-up artists, producers—everyone without whom it is impossible to imagine television. Everyone who united and together with other defenders of our people provides Ukrainians with truthful information and, last but not least, confidence 24/7.

I am grateful to all of you! And I'm sure, I can say this on behalf of all Ukrainians.

Glory to you all!

Glory to all our heroes! Glory to Ukraine!

## Speech by Head of the Office of the President of Ukraine Andriy Yermak during the participation in the video meeting of the Atlantic Council
## 25 March 2022—22:27

Dear Ambassador, Herbst, dear ladies and gentlemen.

Thank you for having me here. I'm grateful for the chance to talk to you. People of Ukraine are grateful to our American friends for all the help you provide. Both military and humanitarian. Thanks for your support. It's really vital for us.

Yesterday, after the NATO summit I was told a joke. The NATO acronym stands for Never Act, Talk Only!

They say the joke is so old that it should be called vintage.

And now allow me to get to Ukrainian. Today, it's the language of freedom. The language of victory.

If this is true, then things are bad for us. More precisely, they are bad for NATO. Because if it reacted to Russia's aggression against itself in the same way as it had reacted to the invasion of Ukraine, Russian tanks would be standing near Dunkirk for a couple of weeks already.

And someone—we know for sure, who exactly—would probably have to land in Normandy again soon.

But NATO is lucky—these tanks are now being disposed of in Ukraine. But the thing is Ukraine is not made for this.

Ukraine has other plans, its own plans. To develop. To build. To continue reforms. To improve life. These plans are not just paused. For thousands of people, they will never come true. They may never come true for our entire state.

After all, the war that Russia is waging against us is not just a war for territory or resources. This is a punitive war. Caused by the desire to return the apostates who rebelled against the "Russian world". Or to destroy them.

For the Putin regime, Ukraine is a heresy. Literally. And the war against it is a religious war.

So, this is a war of annihilation. Russia's goal is to destroy Ukraine. As a people living by their own customs. As a political nation that chooses its own values. As a sovereign state that determines its own path.

There is no exaggeration in these words. They must be taken literally. Because this is exactly what the Russian leadership meant when it has been talking about "one nation" for years. About Ukraine as a "historical phantom" and "not even a state".

Henry Kissinger, a man I respect very much, has grasped

very clearly the essence of Russia's attitude toward Ukraine.

I quote in the original language: "The West is trying to establish the legality of any established border. For Russia, Ukraine is part of the Russian patrimony".

Now the world is promoting the "Give Peace a Chance" campaign, and there are calls for reconciliation between Ukraine and Russia. We did not start this war. We want its end more than anyone in the world. We are making an incredible effort to do so. In particular, the diplomatic one.

However, the word "reconciliation" is completely inappropriate here. It indicates parity and equality of the parties. We see an emphasis on supremacy on the part of Russia. And the intention to continue on the path of violence and destruction.

The Kremlin's aggressive plans are failing. The blitzkrieg failed. No strategic task of the invading force was fulfilled even during the month of fighting.

They believed that the invasion of Ukraine would be an easy walk. They believed that they would quickly stifle our desire for freedom. Well, they have a lot of experience in this. They have Berlin 53rd, Budapest 56th, Prague 68th... But they have forgotten that the CSTO is a pale shadow of the Warsaw Pact. Russia is a pale shadow of the USSR. But it still has very large resources. In particular human resources.

Half a million soldiers subdued Czechoslovakia. 200,000 have been sent to seize Ukraine. Yet. And a new wave of invasion is approaching. And maybe it will be bigger. In Russia, covert mobilization continues. Russia's allies are trying to avoid participating in its aggression. But blackmail and provocations can still force them.

And this means we will have to defend ourselves further.

But it is already quite obvious: the Russian leadership has miscalculated about Ukraine. Miscalculated at each point. Because the line "we will lay down our souls and bodies for our freedom" is not just solemn words from our national anthem.

This is the Ukrainian national idea. We do not just believe that freedom is the highest value. We know that. In 2014, this knowledge was embodied in the slogan "Ukraine is Europe".

Of course, this is not about geography—everything is obvious about it. It's about values.

But today Ukraine is the Grail of Europe. Without exaggeration. Because it is Ukraine who revives the principles that gave life to the current civilization of the West. You can't exchange freedom for comfort. You cannot buy resources for justice and human rights. Cannibalism cannot be justified by originality. You cannot be afraid to call evil. You can't be afraid of evil.

We are not afraid. And this is what makes Ukraine an antagonist of Russia. The anti- Russia that Putin talks about all the time. And in this sense, our state is an indisputable existential threat to him. Because his loss in Ukraine will mean the collapse of the regime. And success will only strengthen it.

Terror is the basis of his regime. Terror is the basis of Russian statehood. Terror is the basis of Russia's military strategy. Russia is a terrorist state.


The Russian armed forces are destroying our cities not only because of technical backwardness and lack of high-precision ammunition. They are doing it to cause horror. Phosphorus bombs dropped on the Kyiv region are not about military superiority. The methodical destruction of Mariupol is not about military superiority.

There were more people in Mariupol before the war than in Miami. Imagine Miami without water. Without access to medication. Without food. Imagine Miami being turned to dust every day. Together with residents who are not allowed to evacuate. Neighbourhood after neighbourhood. Schools. Theatre. Maternity hospital. Without any military sense. Just to intimidate.

They are destroying civilian infrastructure and using unconventional weapons to cause a humanitarian catastrophe. They resort to chemical and nuclear blackmail—the threat of environmental catastrophes due to sabotage at the captured Chornobyl and Zaporizhzhia nuclear power plants remain extremely high.

They are hiding behind civilians. Tens of thousands of them are being taken hostage and taken to work in the depressed regions of Russia. They call it evacuation. In fact, it is an abduction.

That is why I call on the partners: it is time to recognize the Russian Federation as a terrorist state. Officially. It is time to recognize the Armed Forces of the Russian Federation as a terrorist organization. It is time to recognize them as a criminal organization.

But this, apparently, will not happen as long as the seat in the UN Security Council is illegally occupied by a state that has carried out aggression against one of the founding states of the United Nations.

This will not happen as soon as the world's largest and most powerful defence alliance is most concerned about avoiding confrontation with a regime that has been breaking the world's security system for years.

The attack on Ukraine has become a vivid completion of this process.

That's why we have to endure. For ourselves. And for the world. Because it will only get worse. Unpunished tyrannies multiply lawlessness. They do not need the rule of law.

They recognize only the rule of force.

Russia understands only the language of power. Its success in Ukraine will only strengthen the Kremlin's claims. On the territory. On the restoration of the Soviet sphere of influence. On the right to dictate to other nations how to live.

Ukraine will hold on. For us, this war is a people's war.

Therefore, we will not give up our sovereignty or territories.

But we cannot afford Pyrrhic victory. You can't afford that. Destroyed and bloodless Ukraine will cease to be what it is today. It will cease to be an advanced bastion of the European fortress.

To survive, we need very specific things. You know what I'm talking about. But we have to remind people about it every time.

I'll start with the simplest. It is very important to be in time in war. It is important to have time. The more the better. Give it to us. We really need to share intelligence in real time. A clear and complete picture of Russia's actions is very much needed. This is extremely important for our defence.

Two factors are bringing our victory closer. The first is our resilience. Courage of every fighter. Every volunteer. Every citizen. The second has many names—Javelin, Stinger, Mark-19 and so on.

But small arms and portable weapons, no matter how modern, are of limited effectiveness. Without a full-fledged Lend-Lease, without heavy weapons—long-range artillery, MLRS, etc.—the defensive war against Russia will turn into a guerrilla war.

Simply due to the number of its mobilization reserves. This increases the risk of a humanitarian catastrophe and is guaranteed to increase the outflow of refugees. We must avoid this at any cost.

Finally, we need to close the sky. Here we see several options. And they all depend primarily on the political will of the parties. The basic option is to transfer Soviet and Russian-made fighter jets and long-range air defence systems to Ukraine. Relevant reserves are in Poland, Slovakia, Bulgaria, and Greece. They could hand them over to us, and the United States could strengthen their defence by providing a replacement. The temporary deployment of Patriot systems and air police missions could protect these countries from hostile actions and provocations from Russia due to the transfer of weapons to us.

The vast majority of citizens of the United States and other countries stand for increasing support for Ukraine. Including the military support. And the number of such people is growing every week. It is time for politicians to listen to the opinion of their own people as soon as possible.

Russia's success is ensured by fear. It is fear that motivates it to further aggression. It is restrained only by determination. And it's time to show it. Do not give in to blackmail. Don't give in to panic. Don't give in to terrorists.

Ukraine will resist. Ukraine will continue to fight. Not only against the aggressor. But also for the future. For reliable guarantees of post-war security. We are not satisfied with any configuration that threatens the sovereignty and territorial integrity of Ukraine. We will not be satisfied with a compromise on Russian terms. The victim of aggression must not pay for peace. The aggressor must be deprived of the opportunity to attack again. That is why we call on our partners and allies to find a format that will work effectively and for a long time. We have learned the lessons of the Budapest Memorandum. We have paid very dearly for them. This war has totally destroyed the entire old system of international security. We need to build a new one now. And Ukraine has proved that it deserves to be not only its participant and founder, but also its leading participant. And we continue to pay dearly for this right.

And now it's time for the aggressor to pay. We call for the sanctions regime to be strengthened. We call for the strict observance of sanctions. We call for the introduction of mechanisms that will make it impossible for international companies to circumvent sanctions. Give the world a model that will deprive Russia of the opportunity to pursue an aggressive policy for many years to come. Not only after the end of the active phase of hostilities on the territory of Ukraine.

We call for an embargo on Russian energy. We call for the reduction of opportunities of gray and black imports to Russia through the CSTO and the Eurasian Union.

Russia is not a trade or agricultural state, but a military one, and its vocation is to be a menace to the world. These words belong to Emperor Alexander II. But every ruler of Russia could say them. And especially—the current ruler.

It's time to stop this wheel of history. Before he does that. Everything will be Ukraine.

## Russian troops are destroying everything that makes us a nation, but they will be held accountable for that
26 March 2022—23:31

Free people of a free country!

Free Slavutych who will not be conquered by the invaders!

Today we were all with you—on your streets, in your protest. And all together we tell the occupiers one thing: go home while you can still walk.

The Russian invaders entered Slavutych and faced the same reaction there as in the south of our state, as in the east of our country.

Ukraine is united in its desire to live freely, to live independently and for the sake of its own dreams, not other people's sick fantasies. Every day of our struggle for Ukraine, every manifestation of our resistance in all areas the occupiers have entered so far proves that Ukraine is a state full of life, which has historical roots and moral foundations throughout its territory.

Nothing they do will help the occupiers in the Ukrainian territory they temporarily entered. Disconnection of our television and activation of passionate nonsense speeches by Moscow TV presenters, leaflets with propaganda, distribution of rubles. Rubles, which in Russia will soon be weighed instead of assessing them at face value.

Bribing outcasts whom the occupiers are looking for in all the dumps to portray the allegedly pro-Russian government will not help as well.

The answer to Russian troops will be one—hatred and contempt. And our Armed Forces of Ukraine will inevitably come.

That is why ordinary Ukrainian peasants take captive the pilots of downed Russian planes that fall to our land. That is why our "tractor troops"—Ukrainian farmers take Russian equipment in the fields and give it to our Armed Forces of Ukraine. In particular, the latest models that Russia has tried to keep secret. And now the occupiers leave them on our land and just run away...

Actually, they do the right thing. Because it is better for them to escape than to die. And there are not and will not be other alternatives.

Everyone in Ukraine has united and has been devoting all their energy to the defence of our state for more than a month already. Together with the Armed Forces, together with all our defenders, together with our National Guard.

I would like to once again congratulate the National Guard of Ukraine on its day with great respect. I am sincerely grateful for everything you do to protect the state, to protect Ukrainians! Thank you for all the steps to victory that will come and that were made possible thanks to you.

Today I presented awards to soldiers of the National Guard who distinguished themselves in battles with the Russian occupiers. I also awarded the rank of brigadier general to five colonels of the National Guard of Ukraine.

In total, during the full-scale war since February 24, 476 soldiers of the National Guard have been awarded state awards already.

I also spoke today with Polish President Andrzej Duda. Twice. About our people who found protection in Poland. And the need to strengthen our common security. Security of our states. Security for all Europeans actually.

What is the price of this security? This is very specific. These are planes for Ukraine. These are tanks for our state. This is anti-missile defence. This is anti-ship weaponry. This is what our partners have. This is what is covered with dust at their storage facilities. After all, this is all for freedom not only in Ukraine—this is for freedom in Europe.

Because it cannot be acceptable for everyone on the continent if the Baltic states, Poland, Slovakia and the whole of Eastern Europe are at risk of a clash with the Russian invaders.

At risk only because they left only one percent of all NATO aircraft and one percent of all NATO tanks somewhere in their hangars. One percent! We did not ask for more.

And we do not ask for more. And we have already been waiting for 31 days!

So who runs the Euro-Atlantic community? Is it still Moscow because of intimidation? Partners need to step up assistance to Ukraine. These are the words: partners need!

Because this is the security of Europe. And this is exactly what we agreed on in Kyiv when the three prime ministers of Eastern European countries, as well as Mr.

Kaczynski, arrived in our capital. It was in mid-March. Today, immediately after the conversation with the President of Poland, I contacted the defenders of Mariupol. I am in constant contact with them. Their determination, their heroism and resilience are impressive. I am grateful to each of them! I wish at least a percentage of their courage to those who have been thinking for 31 days how to transfer a dozen or two of planes or tanks...

And, by the way, we talked today with our military in Mariupol, with our heroes who defend this city, in Russian.

Because there is no language problem in Ukraine and there never was.

But now you, the Russian occupiers, are creating this problem. You are doing everything to make our people stop speaking Russian themselves. Because the Russian language will be associated with you. Only with you. With these explosions and killings. With your crimes. You are deporting our people. You are bullying our teachers, forcing them to repeat everything after your propagandists. You are taking our mayors and Ukrainian activists' hostage. You are placing billboards in the occupied territories with appeals (they appeared today) not to be afraid to speak Russian. Just think about what it means. Where Russian has always been a part of everyday life, like Ukrainian, in the east of our state, and where you are turning peaceful cities into ruins today. Russia itself is doing everything to ensure that de-russification takes place on the territory of our state. You are doing it. In one generation. And forever. This is another manifestation of your suicide policy.

Our representatives—the Minister of Foreign Affairs and the Minister of Defence of Ukraine—met today in Poland with colleagues from the United States. They were joined by US President Joseph Biden. As I was informed, the negotiations concerned, in particular, these vital interests, which I mentioned above. Concerned what we really need while this ping-pong continues—who should give us planes and other protection tools and how. Ukraine cannot shoot down Russian missiles using shotguns, machine guns, which are too much in supplies.

And it is impossible to unblock Mariupol without a sufficient number of tanks, other armoured vehicles and, of course, aircraft. All defenders of Ukraine know that. All defenders of Mariupol know that. Thousands of people know that—citizens, civilians who are dying there in the blockade.

The United States knows that. All European politicians know. We told everyone. And this should be known as soon as possible by as many people on earth as possible. So that everyone understands who and why was simply afraid to prevent this tragedy.

Afraid to simply make a decision. Vital decision.

Of course, we have already seized a number of Russian tanks, which the military command of this country keeps sending to be burned here.

However, the nations of the world will not understand for sure if the battlefield in Ukraine will be a larger supplier of tanks to protect freedom in Europe than our partners.

Ukraine's position must be heard. I want to emphasize this is not only our position.

This is the position of the vast majority of Europe's population, the majority of Europeans.

If someone does not believe me, look at current public opinion polls in the world.

And if you do not want to hear the opinion of the people, then hear the strikes of Russian missiles hitting right next to the Polish border. Are you waiting for the roar of Russian tanks?

I also spoke with Prime Minister of Bulgaria Kiril Petkov. In particular, about the humanitarian catastrophe due to the actions of Russian troops and how to save our people.

I spoke today at the Doha Forum in the capital of Qatar. This is a respectable meeting that is important not only for the Islamic world, but also for many other countries in Latin

America and Africa. These are the regions where Russian propaganda still has great influence. But we are working against lies all over the world. Let Russia know that the truth will not remain silent. And let every nation in the world feel the depth of Russia's injustice against Ukraine. Against everything that keeps the world within morality and humanity.

The occupiers committed another crime against history. Against historical justice.

Near Kharkiv, Russian troops in their branded inhuman style "de-nazified" the Holocaust Memorial in Drobytsky Yar.

During World War II, the Nazis executed about 20,000 people there. 80 years later they are killed a second time. And Russia is doing it.

The menorah in Drobytsky Yar destroyed by Russian projectiles today is another question to the entire Jewish community of the world: how many more crimes against our common memory of the Holocaust will be allowed to be committed by Russia on our Ukrainian land?

Russian troops are deliberately killing civilians, destroying residential neighbourhoods, targeting shelters and hospitals, schools and universities. Even churches, even Holocaust memorials!

Russian troops receive just such orders: to destroy everything that makes our nation, our people—people, our culture—culture. This is exactly how the Nazis tried to capture Europe 80 years ago. This is exactly how the occupiers act in Ukraine. No one will forgive them. There will be responsibility. Just like 77 years ago. Most likely not in Nuremberg. But the meaning will be similar. You will see.

Everyone will see. Everyone. We guarantee.

Glory to all our heroes! Glory to Ukraine!

# The week is planned to be very busy, so no one will be able to hide the Ukrainian interest somewhere in political offices

## 28 March 2022—00:38

Strong people of our strong country!

Today is the day when we see again and again how far we are from the Russian Federation. Imagine, they were frightened there in Moscow because of my interview to Russian journalists. To those of them who can afford to tell the truth. When journalists were preparing to publish our interview—and we spoke with them this afternoon—the Russian censorship agency came out with a threat. That's what they wrote—they demand not to publish the conversation. It would be ridiculous if it wasn't so tragic.

They destroyed freedom of speech in their state, they are trying to destroy the neighbouring state. They portray themselves as global players. And they themselves are afraid of a relatively short conversation with several journalists.

Well, if there is such a reaction, then we are doing everything right, then they are nervous. Apparently, they have seen that their citizens have more and more questions about the state of affairs in their country.

The maximum contrast is my conversation with our favourite Ukrainian TV media representatives. I held a zoom conference with almost five hundred of our media representatives who are creating a telethon "United News". I am grateful to them.

Although we were limited in time, we talked quite thoroughly. I felt that everyone cares about Ukraine, cares about us and you, cares about our future. I wrote down a lot of questions and suggestions—we will work them out.

Today I supported the global marathon for peace in Ukraine. Not just a television one. In dozens of cities around the world, people gathered in support of our state, in support of freedom. That's a pleasure!

An impressive number of people in the squares of Europe, on other continents. And this is extremely important. Because when people are in the square, politicians will no longer pretend not to hear us and you, not to hear Ukraine.

I will continue to appeal to the parliaments of other countries. The week is planned to be very busy from a diplomatic point of view. Therefore, no one will be able to hide the Ukrainian interest somewhere in political offices or in bureaucratic loopholes.

We will not let anyone forget about our cities, about Mariupol and other Ukrainian cities that the Russian militaries are destroying. More and more people in the world are on the side of Ukraine, on the side of good in this battle with evil. And if politicians don't know how to follow people, we will teach them. This is the basis of democracy and our national character.

Once again, I want to thank our people in Kherson, Kakhovka, Slavutych and other cities who do not stop resisting the occupiers. If the occupiers had temporarily entered Ukrainian cities, it only means that they would have to leave.

And I want to remind those phenomenal fools who are trying to cooperate with Russian troops that they are leaving their own people behind. What will they do to other people's traitors? I would tell them: think about it. But I know that these people don't have anything to think with. Otherwise, they would not have become traitors.

Of course, this week we will work for new sanctions against the Russian Federation, against the aggression, sanctions that are needed as long as Russian troops remain on the territory of Ukraine.

A new round of negotiations is ahead, because we are looking for peace. Really. Without delay. As I was informed, there is an opportunity and a need for a face-to-face meeting already in Turkey. This is not bad. Let's look at the result.

Our priorities in the negotiations are known. Ukraine's sovereignty and territorial integrity are beyond doubt. Effective security guarantees for our state are mandatory. Our goal is obvious—peace and the restoration of normal life in our native state as soon as possible.

The Armed Forces of our state are holding back the occupiers, and in some areas, they are even taking steps forward. Well done. The courage of our defenders, how wisely they behave on the battlefield... This is so important that no words of gratitude will be enough. But again, and again I never tire of thanking. To each of our defenders... To all who fight for our future, for our children, for our people.

I signed decrees conferring the title of Hero of Ukraine upon 15 servicemen of the Armed Forces of Ukraine, 3 of them posthumously.

As well as a decree on state awards to 142 servicemen of the Armed Forces of Ukraine and 5 servicemen of the Department of State Protection of Ukraine.

It is a great honour for me to sign such decrees.

May the memory of all our heroes live forever. May the memory of everyone who gave life for Ukraine, for us, live forever.

Glory to you all!

Glory to all our heroes! Glory to Ukraine!

## We have to fight; we can't burn emotions so as not to burn out
28 March 2022—23:55

Wise people of a strong country!

Today we have good news. Our defenders are advancing in the Kyiv region, regaining control over Ukrainian territory.

Irpin was liberated. Well done! I am grateful to everyone who worked for this result. The occupiers are pushed away from Irpin. Pushed away from Kyiv.

However, it is too early to talk about security in this part of our region. The fighting continues.

Russian troops control the north of Kyiv region, have the resources and manpower. They are trying to restore the destroyed units. The level of their losses, even at 90%, is not an argument for them to stop. Hundreds and hundreds of units of burned and abandoned enemy equipment do not convince them that this will happen to everyone.

Chernihiv, Sumy, Kharkiv regions, Donbas, southern Ukraine—the situation everywhere remains tense, very difficult.

This is a ruthless war against our nation, against our people, against our children.

As of today, 143 children are known to have died. Mariupol remains blocked. Russian troops did not allow any humanitarian corridor to be organized today, they did not allow "silence". Therefore, the situation must now be perceived in a balanced, wise way. As much as possible. Without excessive euphoria from success. But also, without getting yourself worked up. We still need time. We still need weapons. We still have to fight; we have to be patient. We can't burn emotions right now. We can't set expectations too high. Just so as not to burn out.

I spoke with the leaders of the partner countries. It was a very active diplomatic day.

Prime Minister of the United Kingdom Johnson, Prime Minister of Canada Trudeau, Chancellor of Germany Scholz, Prime Minister of Italy Draghi and President of Azerbaijan Ilham Aliyev.

We agreed with Britain to further support our defence and strengthen sanctions against the Russian Federation. Canada also supports a tougher response from the world to the catastrophe created by Russian troops in Ukrainian cities.

In a conversation with German Chancellor Scholz, I also paid considerable attention to the need to increase sanction pressure on Russia.

I thanked the President of Azerbaijan for the humanitarian support provided to Ukraine, informed about the state of affairs in the territories where Russian troops entered.

Italy has agreed to become one of the guarantors of Ukraine's security in the relevant new system of guarantees that we are elaborating.

I will continue this activity tomorrow. I will talk to other world leaders. I will work with international organizations, with the nations of Europe and the world.

Ukraine cannot and will not agree with the passive sanctions position of some entities towards Russia. There should be no "suspended" sanctions packages—that if the Russian troops do something, then there will be some answer...

We went through this story last year when we said that strong preventive sanctions against Russia were needed to prevent an invasion. The preventive package was not made. A full-scale war has begun. There are now many hints and warnings that sanctions will be tightened, such as an embargo on Russian oil supplies to Europe, if Russia uses chemical weapons. There are simply no words.

Just think about what it all came down to. Waiting for chemical weapons... We, living people, have to wait... Doesn't everything that the Russian military is doing and has already done deserve an oil embargo? Don't phosphorus bombs deserve that? Don't the shelled chemical production or nuclear power plant deserve that?

It is important for us that the sanctions packages are effective and substantial enough, given what is already being done against Ukraine by the Russian Federation.

If the sanctions packages are weak or do not work enough, if they can be circumvented, it creates a dangerous illusion for the Russian leadership that they can continue to afford what they are doing now. And Ukrainians pay for it with their lives. Thousands of lives.

Therefore, starting this week, we are creating a group of experts at the President's Office—Ukrainian and international, who will constantly analyse the sanctions against Russia—what they really influence.

Our goal is for the sanctions to work as intended. And so that there is no possibility to circumvent them. This must be a goal for the whole democratic world, without exception. No exception.

During the week I will speak in the parliaments of the partner countries: Denmark, Norway, the Netherlands, Greece, Australia. It is important that these are speeches not only in front of politicians, but also in front of societies.

In front of millions of people who want to hear Ukraine and are ready to hear it to help and support. Who feel that we are fighting for our common freedom? One for all people on our earth.

I will emphasize everywhere that no one has the right to use the lives of Ukrainians to save any income in Russia or income common with Russia. And Ukrainians should not die just because someone cannot find enough courage to hand over the necessary weapons to Ukraine.

Fear always makes you an accomplice. If someone is afraid of Russia, if he or she is afraid to make the necessary decisions that are important to us, in particular for us to get planes, tanks, necessary artillery, shells, it makes these people responsible for the catastrophe created by Russian troops in our cities, too.

Because if you could save, you had to save.

The peoples of Europe, the peoples of the world will definitely hear and support me. And all politicians should think now what they will have left if they do not correspond to the position of their people.

And finally. Already traditional.

Just before delivering this address to you, dear Ukrainians, I signed two important decrees on awarding servicemen of the Armed Forces of Ukraine with state awards. At the request of our Commander-in-Chief, 302 of our defenders are awarded.

I am grateful to all of you for your service! Glory to all our heroes!

Glory to Ukraine!

# Speech to the Folketing
## 29 March 2022—15:45

Mr. Speaker!

Mrs. Prime Minister!

Members of the Government and the Folketing! Danish people!
40 missiles.

Every day, Russian troops use so many different but equally deadly missiles against our state, against Ukraine.

This is the average number per day. 40. More than 1,370 missiles have been used in just over a month of Russia's full-scale invasion of our land.

This morning the Russian missiles hit one of our southern cities—Mykolaiv. The city of shipbuilders.

Absolutely peaceful city, which dreamed of only one thing—to regain the glory of the center of shipbuilding in the Black Sea region.

As a result of this strike, the building of the regional administration was destroyed. It is known that seven people were killed and 22 were wounded. Debris removal continues.

The Mykolaiv region residents didn't have any military dreams. They posed no threat to Russia.

But they, like all other Ukrainians, believe me, have become a target for Russian troops. For missiles, bombs, rocket artillery, mortars.

The total number of means of destruction that Russian troops have already used against our people on our land is simply impossible to count.

But we can say that the intensity and brutality of the hostilities against us have reached a level even higher than during World War II. The most devastating war for Europe.

A month of hostilities—and we already have not one or two, but a whole blacklist of cities that were completely destroyed by Russian bombing.

In dozens of other cities, towns and small villages, residential areas were partially burned, infrastructure was destroyed and enterprises where people worked were blown up. Living, ordinary people.

773 educational institutions—universities, schools, kindergartens—were destroyed. 773. Imagine! And dozens of hospitals, churches, even memorials to Holocaust victims have become targets...

The goal of Russian troops in this war is to completely destroy any basis for the normal life of the Ukrainian people. The occupiers are deliberately making sure that nothing is left of Ukraine. Only ruins. Only refugees.

More than 10 million Ukrainians have already fled their homes due to the hostilities. Almost 4 million Ukrainians have left our country, most of them women and children.

The stories of these people are full of horror.

There are still many burned and shot cars on the roadsides in the areas where the Russian military came. Hundreds and hundreds of such cars, what's left of them. The occupiers were killing civilians even when they were just trying to escape!

Along with our immigrants in Europe and the western regions of Ukraine, there are children who were simply picked up on the road near the corpses of their parents.

Up to 100,000 people remain in our city of Mariupol, which has been blocked by Russian troops for more than three weeks. While there was snow people melted it to get water. All this time we can't deliver humanitarian goods to the city—they are simply blocked. Water, food, medicine. Everything is blocked by the Russian military.

More than 90 percent of all buildings in Mariupol were completely destroyed by shelling and bombs. But Russian aircraft strike without stopping. They purposefully blow up even shelters, although they know for sure that peaceful people are hiding there—women, children, old people.

What Russian troops are doing to Mariupol is a crime against humanity that is being committed live in front of the eyes of the entire planet.

Why is this even possible? Why can't the world stop this flow of Russia's war crimes ongoing since February 24 this year?

The answer is very simple and cynical.

People who make decisions in Russia hope that they will get away with it. Sanctions? They think they can be bypassed. An embargo on Russian oil? They see that this is still nothing more than just talking about this important topic. And concern, constant concern. An international tribunal? They know that it takes years to bring specific perpetrators to justice.

That is why we appeal to you and to the entire democratic community of the world: sanctions against Russia must be strengthened! Constantly. We need to give up Russian oil, we need to block trade with the Russian Federation, we need to close ports for Russian ships. And this must be the solidarity policy of the European Union, of all the member states. Everyone.

It is you, in Denmark, in the country where the basic principles of the European Union, the Copenhagen criteria, come from, who can feel most of all how important it is for all-European solidarity to work for pressure on Russia.

Because this pressure is for Russia to seek peace. This is pressure to give the necessary protection to all the basic values on which life in Europe is built and which are now completely trampled by Russia in Ukraine.

What can be said about the protection of human rights or freedom on the European continent, if there is no such crime against people and humanity in general not committed by the occupiers?

They deport our people to Russia by force, rape women, underage girls, and engage in looting.

They have already taken more than two thousand children to Russia, and we do not know where they are, we do not even have a complete list of these children. Do they have families? How will they then find their loved ones?

It would be simply impossible for a normal person to imagine the level of evil that was brought to our land!

That is why I call on you to raise the issue of solidarity in the defence of freedom, in the defence of humanity at the level of the European Union.

There can be no Russian branches in Europe that split the EU from within, that are trying to help Russia make as much money as possible even now.

Everyone knows very well who in the European Union opposes humanity and common sense. Who does nothing at all to help establish peace in Ukraine? This must stop, and Europe must stop listening to any excuses from official Budapest.

I am grateful to Denmark for its principled position. Thank you to everyone.


I am grateful to your people who help Ukraine and help Ukrainians. To your companies that have decided to leave the Russian market. Maersk, Jysk, Lego, Vestas, DSV, Arla Foods, Carlsberg and many other companies who have made this important decision.

But I ask you not to stop, to be leaders in Europe in promoting the decisions we really need.

Long before this war, it was clear that humanity should reduce the use of fossil fuels. The era of coal and oil has caused huge damage to the environment, to our planet as a whole. Green technologies and green energy have become a logical and just answer to this challenge.

European policy is already aimed at reducing the consumption of environmentally hazardous resources. But Russia's aggression against Ukraine and against everything that life in Europe is built on is an argument to accelerate green transformation on the continent. Europe must give up Russian oil, give up as soon as possible!

Because it is the crazy income from energy resources that allows the Russian leadership to be bold. Violate generally accepted rules. Promote hatred against other nations, against us and destroy the lives of neighbouring countries.

If you had to find the complete opposite of what is called the "Law of Jante" in your country, it would be the "Law of Russian Oil".

I am confident that together—only together with all Europeans, with all responsible states on the planet—we will be able to overcome this catastrophe.

We will be able to return to peace.

We will be able to live together in a European family.

I hope this will happen very soon. But it depends on how consistent and principled we remain at this time.

At a time when the war continues.

However, we have no right now to think only of war. We know there will be peace. We know that we will be able to return to a normal, peaceful life.

That is why I want to invite you to join our initiative to rebuild Ukraine after the war, after our victory.

We invite your companies, your specialists, your state.

Knowing your potential, your creative economic power, I offer your country to take patronage over one of our beautiful regions—after the war. Of course, after the war.

Mykolaiv, the city of shipbuilders, can become such a city, such a region, which will unite you and us even more. Which Denmark can help rebuild?

Ladies and Gentlemen! Danish people!

Now is the dark time in Ukraine.

Thousands of candles are placed in our churches in memory of the people whose lives were taken by this war.

I know that for you the warm light of candles is a synonym of home comfort, ordinary good human life.

Life, which today has become an unattainable dream for many in Ukraine. The Russian invasion continues.

But I believe, I know, that we can return to peace.

And I ask you to light a candle at home tonight in memory of all Ukrainians whose lives were taken by Russian aggression.

May the memory of all who gave their lives for our freedom, world freedom, live forever!

Glory to Ukraine!

# Signals from the negotiations can be called positive, but they do not silence the explosion of Russian shells
## 29 March 2022—22:53

Wise people of a strong country!

The 34th day of the full-scale invasion of Russia and our full-scale defence is coming to an end. Successful defence.

I'm sure you saw the news today that the Russian military command allegedly decided to "reduce hostilities in the directions of Kyiv and Chernihiv."

Well, the same can be said about Chornobaivka—as if the Russian aviation simply decided to fly less, and the Russian military vehicles—to drive less. I am grateful to all our defenders, to all those who ensure the defence of Kyiv. It is their brave and effective actions that force the enemy to retreat in this direction.

However, we should not lose vigilance. The situation has not become easier. The scale of the challenges has not diminished. The Russian army still has significant potential to continue attacks against our state. They still have a lot of equipment and enough people completely deprived of rights whom they can send to the cauldron of war.

Therefore, we stay alert and do not reduce our defence efforts. Both in the north of our state and in all other regions of Ukraine, where Russian troops have temporarily entered. The defence of Ukraine is the number one task now, and everything else is derived from it.

It is on this basis that I consider the messages on the negotiation process, which is underway at various levels with representatives of the Russian Federation.

The enemy is still in our territory. The shelling of our cities continues. Mariupol is blocked. Missile and air strikes do not stop. This is the reality. These are the facts.

That is why the Armed Forces of Ukraine, our intelligence and all those who have joined the defence of the state are the only guarantee of our survival today. As a nation. As a state.

The guarantee that works.

Yes, we can call positive the signals we hear from the negotiating platform. But these signals do not silence the explosion of Russian shells.

Of course, we see all the risks. Of course, we see no reason to trust the words of certain representatives of a state that continues to fight for our destruction. Ukrainians are not naive people. Ukrainians have already learned during these 34 days of invasion and over the past eight years of the war in Donbas that only a concrete result can be trusted. The facts—if they change on our land.

Of course, Ukraine is willing to negotiate and will continue the negotiation process. To the extent that really depends on us. We expect to get the result. There must be real security for us, for our state, for sovereignty, for our people. Russian troops must leave the occupied territories. Ukraine's sovereignty and territorial integrity must be guaranteed. There can be no compromise on sovereignty and our territorial integrity. And there will not be any.

These are clear principles. This is a clear vision of the possible outcome. And to those on social networks who perceive words as if they are facts already, I want to remind one thing: we live in a democratic state and fight for our freedom. For freedom for our people.

Therefore, any decisions that are important for all our people must be made not by one person or a group of people with any political views, but by all our people. The wise people of Ukraine.

And certain countries should not even expect that certain negotiations will facilitate the lifting of sanctions against the Russian Federation. The question of sanctions cannot even be raised until the war is over, until we get back what's ours and until we restore justice.

On the contrary, sanctions must be strengthened. Intensified weekly. And they must be effective. Not just for headlines in the media that sanctions have been imposed, but for real peace. Real.

And to ensure this, a team of Ukrainian and international experts has already begun work to assess the effectiveness of the sanctions imposed on Russia. On the Ukrainian side, this area is coordinated by Head of the President's Office Andriy Yermak, and on the international side by Michael McFaul.

During the day the rescue operation was ongoing in Mykolaiv. The debris of the building of the regional administration destroyed by Russian missile strikes was dismantled. As of now, 8 people have been reported killed and 30 wounded. It is likely that these are not final figures.

The Russian troops hit Mykolaiv very insidiously. At a time when people came to their workplaces in the morning. Thank God, most of those in the building managed to evacuate when they heard an air alarm.

This one more act of the Russian so-called denazification of Mykolaiv took place in the morning after the anniversary of liberation of the city from Nazi invaders. Mykolaiv residents remember the day of March 28, 1944. And they see who the Russian troops trying to capture their city now look like.

I spoke about Mykolaiv today in my address to the Danish Parliament and the Danish people. I invited the society of this country to take part in the reconstruction of the city and the region after the war. In the framework of our program of Ukraine's reconstruction, we involve partner states, leading companies and the best specialists in order to guarantee the speed and quality of the reconstruction of our state.

As I was told, this proposal was very positively received in Denmark.

There is also important news from our government officials. As of today, the new functionality of our "Diia" state service will be available. As I promised, the state will compensate for the loss of a house or apartment as a result of hostilities. Every citizen of ours can already submit an application in "Diia".

Applications are already available in the mobile application. You need to update the app to see this new service. And in a week, it will be available offline—in the centres of administrative services. In itself, the functionality in "Diia" is quite convenient. But all the necessary details will still be clarified by our government.

The main thing is that the state will compensate for every meter of lost real estate.

In addition, government officials today expanded the program to help those institutions that support IDPs from the areas of hostilities.

Another important decision was to allocate 426 million hryvnias to pay the miners' salaries.

Traditionally, I signed several important decrees before delivering this evening address. The first is about awarding communications service employees. I am sincerely grateful to everyone who provides the fundamental basis of our lives. Who gives us connection?

By the way, on the day of the beginning of the Russian invasion, the first missile strike in the JFO area was made against them.

12 people were awarded state awards, 4—posthumously.

The second signed decree is on awarding 126 servicemen of the Armed Forces of Ukraine, 34 of them—posthumously.

We will always be grateful to each of our defenders for the defence of our state in the Ukrainian Patriotic War against Russia.

May the memory of everyone who gave life for Ukraine live forever!

Glory to each of our heroes! Glory to Ukraine!

# Speech in the Norwegian Storting
30 March 2022—17:22

Mr. President of the Storting! Mr. Prime Minister! Members of the Government, dear deputies! Norwegian people!

It is a great honour for me to address you on behalf of the Ukrainian people.

Today is the 35th day of Russia's full-scale invasion of Ukraine. After 8 years of war in the east of our state, in Donbas, Russian troops went on the offensive from three directions at once—from the north, east and south. They attacked us on land, in the air and from the sea.

Russian missiles and air bombs hit our cities and civilian infrastructure every day and night. There are no forbidden targets for Russian troops. They attack everything. They attack hospitals and airports, food warehouses and residential areas.

Ukraine's losses are enormous. Tens of thousands of houses were destroyed, dozens of cities and villages were burned, millions of people were left without the opportunity to live normally.

The columns of Russian armoured vehicles are not decreasing. Although we have already destroyed more Russian tanks and other combat vehicles than Moscow has lost in any war in the last 50 years.

Russia's treacherous actions at sea deserve special attention, as it is one of the greatest threats to international security of all that has emerged since World War II. Ukrainian ports in the Black Sea and the Sea of Azov have been blocked by Russia since the first day of their invasion. About a hundred ships cannot enter the Mediterranean Sea.

Some ships were simply hijacked—this is piracy for theft of cargo. Several ships were fired at. But the blockade of ports was implemented by Russia not just by the navy.

They mined the sea. And now the mines planted by Russian forces are drifting at sea. And this is a danger for anyone: for any ships and ports of any country in the Black Sea region.

One of these mines was recently cleared in time in the Bosphorus. Another—near the Bulgarian border. Another—near the coast of Romania. I don't even want to imagine what will happen if some of these mines are not cleared in time. Who will be affected then? Maybe ferries, God forbid. Or passenger liners. Or merchant ships. Or possibly tankers, the explosion of which could lead not only to human casualties, but also to a large-scale environmental disaster. And then Russia will say again, as always, that it is not them. As it has said many times when killing critics of the Russian government in Europe or even shooting down the Malaysian Boeing in the sky over Donbas.

The war is not limited to our borders now. No other state since World War II and the Nazi aggression at sea has posed such a threat to free navigation as Russia has already posed.

Think about it—how do they look at it in those regions of the world where there are potential aggressors and new wars with neighbours are quite possible? They are waiting there to see if Russia will be punished enough for its actions. These horrible, aggressive actions. If not, you will see everything we are experiencing now will be repeated in other regions.

Ladies and Gentlemen!

Norwegian people!

We have no common borders with you, but we have a common neighbour who denies all our common values. For the Russian state in its current condition neither the freedom of nations nor the freedom of human matters.

In Russia, universally recognized human rights are denied. It's not that there is no security for minorities, they can just be killed there. And they are being killed.

I'm sure you know all about it. You know that there is no rule of law and fair trial. You know that splitting and destroying European democracies is a long-standing policy of the Russian Federation. Russia's war against Ukraine simply continues all this. It is an attempt to destroy everything that Europe is holding on to, what we are holding on to. Therefore, it is an aggression that aims to go beyond our borders.

I think you are experiencing new risks near your border with Russia. A number of Russian troops that has no normal explanation has already been amassed in the Arctic region. For what? Against whom?

The future of Europe—the whole continent from north to south, from west to east—is being decided right now. On our land, on Ukrainian soil, in Ukrainian air, in Ukrainian sea. So that your soldiers do not have to defend NATO's eastern flank, so that Russian mines do not drift to your ports and fjords, so that your people do not have to get used to the sound of air alarms and so that Russian tanks are not amassed at your border, we must stop the aggression of the Russian Federation together and only together.

I am grateful to your government and to the whole of your society for the tangible support you have already given to our state. Including for the help with weapons. You have taken historic steps by giving us what we need in the struggle for freedom and against tyranny.

But the war continues. Russia is sending new forces to our land to continue to destroy us, to destroy Ukrainians. We must do more to stop the war!

The first and most important thing is weapons. Freedom must be armed no worse than tyranny. I will be very specific in these walls, in your walls. Believe me, we are losing specific people, specific cities are being destroyed. So, I want to make it clear what we need. In particular, anti-ship weapons—Harpoon missiles, as well as air-defence systems—NASAMS. In addition, we need weapons to destroy armoured vehicles and artillery systems.

All the weapons you can help us with will be used only to protect our freedom, your freedom. Only to protect the freedom and security you enjoy with other Europeans.

The second thing is sanctions. The only way that can motivate Russia to seek peace. I am convinced that the country that annually awards the Nobel Peace Prize understands better than anyone else what peace is worth and how we need it. How valuable every effort on the way to peace is. Therefore, new sanctions packages must be introduced weekly, without pauses. The stronger they are, the sooner we will restore peace.

I am grateful to Norway for joining the EU sanctions. But I ask you to do something else as well. It is important that European companies do not help this military machine, which has already killed thousands of our people, destroyed dozens of cities completely. No krone, I beg you, no euro of taxes that help Russian aggression!

For example, your company MOTUS TECH and other companies must stop supporting Russia's ability to destroy neighbours. How can one supply ship equipment to Russia when it uses its fleet to mine the sea and destroy any opportunities for free navigation?

Also, the European Union, and therefore, I hope, Norway, must finally implement a ban on Russian ships using ports on the continent. As long as Russia blocks our ports, it has no right to use all the ports of the free world.

I want to emphasize this is not a question of money, no! This is a question of freedom and security of navigation in the world.

Third, you are one of the most responsible suppliers of energy resources in the world. Confidence of the whole world in Norway has always been and I am sure will be at the highest level. This contrasts sharply with Russia's behaviour in energy supplies.

It is you who can make a decisive contribution to Europe's energy security by providing the necessary resources for both the European Union and Ukraine. We have already started a dialogue on the supply of about 5 billion cubic meters of gas to Ukraine for the next heating season. I hope this will be the basis for our long-term cooperation in this area.

Ladies and Gentlemen! Norwegian people!

Looking at our common path, we always meet in history in difficult yet defining moments for Europe.

Like a thousand years ago, when the Norwegian Vikings were frequent visitors in Kyiv and participated in the formation of the first Kyiv state. Or—Garoaríki. This is what the lands of Rus'-Ukraine were called in Scandinavian sagas. The country of fortresses.

The country of cities. Both our and your ancestors lived in them more than a thousand years ago.

Today, Russian bombs are flying at our land and our people. At the land where the Ukrainian Princess Elisiv of Kyiv was born and grew up. Wife of King Harald III of Norway, mother of King Olaf the Peaceful, grandmother of Magnus III, great- grandmother of Eystein I and Sigurd the Crusader.

These are the pages of our common history! History of Kyivan Rus'. And this history was created on this land and by our people. And we are defending it together again.

This was the case 77 years ago, when Ukrainians, along with other peoples of the anti- Hitler coalition, liberated European land from Nazi invaders. Fedir Kompaniyets, a Ukrainian from the Sumy region, was the first soldier to enter the liberated Kirkenes in October 1944 at the head of his unit. Now in his small homeland—in the Sumy region—fierce battles with Russian invaders are taking place.

Ukrainians united as much as possible to repel this aggression. To protect our state and our way of life—democratic, free, with full protection of rights and freedoms for everyone.

The price is horrible for us—today we know about the death of 145 children, and this is only an officially confirmed number. It is not possible to establish the full number of dead in the occupied areas. It is likely that we have lost hundreds—think about it!—hundreds of children. Just children.

After this war we will have not only to rebuild the country physically—rebuild our cities, demine our land, our sea. We will have to rehabilitate people, both military and civilian. Heal after injuries, after everything they had to go through.

I know that your country has a lot of experience in rehabilitation. And this is something you can also help us with.

And now I invite you to join our project of reconstruction of Ukraine. The colossal losses we have suffered mean that the amount of recovery, the amount of investment required will also be colossal. As one of the world's most responsible investors, Norway can do much to restore stability in Eastern Europe.

And then, I am sure, we in Ukraine will be able to adopt one of your extraordinary traditions. A wonderful tradition. The one that characterizes you the most—peaceful people, a society built on the principles of good.

Every year on May 17, on Constitution Day, you organize an extremely sincere celebration—a parade of schoolchildren. Children from all over Norway take part in it. This year, our children will go with your children—Ukrainians who came to you for protection and security.

And I hope that soon, when we manage to restore peace in Ukraine together, and it will happen, I will be able to invite you, to invite you and your children to take part in such a parade in Kyiv on one of our holidays. To celebrate our common freedom, our common right to a happy future for our children. In peace. In Ukraine. In Europe.

Because, as they say, if a rock breaks off from Europe, Europe becomes smaller. So, we must do everything to ensure that a rock like Ukraine is always with Europe. Only together.

Thank you, Norway! Glory to Ukraine!

# We will not give up anything and will fight for every meter of our land, for every person
## 30 March 2022—23:53

Dear Ukrainians!

Today I have few words, not much time, a lot of emotions and even more tasks. It is that kind of moment. A turning point, when we can and should talk only about the most important thing.

Yes, there is an ongoing negotiation process. But these are still words. So far, no specifics.

There are also other words about the alleged withdrawal of Russian troops from Kyiv and Chernihiv. About the alleged reduction of activity of occupiers in these directions. We know that this is not a withdrawal, but the consequences of exile. Consequences of the work of our defenders. But we also see that at the same time there is an accumulation of Russian troops for new strikes in Donbas. And we are preparing for this.

We do not believe anyone—we do not trust any beautiful verbal constructions. There is a real situation on the battlefield. And now—this is the most important thing. We will not give up anything. And we will fight for every meter of our land, for every our persons.

In the current situation of our state, there should be no such discussions to which society and our politicians are accustomed in peacetime.

If someone pretends to be able to teach our Armed Forces how to fight, how to resist the enemy, the best way to do it is to go to the battlefield directly.

Not from a chair at home or from the place where you left for safety. But from the area of real hostilities. If you are not ready for this, you should not even start teaching our defenders.

Today was a very active diplomatic day for me. A difficult one. Priorities are known. There are three of them: weapons for Ukraine, new sanctions against Russia and financial support for our state.

A conversation took place with US President Biden. Very detailed, lasted an hour.

Of course, I thanked the United States for a new $ 1 billion humanitarian aid package and additional $ 500 million in direct budget support. And I stressed that right now is a turning point.

I told President Biden what Ukraine needs. And I was as sincere as possible with him. The support of the United States is vital for us. And now it is especially important to lend a hand to Ukraine, to show all the power of the democratic world.

And if we want to fight for freedom together, then we ask our partners ... And if we really fight for freedom and protection for democracies together, then we have the right to demand help in this crucial difficult moment. Tanks, planes, artillery systems... Freedom must be armed no worse than tyranny.

I also spoke about this today in an address to the Norwegian parliament and people. To one of the states that supported us significantly. I called for more help to Ukraine.

With weapons and sanctions against Russia as well.

I spoke today with the President of Egypt and the Crown Prince of the United Arab Emirates. I have done, am doing and will do my best so that our people can defend themselves until justice is restored.

On Ukrainian soil and in the Black Sea region. This is our

fundamental interest. This is our survival. It is for the survival of the Ukrainian people that we are now fighting. In this war, without exaggeration, the Patriotic War against Russia.

And now I want to mention a few more important things.

First. There are those who work together with everyone to defend the state. So that Ukraine can gain its future. We appreciate the work of each such person. And there are those who waste time and work only to stay in office. Today I signed the first decree to recall such a person. Such an Ambassador of Ukraine. From Morocco. The Ambassador from Georgia was also recalled.

With all due respect: if there are no weapons, no sanctions, no restrictions for Russian business—please look for another job.

I look forward to concrete results in the coming days from our representatives in Latin America, the Middle East, Southeast Asia and Africa.

I expect the same results from military attaches in the coming days. The diplomatic frontline is one of the key frontlines. And everyone there must work as efficiently as possible to win and help the army. Each on the diplomatic frontline must work just as each of our defenders on the battlefield.

And the second point. Traditionally, today, before delivering this address, at the request of the Commander-in-Chief, I signed a decree on state awards to our military. 122 defenders, 23 of them posthumously.

Eternal memory to all who died for Ukraine! Eternal glory to all our heroes!

Glory to Ukraine!

# Speech in the Australian Parliament
## 31 March 2022—11:38

Distinguished Mr. Prime Minister!

Dear Mr. Speaker of the House of Representatives! Dear Mr. President of the Senate!
Dear leader of the opposition!

Ladies and gentlemen, members of the government, senators, and members of the parliament!
Australian people!

Thank you for the great honour of speaking to you today.

In May 2016, thousands of Australians gathered at Perth Airport to see the Ukrainian "Mriya" for the first time. "Mriya" is the name of our An-225 aircraft. "Mriya" is a dream in English. After covering almost 15,000 kilometres, it delivered to Australia an urgent cargo—a 130-ton electric generator, which your enterprise desperately needed. Delivery by sea would take several months. And the Ukrainian plane did it in a few days.

We have always been proud of our "Mriya". Not because it is the largest on the planet. First of all because it helped people from all over the world by delivering food, drinking water, equipment for peacekeeping and humanitarian missions.

In 2019, after the beginning of the COVID-19 pandemic, our "Mriya" constantly delivered the most necessary medical supplies. That saved people. Adults, children—all. In different countries, on different continents. "Mriya" was bringing life. But now it is impossible.

Impossible, because there is a state that has completely different values than we have, than you have, than the whole civilized world has. And this state started a full-scale war against us.

It bombs and shells peaceful cities and villages, killing our peaceful people. Kills children. Arranges blockades of cities, holding hundreds of thousands of people hostage without water, food, light, and heat. Daily. It separates thousands of children from their parents and takes them out, or rather kidnaps them, forcibly relocating to its territory.

And on February 27, as a result of fighting in the city of Hostomel, our plane "Mriya" was burned. Can we say that Russia has destroyed our dream? No. It burned the plane, it burned the iron. It destroyed matter, not soul. The shell, not the essence. Not freedom. Not dignity. Not independence.

We know that our dream cannot be defeated and destroyed. Especially if we can count on the support and help of the free world. On your support, on your help. And as in the story I told above, it is not needed in a few months, it is needed now.

Ladies and Gentlemen! Australian people!

The distance between our states is great, thousands of kilometers. We are divided by the seas and oceans, the territories of dozens of other countries, time zones. But this distance simply does not exist for the cruelty and chaos that Russia has brought to Eastern Europe, to the region of our Black and Azov Seas, to our Ukrainian land.

Everything that is happening in our region due to Russia's aggression and that is destroying the lives of our people has already become a real threat to your state and your people. Because this is the nature of evil—it can instantly overcome any distance and any barriers. Destroy life.

For decades, there has been no such threat of nuclear strikes as there is now. Because Russian officials and state propagandists are openly discussing the use of nuclear weapons against those who do not want to obey Russian demands.

For decades, it has not been the case that one state completely blocked the sea for another state and all merchant ships of any country.

But that is exactly what Russia has done. Our part of the Black Sea and the Sea of Azov is now a completely dead sea. And any ship that tries to enter our waters can simply be destroyed by the Russian fleet. More than a hundred merchant ships under various flags are blocked by Russia in our ports!

For decades, there has never been a state in the world that has started a war against a neighbouring people, openly declaring its conquest or destruction. So that not even the name of this nation remains, so that there is no possibility of free life for this nation.

Russia has already returned to the world the worst pages of the XX century. The greatest threats of that century. It returned the evil that humanity has long hoped to forget.

But the worst thing is that if Russia is not stopped now, if Russia is not brought to justice, some other countries in the world that dream of a similar war against their neighbours will decide that this is possible for them as well.

The fate of global security is being decided now.


No human is capable of controlling the wind and precipitation on the planet, and therefore no one will be able to save one or another part of the Earth from radiation pollution due to the use of nuclear weapons.

No state on the planet should have even a theoretical possibility to block maritime trade routes and even more so to completely close the sea to other states. I repeat once again: there should not even be a theoretical possibility!

No ruler in the world should count on impunity when considering the prospect of war. Ladies and Gentlemen!

Australian people!


After 36 days of Russia's full-scale war against Ukraine, it is safe to say that there is no other way in the world to guarantee global security than to force Russia into silence, into peace. And also, to bring it to justice—this is important—for everything it has done against global security.

A state that does not shy away from nuclear blackmail should immediately receive sanctions that demonstrate that blackmail has devastating consequences for the blackmailer.

Effective tools are also needed to bring to justice any state that blocks maritime trade routes. So that no one even has such a temptation—to make the sea dead.

Now there are simply no such tools in the world. Therefore, Australia's leadership can be indispensable in modernizing the global security architecture. As well as in strengthening our anti-war coalition, which is now working to return peace to Ukraine.

It is also necessary to improve the capacity of international institutions created for the responsibility of war criminals and those who commit any criminal act for which the whole world can punish in solidarity, not just one state alone. If this was done in time, life in the world would be much safer.

I am sure that each of you, as well as each of us Ukrainians, remembers the tragedy of MH-17. Malaysian Boeing shot down by the Russian occupiers in the sky over the Ukrainian Donbas. Then 298 people died. My condolences to all the families who lost their loved ones.

But was it possible to bring to justice those who caused this tragedy? No. They are hiding in Russia. And, obviously, received security guarantees from the Russian state. Has Russia paid compensation to the relatives of the victims? No. It still denies its guilt in the tragedy.

Eight years have already passed, and justice has not been restored yet. And no one knows how much longer it will take for at least one tragedy to receive a worthy response from the international community, from all of us.

And how many more new tragedies has Russia created or will create?

It is often said that unpunished evil returns. I would add unpunished evil returns winged, with a sense of omnipotence. If the world had punished Russia for what it did in 2014, there would be none of the horrors of this invasion of Ukraine in 2022.

We need to fix these terrible mistakes now.

I am grateful to Australia for its bipartisan support for our defence against invaders. For the help that your state has already given us. In particular, for 70 thousand tons of coal for the needs of our energy.

But this is just the beginning. Together we can, and therefore must do more. New sanctions against Russia are needed. Strong sanctions. As long as it doesn't abandon nuclear blackmail, the blockade of the sea, it must pay the highest price. No Russian ship should be allowed into the ports of the free world. Buying Russian oil means paying for the destruction of the foundations of global security. Any business activity with Russia must be completely stopped. Not a single dollar for the elimination of people!

Any attempt by Russia to circumvent sanctions must also be stopped. After all, what kind of sanctions are these, if they can be circumvented thanks to simple schemes?

But above all, we must arm those who are really fighting for freedom. For evil to lose and for Russia to seek peace, Ukraine must have everything it needs on the battlefield.

For example, you have wonderful Bushmaster armoured vehicles that can significantly help Ukraine. As well as other models of equipment and weapons that can strengthen our position. If you have the opportunity—Ukraine will be grateful to you.

Now in Ukraine they will definitely do more for our common freedom, for our common security than being covered with dust on your land. The Ukrainian people have already shown the world how sincerely we value freedom. How consistently we are ready to defend it.

Our heroes are fighting against the army that is considered one of the strongest in the world. But all our people, without exception, are already thinking about the future.

About how we will live after the war. How we will rebuild our country, our Black Sea region.

We invite the world's leading countries, leading companies, and the best specialists to join the project of Ukraine's reconstruction. Take patronage of a region, city or industry of your choice in our country that needs restoration.

Your state has given Ukraine a special status of a like-minded country. But we are not only related in our thoughts—we are also related in our dreams.

Therefore, I invite your beautiful country to look closely at our southern regions, at our coasts of the Black Sea and the Sea of Azov. Restoration of our ports, development of such cities as, for example, Kherson, which is fighting for its freedom today, restoration of the maritime industry of Ukraine can be a special contribution to stability for you after this terrible war.

Together with the fundamental protection of free navigation, this will restore the strength of the old but correct words: whoever is able to defend freedom at sea, is able to defend freedom in the world. I believe you can do it!

And I hope that the Ukrainian community of Australia, our strong Ukrainian community, will join this common work. It will support us now as much as in previous years.


Dear friends, the geographical distance between us is insane. Thousands of kilometres. But what does this distance mean for those who have a common understanding, who see the world the same way, who are bitterly disturbed when the enemy comes, when children are killed, when cities are destroyed, when refugees are shot on the roads, when a peaceful country is turned into a burned territory? Then any distance disappears. Geography means nothing. Only humanity matters. Only a dream of returning to a peaceful life.

A dream we will fulfil.

Definitely. And definitely together.

Thank you!

Thank you, Australia! Glory to Ukraine!

## Speech in the States General of the Netherlands
## 31 March 2022—13:31

Mrs. Speaker!

Dear members of parliament! Mr. Prime Minister! Mark!
   Dear Minister of Foreign Affairs, Minister of Defence!

Dutch people!

I have the great honour of becoming the first foreign head of state to address the House of Representatives of the Netherlands and your people. In this format, at such a time.

I am sincerely grateful for this opportunity. For the fact that in these critical circumstances in which my country and our entire continent found themselves, I can explain to you directly what is happening and why it is so important to be together now for all of us, for all Europeans. For all who value peace on our planet. Peace for which millions of people have fought, generations of Europeans. And which was destroyed by one decision, in one moment.

So much has been done since World War II so that what

Ukraine is experiencing right now never happens again. But everything repeats. Unfortunately. Only so far for one European country, not for the whole continent.

But World War II began with the destruction of individual states as well. And then it led to the tragedy of Rotterdam, the terrible bombing of London and the massacre that engulfed all of Europe.

If peace on the continent had not been preserved, if the great war had returned with no less brutality than 80 years ago, no one could have a reason to believe that certain state borders would manage to deter aggression.

Especially since many in Russia want to carry this aggression further, further to Europe. The shadow of those ruins of Rotterdam is already hanging over many European cities. Ukraine is just the beginning if Russia isn't stopped. If we don't stop it immediately!

36 days! 36! That is how long our state, our people have already been fighting alone against the army, which was considered among the strongest in the world. Russia has been preparing for this campaign against us, against freedom, against our people for decades. They have accumulated as many resources to spend on war, on death, as not every European country can spend on life.

And now these Russian resources are working at full capacity and, by the way, tirelessly. They work in such a way that... No matter how scary it may sound, people are already getting used to it. The world is beginning to adapt. They start to ignore everything they hear about the war. They are getting used to the news about the new bombing of our peaceful cities. About new missile strikes. They are getting used to the updated lists of those killed. Daily reports of the number of destroyed houses and shelled cities and communities no longer evoke emotions.

For many others, the war in Ukraine is becoming routine. Unfortunately, this is true. Routine. But not for those whose lives are in danger every minute.

Who, as residents of our city of Mariupol, has been under complete blockade for more than three weeks already? Without everything: without life, without food, water, basic medicines, without communications. Who is forced to stay in basements, hide anywhere just so as not to die under fire.

But not for those whom Russia has taken to its territory. Simply deported, as the Nazis did in the occupied countries. Thousands of Ukrainian children and tens of thousands of adults were forcibly transported to the territory of the occupying state.

Unfortunately, we do not know anything about the fate of most of them.

How to return them? Will they lose touch with their relatives? Will Russia give back these people, these children? These are horrible questions for us. And for some it is becoming a routine that one should not even pay attention to.

We are now at a time when we need to act even faster, even more powerfully than during the first month of the war. When the peoples of Europe, the peoples of the world saw what Russia was doing. And they are all full of indignation, full of desire to help. It's true.

But people's attention and emotions do not focus on the same thing for long. If the situation is not resolved, people may switch to something else.

We have no right to give this war another 36 days! We must all work together to make Russia seek peace as soon as possible!

Hundreds of children were killed. Thousands of people were killed. Tens of thousands of houses were destroyed. Burned cities, villages. Russian occupiers rape women in occupied areas. They loot everything they can, everything they find. They even kill not to achieve any military success anymore. Not to sow terror. They started killing because it is fun for them! Entertainment for people who have as many weapons as they want and no deterrents.

We will never accept this! And we will never stop defending ourselves! Ladies and Gentlemen!

Dutch people!

I know that tomorrow your country will celebrate 450 years since the beginning of the armed uprising against tyranny. A fundamental event for your state, for your society.

Under normal circumstances, in my address to you, I would talk about it as you are used to hearing it. As about history, a historical moment. As about your heritage. As about the achievements of generations of people who lived 450 years ago.

But today, as my country struggles against tyranny, I will speak about it solely as about a current event, as about something that must happen here and now. The faster the better.

What was the goal of the founders of the Netherlands? Obviously: freedom, democracy, human dignity, cohesion, cultural, religious diversity.

Since then, the path to everything that shows modern Europe has continued. To the free life of dozens of different nations together—in a single space. To tolerance, which provides an unprecedented level of human respect for each other in human history.

And all this is now under attack again. All this now needs to be defended again. To be defended in the east of Europe, to be defended in our state, in Ukraine. So far only in Ukraine… So far there is a chance to stop the tyranny on our land and drive it back, beyond our Ukrainian border.

I am grateful to you, politicians, I am grateful to all ordinary people for the extremely strong support of my state, our people at this time. For leadership in sanctions. For the principled stance in business activity related to the Russian Federation. For the help you provide to Ukrainian immigrants who have felt family care in your society. This is all extremely valuable!

But Russia does not cease hostilities on the territory of Ukraine. Exactly on the territory of Ukraine. And we have to do much more to restore peace. To protect freedom. To save us as a state. And to really ensure one vital fact: there will never be another war in Europe. Never again!

In 2014, the world did not fully understand why the Russian occupiers came to our land. Then—to the land of Crimea, partly—to the land of Donbas. And you felt it. After they shot down a Malaysian Boeing flying from Amsterdam.

There can be no doubt that this is a totally unjust war. This is a war that the Russian state cannot be forgiven. Hundreds and hundreds of crimes for which everyone must be held accountable. All those who gave criminal orders. Everyone who carried out these criminal orders. And all those who provided political cover for these criminal orders.

Your city, The Hague, the capital of international justice, knows exactly how to do it. I'm sure they will do it! To assert international law. To assert the rule of law. To assert justice that is clear to everyone on Earth.

But for that to happen, sanctions need to be stepped up. Together with other EU countries, you have to do everything possible so that Russia does not have the resources to continue this war, the war in Europe, and so that there is no political opportunity to hide criminals.

Close your ports to Russian ships! Together with all other EU countries. Stop any trade with this country that has forgotten all the lessons of World War II!

Get ready faster to give up Russia's energy resources, so that billions, billions of euros for them do not go to arms production and mass killings in Ukraine.

Ladies and Gentlemen! Dutch people!

Tyranny must lose. Tyranny must always lose.

And for that to happen, freedom must get all the weapons it

needs to win, to defend itself. The weapons that are available on the continent. The weapons you have.

Ukraine is grateful for the support it has already received from you. From your society. From your state. This support is truly unprecedented. It is truly the support of a leader. But the war is so intense, Russian troops are so active that we need more.

"Stingers" and "Panzerfausts" allow you to hold on, to fight. However, this is not a weapon of victory. We desperately need weapons that can make our skies safe, that we can use to un-block our cities where Russia is artificially creating famine.

We need weapons that can drive the occupiers out of our land. Aircraft, tanks, NASAMS air-defence systems and Spike anti-tank systems, shells, missiles and more. You have this list. And I hope you will find an opportunity to help us as much as you can, to help us with that.

The second point. I urge you to influence international institutions! The crimes of the Russian occupiers must be punished. Deportations, massacres, destruction of civilian in-frastructure, bombing of hospitals—all this must be answered by the democratic community.

Imagine: Russian troops are deliberately destroying our agricultural sector! They are mining fields; they are blowing up agricultural machinery now. They are doing everything to destroy our potential, agricultural potential, and provoke a food crisis. Not only in Ukraine—in the world.

And they are doing it in a country that could become one of the most powerful agricultural centres in Europe and the world.

But I am confident that we will be able to overcome all this. I am confident that together we will be able to build even more potential. And become a truly global agricultural power.

Third. We already have to think about rebuilding Ukraine. About how we all—not only Ukrainians, but all Europeans—will return to a peaceful life.

I dream of this day. The day when Ukrainian immigrants

who arrived in the European Union after the beginning of the Russian aggression will be able to say, "thank you" and return home. Return to rebuilt cities, to restored Ukraine.

And I invite your country to join this project—the project of reconstruction of Ukraine. I urge you to choose a city, a region of our state that can see your care, can feel what you can do.

And for everyone in your country who still has doubts to definitely feel that we, Ukrainians, can be with you—in the European Union.

I am convinced that this will reinforce our common European home. And will make the European project even more perfect.

I believe that this will happen very soon! Because it is absolutely rational. With our potential, with our people, with our ability to defend freedom. And you know this perfectly well! And you know very well, my friend Mark, that our accession to the European Union depends very much on you, on your country.

I want to thank you for everything! Thank you, the Netherlands! Glory to Ukraine!

# Speech in the Federal Parliament of Belgium
## 31 March 2022—16:55

Dear Mrs. President of the Chamber of Representatives! Dear Mrs. President of the Senate!

Dear Mr., Prime Minister!

Dear Ladies and Gentlemen, deputies, and members of the government! Dear Belgian people!

Eight years of war. 36 days of full-scale invasion of the Russian Federation. Did many people expect that our state and our people would be able to resist Russian troops for so long?

Let's be honest: no. Few. They thought we would fall under the blows of Russian troops. But we withstood. Our people endured. We are fighting. We are defending our freedom, amazing the world with the courage of Ukrainian heroes, our Armed Forces of Ukraine and all citizens of Ukraine who do not surrender, who believe in victory.

In the south of our state there is a city of Mariupol, which you mentioned today. I am very grateful to you, Madam Speaker. One of the most promising and economically powerful cities in Ukraine. That was before this war. And now more than 90% of all buildings in this city are completely destroyed by Russian strikes—aircraft, artillery, mortars, tanks. Thousands of peaceful Mariupol residents died. People are buried just in the city. In the courtyards of high-rise buildings. Or rather, what is left of the high- rise buildings.

Mariupol has been under complete blockade for more than three weeks. The Russian military closed all entrances to the city and blocked access from the sea. You all know these details, there is nothing in the city: no water, no food, no medicine, no life. There is nothing you need to sustain any life.

But Mariupol does not give up. Mariupol continues to fight the occupiers. Its defenders had a choice—they could leave the city and give it to the Russian invaders. They did not.

Every day we try to do everything to make the humanitarian corridors from Mariupol work! To save civilians who still remain in the city. Women and children, the elderly... In part, we succeed. But in most cases, the Russian military does not release people into the free territory of Ukraine. And does not allow any humanitarian cargo into Mariupol.

Today it is the most horrific place in Europe. It is hell. It is a catastrophe that everyone knows about, the whole world. But no one is determined enough to help stop the catastrophe in this city and in other cities in our country.

And now I want to ask everyone—I want to ask you, I want to ask all Europeans who hear me now. What do the defenders of Mariupol hope for? What do the defenders of other cities, towns and villages of Ukraine hope for? In all those areas where the battles are no less appalling than you had near Ypres. Or maybe it's even worse in Mariupol... I don't know.

Do the defenders of our cities hope for the closure of the skies over Ukraine to Russian missiles and aircraft? They know there is no courage to do so.

Do they think about whether our state meets the criteria for joining the European Union? Our state, which has already given thousands of lives in the war for freedom in Europe...

Do Mariupol residents or defenders of any other city in Ukraine calculate the level of losses of European companies from the termination of business in the Russian market? Do they think about money at all?

No. They do not hope for it. Do not calculate it. Because that's exactly what they deserve.

Agree, these are completely different worlds. The world of those who really fight for freedom. Here and now. Against tyranny. Against a tyranny that wants to split Europe and destroy everything that unites us.

Everything that unites you... And the world of those who are so used to freedom that they don't even want to notice what the struggle for it is worth. The world of those who believe that Russian diamonds in Antwerp, for example, are more important than the war in Eastern Europe.

Or the world of those who believe that the accessibility of European ports to Russian ships is more important than the Russian military machine's attempt to destroy the entire nation around you. 40 million Ukrainians!

The main question in the life of every person is not what this person hopes for, what this person thinks or calculates... The main question is what this person is worthy of.

And I, as the President of a worthy country, address you with quite logical statements. With what is clear to the vast majority of the world, Europe, Europeans in different countries. We have seen these polls; we know how people support us.

Our defenders deserve to receive from Europe for the freedom of which they are fighting the weaponry that will definitely stop Russia's offensive, and therefore the onset of tyranny.

When we are talking about aircraft, tanks, artillery systems, anti-ship weapons, we are talking about what is really needed. And what the countries of the European Union, the countries of NATO have.

Our defenders deserve that European companies finally stop making money together with those who are trying to destroy us.

Our defenders deserve not to think about the criteria, but to know that Ukraine will be a member of the European Union. Because if they lose, if we lose Mariupol and other Ukrainian cities, there will be no strong European Union anymore. Because tyranny will come to take away from you everything you possess and are proud of.

Of course, we do not wish you this. And this is by no means a threat. This is the reality. We feel it. This is a statement of all the facts we live in. A statement of what is clearly visible from Mariupol—the headquarters of the European resistance. Of what is clearly visible from Ukraine—the headquarters of European dignity.

And I am sure that those esteemed headquarters that are located on your beautiful land are fully aware of everything I am telling you. They realize it. Although, perhaps, they do not speak aloud. So let us all together in Europe be worthy of the feats that Ukrainians demonstrate in the war for freedom. For a free Europe and against tyranny. Against Russia.

We are grateful to you, very grateful to your state for the support you have already provided. Belgium was one of the first to provide us with defensive assistance. This is a historical moment, a historical gratitude. We will never forget that.

You have already warmly welcomed more than 30,000 Ukrainians who left their homes because of this war. But it is you, as the heart of Europe, who can inspire all other Europeans to do more. To help us drive the occupiers out of Ukraine and restore the precious peace.

Peace that is worth more than anything, more than any values, more than any diamonds. More than any agreements with Russia. More than any Russian vessel in European ports. More than any barrel of Russian oil.

Each of you knows what needs to be done to restore peace. To be truly worthy of Europe. So help us, do it! Weapons. Sanctions. EU membership.

And soon the future will thank you.

Glory to all our heroes!

Glory to the heroic city of Mariupol! Thank you sincerely to your state!

Glory to Ukraine!

www.lmverlag.shop

Made in the USA
Las Vegas, NV
06 January 2024

83912872R10184